Writing Themes
About
LITERATURE

Writing Themes About LITERATURE

SECOND EDITION

Edgar V. Roberts
Herbert H. Lehman College,
The City University of New York

PRENTICE-HALL, INC., *Englewood Cliffs, New Jersey*

PE1479
.C7
R59
1969

Library of Congress Catalog Card No.: 69-10870

Current printing (*last number*):
10   9   8   7   6   5   4   3   2   1

Printed in the United States of America

PRENTICE-HALL INTERNATIONAL, INC., *London*
PRENTICE-HALL OF AUSTRALIA, PTY. LTD., *Sydney*
PRENTICE-HALL OF CANADA, LTD., *Toronto*
PRENTICE-HALL OF INDIA PRIVATE LTD., *New Delhi*
PRENTICE-HALL OF JAPAN, INC., *Tokyo*

for Nanette

Acknowledgments

I present this revision of *Writing Themes About Literature* with gratitude to the many instructors and students who have spoken kindly about the first edition. Their reception of the book has made the second edition possible. The excisions, additions, and modifications made here have resulted from my own experience with the book and also from the experience and wisdom of a number of instructors throughout the United States. To these people I am especially grateful. They are, Professors Peter W. Dowell, Emory University; Robert F. Dunn, Saint Joseph's College; Donald B. Halog, College of Saint Teresa; E. H. Johansson, Ohio University; Jean E. Lafreniere, Macomb County Community College; Milton C. Petersen, Washington State University; Roy G. Pickett, The University of New Mexico; Morton D. Rich, Montclair State College; Ian Ross, The University of British Columbia; and Mrs. Barbara Swords, Elmhurst College. In each step of revision I have had their comments before me; they will see the extent of my indebtedness to them. I should like to thank Mrs. Catherine Walter and especially Mrs. Benita Shaw, who assisted me in preparing the manuscript of the second edition for the press. I should also like to thank Paul O'Connell of Prentice-Hall for his encouragement and assistance over the years and Janice Medlock of Prentice-Hall for her diligence and creativeness in the preparation of the second edition.

EDGAR V. ROBERTS

Contents

To the Instructor

This book provides a fresh and interesting approach to the writing of themes on literary topics. Each assignment is about a phase of literary study that is usually considered in literature and composition courses. The book is different from handbooks, rhetorics, textbooks on poetry and prose, and collections of critical essays because it concentrates on literary problems *as* they bear on the writing of themes. I have tried to keep in focus the needs of the student with a difficult assignment on a work of literature, and I have emphasized how the assignment may be treated within the confines of a theme. This approach is new; it has the virtue of making the theoretical discussion of a technique of literary criticism immediately vital to the student. If he can see a literary problem in the light of his necessity to write about it, he is more likely to learn his lesson well. This book might be called a rhetoric of practical criticism for students.

Students need guidance before they write a theme about literature. It is a common complaint among teachers that papers on literary topics written by their students are not really to the point. The reason is simple: the majority of students asked to "analyze the structure of X play, or Y poem, or Z short story" do not really understand what structure is or how to go about analyzing it. Students asked to discuss "point of view in X literary work" are similarly handicapped, and so on through most themes they write about literature. Under these conditions, instructors either waste valuable time explaining theme assignments or else continue to receive inadequate student writing about literature. This book is offered as a solution. Its aim is to free instructors from the drudgery and lost time of making assignments and to help students by explaining and illustrating many approaches to literary technique in order to provide a sound basis for analysis. The practical aim of the book is to aid students in improving their reading and writing skills.

Many other books have been published with these ends in view, but I have not found them satisfactory. They present works by distinguished literary critics like I. A. Richards and Virginia Woolf and deal with subjects like "Badness in Poetry" and "The Novels of Thomas Hardy." Presumably, after reading these masters, the student is expected to imitate them.

I believe that this approach is not practical for the college classroom. The examples from the professional critics and scholar-teachers may exemplify many literary techniques, but their main concern is not to assist the student who has a composition to write. Examples of this sort are anywhere from five to twenty times longer than the composition expected from the student; they are usually subtle and sophisticated, referring with easy familiarity to writers unknown to the student; and the technical approaches are often either too complex or too advanced for the student's use. The result is that he is confused, not helped. At his age he cannot be expected to write as the critics do, nor can he be expected to receive more than limited benefit from the critics. He needs clear directions and short examples that are not only in accord with his understanding but similar to the theme he is expected to write. The assignments in this book fit this need. All have been worked out in the classroom and have demonstrably helped students improve their themes about literature.

Even though the assignments can stand alone, they may be used as bases for discussions before assignments are due or as supplements to the discussions. Of course, the assignments may be modified if you so desire. In their present form, however, they can assist you immeasurably in the assigning of themes. Too frequently, when assignments are made orally, students lose important directions; many a slip occurs between your words and the student's notebook. This book is therefore designed to make assignments clear and unequivocal so that no questions should arise late on the night before an assignment is due.

Each chapter is devoted to the consideration of a separate literary approach that creates a problem in composition. There is first a discussion of the problems caused by the particular assignment and then a sample theme that should be within the scope of the undergraduate. The discussions are always focused on critical techniques as they bear on writing assigned to students. The sample themes show how a student might handle the various assignments. Although some students will follow the patterns closely, others will wish to adapt the discussions and samples to their own needs. The result in either case should be superior student writing.

The samples have been conceived and written in the belief that the word *imitation* does not need to be preceded by words like *slavish* or *mere*. Much poor composition results from uncertainty about what is expected in the way of imitation. While the student seeks a *form* in which to express himself, he dissipates his energies and does not devote enough attention to a careful study of the literary text that has been assigned. If the student can learn from the discussion of a technical problem and can compare this discussion with a sample theme, he will set his mind working in the right channels and produce superior themes.

For illustrative purposes, the sample themes are slightly long, yet they are within the approximate lengths of most undergraduate themes. Although the various lengths cannot always coincide with the word-limits set by individual instructors, the organization and method of the samples should be, and have been demonstrated to be, helpful. These samples should be regarded both as goals toward which the freshman can work and as guides for more advanced students.

In order to make the sample themes as meaningful as possible, the present edition of *Writing Themes About Literature,* like the first, includes the passages from works on which there are analytical and stylistic themes. To do the same for as many of the other sample themes as possible, a new appendix (C) is included in this edition. This appendix contains the complete texts of five poems and also the texts of Swift's "Digression on Madness," Lawrence's "The Horse Dealer's Daughter," and Hardy's "The Three Strangers." Obviously, the other works on which there are sample themes would lengthen the book beyond reason. The stories not included here are frequently anthologized, however, and the novels are readily available in paperback editions. The play by Pinter, *The Homecoming,* might be made available in the library reserve room.

There are, of course, frequent references throughout the book to many literary works, and it is unlikely that any student will yet have encountered all. Because references cannot be justified unless they clarify, I have tried to make each one self-explanatory and have included enough details to achieve this end. Lack of familiarity with the particular work being discussed therefore should not deter a student from understanding the point of the reference. In addition, I have tried to refer to works that a college student is likely to encounter, if not in freshman English, then in survey or other upper-level courses, or even, let us hope, in his own independent reading. Thus, there are many references to Shakespeare's plays and sonnets, to Joyce's *Portrait of the Artist,* and also to Dreiser's *Sister Carrie.*

The chapters have been arranged in an order of increasing difficulty and technicality. Although a full-year course could be devoted to the progression of themes from beginning to end, you may wish to assign the same type of theme on different works of literature until the students show mastery of that particular type. You might also base theme assignments on single aspects of any one chapter. Thus, a single-paragraph theme might be written on the images in only a single stanza of poetry; an entire theme might be devoted to only the rhythm (or the segmental poetic devices) in a poem or to the diction (or the grammar) in a passage of prose. The same might be done for a certain trait of a character, for the effect of point of view on the reader's understanding of a character, and so on. In whatever way the assignments are used, they offer a thematic unity to an entire year's course in composition—namely, writing themes about literature. In addition, I believe that the student beyond the freshman year will continue to find the book useful, because the advanced assignments here are as difficult and technical as those for upper-division courses.

The book offers a practical solution to a very real problem in many composition courses. Composition is frequently regarded as a service, for it teaches writing techniques essential in all college work. This need has forced the content in composition to cover too wide a range of subject matter. There can be little unity when students write themes on topics derived from many unrelated fields. All this material is usually taught by instructors who have been prepared by years of literary study. Here is the rub: although you yourself may want to teach literature as a discipline and as a pleasure, you know that your students must have intense work on composition for all their other college work. One purpose of this book is to reconcile this conflict by unifying the course and making it challenging to you as well as to the student. Using the assignments here, you can satisfy the needs of your course by teaching composition while you satisfy your own discipline by teaching literature and literary techniques. Although these assignments attempt to integrate the teaching of literature and composition, many have a residual effect on other courses. For example, the lesson learned from the comparison-contrast theme can be applied to the heredity-environment controversy in a psychology or sociology class; or the themes on tone and point of view will benefit the student of political science who must read and analyze speeches.

An almost foolproof solution to another difficulty in teaching composition—plagiarism—is offered. During the semester, for example, you might assign a theme about the main idea in "The Garden Party," whereas during the next you might assign a theme about the main idea in *Macbeth,* and so on. In colleges and universities where a common syllabus is used in all freshman courses, the same procedure could be followed uniformly. This plan, whereby the form of each theme is preserved while the subject material is changed, could render extinct the traditional fraternity-house theme barrel. The possibilities for varied assignments are virtually endless.

Most important of all, however, is that the book is aimed at the appreciation of good literature. Literature is the property of all; its appeal is to all. But literature, as an art, employs techniques and offers problems that can be understood only through analysis, and analysis means work. The immediate aim is to help the student in this work, but the primary object of the book is to promote the pleasurable study and, finally, the love of literature.

To the Student

The chapters in this book are theme assignments based on a number of analytical approaches important in literary criticism. The assignments are presented in the hope of fulfilling two goals of English courses: (1) to write good themes, and (2) to assimilate great works of literature into the imagination. Negatively, the book aims to avoid themes that are no more than synopses of a work, vague statements of like or dislike, or biographies of an author. Positively, the book aims to raise your standards of judging literature—and therefore your ability to appreciate good literature—by requiring you to apply, in well-prepared themes, the techniques of good reading.

No educational process is finished until you have applied what you have learned. The need to apply something forces you to recognize where your learning is complete and where it is incomplete and application forces you to strengthen your knowledge and supplement your deficiencies. Thus, your grasp of a literary concept like *point of view* will not be complete until you write about the point of view in a particular work. As you write, you may suddenly discover that you need to go back to the work, to study your notes on it, and to compare them with what you understand about the problem itself. In writing, you must verify facts, grasp their relationship to your topic, develop insights into the value and artistry of the work, and express your understanding in a well-organized and well-developed theme. After you have finished a number of such themes, you should be able to approach other literary works with more certainty and skill. The more you know and the more you can apply, the more expert and demanding will be your critical taste.

WHAT IS LITERARY ANALYSIS?

Analysis attempts to find truth. The process of analysis is to divide a problem into various parts, for although a whole object is difficult to comprehend at one glance, the parts may be examined more easily, and their natures, functions, and interrelationships may be more fully understood when they are examined one by one. For example, if you have the problem in chemical qualitative analysis of discovering the elements in a chemical solution, you can make only one test on the solution at a time, because if you tried to make all your tests at once you would not be able to control or distinguish your results.

The analysis of literature is based on the same truth. Although the work you have read is an entirety, you must make separate inquiries in order to discover its full meaning and to appreciate it fully. You could not talk about everything in *Paradise Lost* at once, for example, without being guilty of the greatest superficiality. It is better, in your discussion, to narrow the scope of your topic by talking about the diction, epic conventions, theology, or dramatic action. An attempt to discuss everything at once would inevitably distort some things and omit others; results of this sort of investigation are usually wrong or misleading. Truth, however, can emerge only where all possibilities are considered. So your problem in making an analysis is to make the subject small enough to go deeply into it. In other words, you can write a good theme about a relatively restricted part or aspect of the work you have read; but you would find it impossible to discuss everything unless your analysis grew to the length of a book.

A serious objection sometimes arises about literary analysis. Although scientific analysis is necessary, it is said that too much literary analysis "spoils" appreciation of a work, or that in making an analysis, you "murder" literature as you "dissect" it. This objection is not valid, for the purpose of analysis is not to cut up literature like a frog and leave it in pieces. No matter how completely you analyze a work, you cannot do that; the work will remain healthy and untouched. For example, the fourth voyage of Swift's *Gulliver's Travels* has not been changed by all the critical essays that have been written about it. But what has changed is what people *see* in the fourth voyage. It used to be that critics saw evidence in the work that Swift hated mankind. More recent analyses of the work have disclosed evidence that Swift was a humanitarian urging men to change their behavior by steering a course between emotion and pure reason. Other analyses have seen the work as an appeal to follow religion. The effect of these and other analyses of the work has been to uncover its rich complexity and its basic affirmation of life, and ultimately to raise it in critical esteem. Such is the real business of literary analysis. By pointing out the author's insights into problems of life, and by describing various aspects of his skill, literary analysis aims at the appreciation of literary excellence.

It is therefore important for you to keep literary analysis in perspective: analyzing a work is a *means* toward appreciation and evaluation, not an end in itself. It is an honest attempt by you, the reader, to discover the truth about a work and to base your appreciation on your own thought and discovery, not on a vaguely aesthetic reaction. If you analyze the work to know it better and to like it better, you have really dismissed the entire objection.

As you think about what to put into your theme, remember that literary analysis is a way of getting at the heart of the work. To this end, there are four broad areas that literary analysis explores: (1) meaning, (2) structure, (3) style, and (4) background and influences. There is usually overlapping among these; for example, in writing about *point of view*, you would emphasize its impact on both meaning and style. In discussing background and influences, you might emphasize how things seemingly extraneous to the work enable a fuller comprehension of meaning, structure, and style. It is always wise, in fact, to emphasize that your particular topic has a relation to the entire work. In this way you are really demonstrating the relationship of literary analysis to literary appreciation, which is the goal implied in all intelligent discourse about literature and in all themes about literature.

WHAT IS A THEME?

As you begin any of the following assignments, you should consider the following ideas about the nature of themes. A theme should be a short, accurate, and forceful presentation of ideas or descriptions, well contrived as a totality or unity. A theme should not ramble in any way, but should be clearly united around a dominating thought or *central idea*. A theme is a brief "mind's full" on any particular subject; that is, it presents and considers the subject in several of its various aspects. The theme cannot cover all aspects, as might a book or a long essay.

There are two basic needs that you must always remember: the first is for a *central idea* or *point,* and the second is for a *clearly ascertainable organization.*

The Central Idea or Point

Themes are so named because throughout the composition called a *theme* there runs a basic or central idea—a theme—that unifies the paper into a logical whole. On every subject you encounter there should be some dominating idea or mood that will suggest itself to you or one that you will derive from your own intensive concentration. For example, when you look at a room, you might feel that it is cheerful; when you listen to the latest news, you might decide that it is depressing. Were you to write a theme describing the room or another discussing the news, you would have to keep your central idea foremost in your reader's mind *throughout* your theme, or else you would not have a theme.

You should first bring out your central idea in the introduction. State your point clearly, for your reader must be left in no doubt about what you wish to assert. Your point might be that the story is well unified, or that it is about the folly of attempting what is beyond man's power, or about the necessity for dedication regardless of the consequences, and so on. Throughout your theme, you must constantly keep reminding your reader that your material is relevant to the point you have made; you must always emphasize the connection between your dominant idea and whatever you are saying at the moment. Anything not relevant to your point does not belong in the theme.

The need for a central idea will also make you aware of the need for paragraph transitions, because you are proving or showing *one* central idea, not a *number* of ideas. Transitions form bridges to connect one part of the theme with another; having a central idea always in mind makes continuity between paragraphs both essential and natural.

Organizing Your Theme Around the Central Idea

Once you have thought of a central idea, you should make notes of materials that support it. You will need to treat these materials in order, and in your introduction you should write a sentence that describes this order. This sentence is called a *thesis sentence*. Thus the introduction is important for your whole theme: first because it announces the central idea, and second because it announces the pattern of the theme, through which the central idea should be carefully woven.

As the whole theme is organized around the thesis sentence, each paragraph should be organized around a *topic sentence*. Here is a brief outline to illustrate the meaning of these terms. The type of theme is the "Specific Problem," and the question is, "In Katherine Mansfield's story, 'Miss Brill,' is the character Miss Brill worth your sympathy?"

Theme

Miss Brill as a Sympathetic
Character

Paragraph 1   INTRODUCTION containing CENTRAL IDEA and THESIS SENTENCE

CENTRAL IDEA: Miss Brill is worth my sympathy.

THESIS SENTENCE: She is made worthy of sympathy because of her harmless character, because of her loneliness, and because of Katherine Mansfield's skillful treatment of her plight.

Paragraph 2   TOPIC SENTENCE: Because Miss Brill is harmless, the hurt done to her seems unjustified and unnecessarily cruel.

Paragraph 3   TOPIC SENTENCE: Miss Brill's loneliness and vulnerability make her naturally pitiable.

Paragraph 4   TOPIC SENTENCE: Miss Mansfield's restrained, objective treatment of Miss Brill's heartbreak prevents sentimentality and encourages exactly the right proportion of sympathy.

Paragraph 5   CONCLUSION: Miss Brill is pictured realistically as a lonely human being in trouble, and this picture justifies sympathy.

This illustration shows, in its simplest and most rudimentary form, the function of the thesis sentence and topic sentences in organizing a theme, and it demonstrates the relationship between the two. Of course as you become more experienced, you will vary these elements in your theme, making them more subtle and less obvious. They are explicitly stated here for purposes of illustration. Because the thesis sentence and topic sentence are basic concepts in composition and are sometimes regarded as interchangeable, they are constantly distinguished throughout this book. To assist you, these sentences are marked in the first three sample themes. After this point you will have acquired enough skill to distinguish them for yourself.

The Main Problem in Writing

Once you have understood and applied the principles of thematic development and thesis-sentence organization, you will still be faced with the problem of how to write well. There is little difficulty in recognizing superior examples of student writing when you see them, but there is usually much difficulty in understanding precisely what constitutes the superiority. For this reason the most difficult and perplexing questions you will ask as you write are these: (1) "How can I improve my writing?" or (2) "If I got a *C* on my last paper, why wasn't the grade a *B* or an *A?* How can I improve my grades?" These questions are really both the same, with a different emphasis. Your concern is with improvement.

As an undergraduate, you should not be offended if you are told that you probably have not yet acquired a great deal of knowledge and understanding of literature. Your mind is growing, and it still has many facts to assimilate and digest. As you accumulate these facts and develop your understanding, you will find that ease of expression will also develop. But at the moment your thoughts about literature might be expressed thus: "When I first read a work, I have a hard time following it. Yet when my instructor explains it, my understanding is greatly increased. I would like to develop the ability to understand the work without my instructor's help. How can I succeed in this aim? How can I become an independent reader?"

In answer, you started trying to overcome the problem the day you enrolled in college. This action testifies to your desire to improve. Bear in mind also that education is a process, and that what baffled you as a freshman may seem child's play when you are a junior or senior. But in the meantime you want to know how to assist growth. There is no magic answer, no shortcut to knowledge. You must work. In your literature classes, here are some habits that you should develop and always pursue.

1 Study each reading assignment carefully. Look up all words that you do not know.

2 For further study, underline what seem to be key passages. Write some of these passages on cards, and carry the cards with you. Then, when you are riding or walking to class, or at other times, try to memorize key phrases and sentences and lines of poetry.

3 Make notes on interesting characterizations, events, and ideas. If you like a character, say so, and try to describe what you like about him. If you dislike an idea, say so, and try to describe what you dislike about it.

4 Try to see patterns developing. Make an outline of the story or main idea. What are the conflicts in the story? How are these resolved? Is one force, or side, triumphant? Why? Or is the conflict unresolved?

5 Do you see anything in the story that you do not understand? Do not forget the difficulty; write a note about it and ask your instructor in class.

The second major obstacle to writing well is inexperience. As a result, when you start you may be tempted simply to write a *synopsis* of the story or argument. A synopsis of a work is inadequate for your themes, mainly because a synopsis does not indicate real *understanding*.

Your education is aimed first at the *acquisition* of knowledge and secondly at the *digestion* and *use* of knowledge. A synopsis indicates only that you have read the material. Therefore if you wish to show your understanding, you must do something more—you must show that you can put what you have read into a meaningful pattern.

The theme assignments in this book are designed to help you do just that. As you work out each assignment, you will be dealing with particular methods of assimilating and using knowledge. In only one assignment are you asked to provide a synopsis: this is the *summary theme,* but even here, the synopsis is relevant only if it can be related to your central idea. The summary theme (Chapter 1) therefore represents more thought and organization than does a synopsis. In all the other assignments in this book you are asked to concentrate on a particular point raised in the study of literature. In every case it is important that you read and follow the work, but it is more important that you show your understanding of the work.

There are a number of ways in which you may set up patterns of development that can assist you in avoiding mere synopsis. One student may make a deliberate point of discussing the conclusion of a story *first;* in this way he can break the rigid order of following the story from first to last and can thus impose his *own organization* on the theme. Another student may write to a mythical reader who has just finished reading the assigned work but who has not yet had time to think about it and understand it fully. Then, when this student-writer writes, he does not need to tell his imaginary reader *what* happens but can concentrate instead on *why* things happen. This method has proved extremely successful. Let us look briefly at two examples of student writing to see how this writer-reader frame of mind can operate to improve writing. These examples are from themes analyzing Thomas Hardy's story "The Three Strangers."

1

After a short lapse of time, the second stranger enters. He tells the guests that he is en route to Casterbridge, and he relates his occupation by singing a song. The second stranger is the hangman who is supposed to hang a man in Casterbridge for stealing sheep. As he reveals his occupation, an air of dismay is cast upon the guests.

2

Hardy deepens his plot with the entrance of the second stranger—a brash, selfish, demonlike figure who reveals in a grim song that he is a hangman. Since he is going to Casterbridge to hang a man for stealing a sheep, his manner fills the shepherds, poor themselves, with dismay. Their response serves Hardy's purpose of developing both sympathy for the shepherds and anger toward inhumanity in the law.

The first column is adequate but no more, for it illustrates only superficial knowledge. The second column illustrates *understanding* and is therefore superior. Phrases like "Hardy deepens his plot" and "Hardy's purpose" illustrate that the writer of the second column is assuming that his reader knows the story, but wants to read an interpretation. Notice too that the second column is more compressed than the first, even though it is longer (69 words to 62). Its greater length is caused by greater *play of mind* (to borrow a phrase from Matthew Arnold). Compare again the information contained in these two parts of the paragraph:

. . . the second stranger enters. He tells the guests that he is en route to Casterbridge, and he relates his occupation by singing a song. The second stranger is the hangman. . . .

. . . the second stranger—a brash, selfish, demonlike figure who reveals in a grim song that he is a hangman. Since he is going to Casterbridge. . . .

The subject matter of the two passages is essentially the same, but the second column says in twenty-five words more than the first column does in thirty.

The answer to that difficult question about how to make *C* writing into *A* writing is probably to be found in the comparison of the two columns. Besides using English correctly, the superior writer always allows his mind to play upon the materials. The superior writer always tries to give the results of his thoughts to the reader. He dares to trust his responses and is not afraid to go out on a limb. When he refers to events in a story, he embodies observations and interpretations in his remarks. Observe that there is a play of mind operating in this sentence, though the sentence also refers to events:

> Since he is going to Casterbridge to hang a man for stealing a sheep, his manner fills the shepherds, poor themselves, with dismay.

Notice the words "since" and "poor themselves." These have been introduced by the writer to indicate relationships—causes and effects. There is knowledge here, but more importantly, there is also *use* of this knowledge. If the quality of good writing can be located, it resides in the inclusion of words of this sort and in the understanding shown by that inclusion. If you wonder how to improve your writing and your grades, the answer is: work constantly toward writing that will demonstrate your *understanding.* Grammar, organization, central idea—all these are important, but all are subordinate to understanding.

Keeping to Your Point

Whenever you write a theme about literature, then, you must strenuously try to show your understanding. Your greatest problem is that of unity. Once you have gone off on a tangent, you are following the material rather than leading it. If you can stick to your point, however, you will be mastering the material and thereby showing understanding.

Let us look at another example. The following paragraph is taken from a theme on the "Idea of Personal Responsibility in *The Odyssey.*" This is the third paragraph; the writer has stated his thematic purposes in the first paragraph, and in the second has shown that various characters in *The Odyssey* believe men are responsible for their actions and must bear the consequences. In the third paragraph he writes:

More forcefully significant than these statements of the idea is the way it is demonstrated in the actions of the characters in the epic. Odysseus, the hero, is the prime example. Entrapped by Polyphemus (the son of Poseidon the Earth-Shaker by the nymph Thoosa) and threatened with death, Odysseus in desperation puts out the eye of his captor, who then begs his father Poseidon for vengeance. Answering his son's anguished curse, Poseidon frustrates Odysseus at every turn in the voyage back to Ithaca, and forces him to wander for ten years before reaching home.

This paragraph shows how easily a person may be diverted from his objective in writing. The first sentence adequately states that the idea is to be demonstrated in the actions of the epic. That the remainder of the paragraph concentrates on Odysseus is no flaw, because the writer concentrates on other characters in following paragraphs. The flaw is that the material about Odysseus does not go beyond mere synopsis; it does not come to grips with the announced topic of personal responsibility; it does not indicate understanding. The material may be relevant to the topic, but the writer does not point out its relevance. The writer began well, but he did not show how the material illustrates his point, and thus the paragraph is bad. Remember always that in expository writing you should not rely on making your meaning clear simply by implication; you must make all relationships explicitly clear.

Let us see how this problem can be solved. If the ideal paragraph could be schematized with line drawings, we might say that the paragraph's topic should be a straight line, moving toward and reaching a specific goal (explicit meaning), with an exemplifying line moving away from the straight line briefly in order to bring in material, but returning to the line after each new fact in order to demonstrate the relevance of this fact. Thus, the ideal scheme would look like this:

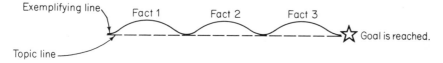

Notice that the exemplifying line, or the example or the documenting line, always returns to the topic line. A scheme for the paragraph on *The Odyssey*, however, would look like this:

How might this paragraph be improved? The best way is to reintroduce the topic again and again throughout the paragraph, in order to

keep reminding the reader of the relevance of the exemplifying material.
Each time you mention the topic you are bringing yourself back to the
line or back to the point, and this practice should prevail no matter
what the topic. If you are analyzing *tone*, for example, you should keep
pointing out the relevance of your material to the tone of the work, and
the same applies to *structure* or whatever aspect of literature you are
studying. According to this principle, we might revise the paragraph on
The Odyssey as follows, keeping as much of the original wording as we
can. (Parts of sentences stressing the relationship of the examples to
the topic of the paragraph are italicized.)

> More forcefully significant than these statements of the idea is the way it
> is demonstrated in the actions of the characters in the epic. Odysseus, the
> hero, is the prime example. When he is entrapped and threatened with
> death by Polyphemus (the son of Poseidon the Earth-Shaker by the nymph
> Thoosa), Odysseus in desperation puts out the eye of his captor. Though
> his action is justifiable on grounds of self-preservation *he must, according
> to the main idea, suffer the consequences.* Polyphemus begs his father
> Poseidon for vengeance. Poseidon hears, *and accordingly this god becomes
> the means of enforcing Odysseus' punishment,* since Odysseus, in injuring
> the god's son, has insulted the god. The Ithacan king's ten years of frus-
> tration and exile are therefore not caused by whimsy; *they are punishment
> for his own action. Here the idea of personal responsibility is shown with
> a vengeance;* despite the extenuating circumstances, *the epic makes clear
> that characters must answer for their acts.*

The paragraph has been lengthened and improved. You might
object that if all your paragraphs were lengthened in this way your
theme would grow too long. The answer to this objection is that it is
better to develop a few topics fully than many scantily. Such revision
might require you to throw away some of your topics or else to incorporate them as subpoints in the topics you keep. This process can only
improve your theme. But the result of greater length here is that the
exemplifying detail points toward the topic, and the paragraph reaches
its goal.

The same need for sticking to your point is true of your entire
theme, for you will not be successful unless you have thoroughly convinced your reader that your central idea is valid or true. The two following themes should illustrate this truth. The theme on the left is only
rudimentary. The writer suggests at the outset that he will explore the
harm the parents cause their children in the two plays being compared.
Although occasionally he gets back to this point, the theme rarely gets
above the level of synopsis. The theme in the right-hand column is
superior because the writer announces his central idea and pursues it
throughout. As in the earlier paragraph, those parts of the following
themes that emphasize the central idea will be italicized. The type of
theme is *comparison-contrast* (Chapter 8), and the assignment was made

specifically on Arthur Miller's *All My Sons* and Tennessee Williams's *The Glass Menagerie.*

Theme 1	**Theme 2**

Theme 1

A COMPARISON OF TWO PLAYS

Theme 2

THE DESTRUCTION OF CHILDREN BY PARENTS IN TWO PLAYS

Miller's *All My Sons* and Williams's *The Glass Menagerie* are the two plays being compared. Both plays have the family as the center around which the characters revolve. In both families, *the parents hurt the children.* Miller writes of a well-off, factory-owning family; Williams of a low-class family.

In both Miller's *All My Sons* and Williams's *The Glass Menagerie,* the family is the center of the action. Miller's family is well off; Williams's is lower class. This difference is not material in view of the fact that both dramatists demonstrate the *destructive effects of parents upon children,* regardless of class. It is true that these parents were once children themselves, and that presumably they were recipients of *equally destructive effects from their parents.* This element gives both plays direct, universal appeal: that is, both plays dramatize the process by which our society is *generally hurt by what,* to the dramatists, *are outmoded economic and social values, transmitted by parents to children.* The fathers, mothers, and children will be discussed in that order.

The comparison of the families may start with the fathers. Joe Keller, of *All My Sons,* is an ambitious, conniving, and good businessman. He allows a defective shipment to go through because, as he says, he could not let forty years' work go down the drain. He also says to Chris that he did what he did because he wanted Chris to have something for his future, a business. Not much is mentioned of the father in *The Glass Menagerie,* but from what is given the reader, we picture him as a worthless drunkard. He had no purpose in life and consequently was a poor provider for his family. One should

The fathers in both plays seem to be the ones *first to do hurt,* because they both lack responsibility and social conscience. Joe Keller is shown as ambitious and conniving—qualities which in America go to form the good businessman. The Wingfield father, never seen except in portrait but only described, is a drifter and worthless drunkard. *Both are irresponsible. Joe's unscrupulousness causes the death of twenty-one boys who flew in airplanes made defective by his deliberate negligence.* The Wingfield father simply *abandons his family.* The trouble is that both characters are simply pawns in a not condone Keller for what he did, but at least Keller had some initiative and foresight whereas the Wingfield father had nothing. *Both fathers hurt their children.*

Next we can compare the mothers in the two works. In Miller's play the mother is a sensitive, unyielding, and loving person. It is she who stands firm in her belief that Larry is still living. By doing this she prevents her other son Chris from marrying Ann. In a sense, she is looking out for her son's interest because if Larry was ever to return, chaos would result. Amanda, the mother in *The Glass Menagerie,* is a very sociable person. Her daughter is unbelievably shy. The mother attempts to help her daughter. She does, also, what she thinks will be in the interests of her daughter. Therefore she concludes that marriage is the answer to Laura's problems. We can see how two different mothers with the same goals—happiness for their children—*achieve the opposite results because they fail to attend to the needs and desires of their children.*

Lastly, the children will be compared. Chris is both an idealistic as well as realistic person. He tries to think the best of people, as he does

game much larger than themselves. Joe's defense of his action, for example, makes good sense. *His motives are not bad* from a short-term point of view. He really did not want to let forty years of work go down the drain, and he really did want to give Chris (and Larry) a thriving business. His means, however, *were selfish and hurtful—primarily economic rather than human and loving—*just as the Wingfield father causes his family *untold damage* by abandoning them for a life that to many might seem very pleasant.

While less *creators of hurt* than *agents of it,* the mothers in both families also *cause much damage.* Kate Keller, while sensitive and unyielding, is nevertheless loving. Her firm belief that her son Larry is still alive is caused, we ultimately learn, by a defense against her awareness of *Joe's great crime,* but *the end result is the unhappiness of her son Chris.* Her love is mixed with a *deliberately unreal outlook.* While superficially different from Kate, *Amanda is similarly destructive.* Attempting to look out for the interests of her daughter, she tries to make a carbon copy of herself, even though her background is dead as far as her daughter is concerned. Her failure is that she does not see her daughter as an individual with separate and distinct needs. Laura's reaction to her mother's manipulation is *withdrawal,* but Amanda cannot see any *harmful effect.* Both mothers, desiring to make their children happy, *produce the same unhappy results.*

The full effects of *these destructive parents are felt by the children.* Larry, we learn, *has killed himself because of shame for his father's* with his father. When he finds out otherwise he is *terribly shocked and disappointed.* Much the same thing happens when Laura finds out that Jim is going to get married; her reaction is one of *disappointment and withdrawal.* Just when she has finally gotten socially involved with someone, he leaves. So we see how both children have to put up with *disappointments;* one finds out his father is a murderer, while the other loses the first person she ever loved.

deed. Chris, we see demonstrated, *is shocked, angered, and embittered by it. Laura is disappointed,* ostensibly by hearing that Jim is going to marry another, but ultimately by having been brought up *without a father and with her mentally disjointed mother.* Tom simply leaves, but he remembers his mother objectively and his father condescendingly. *While a bang marks the destruction* in *All My Sons,* one might say that a sigh— or a whimper—marks it in *The Glass Menagerie.* But the effects of the parents on the children, and beyond that of the society on its members, are the same—*destruction and decay.*

Through comparing and contrasting the members of each family we have been able to see how these families are different and how they are similar. In both *families, however, the children are hurt by well-intentioned* but foolish parents.

Comparing and contrasting the two families in this way finally brings out their basic similarities. The parents in both families are interesting and not particularly abnormal. In both groups of parents there are strongly contrasting values which contend to *the destruction of children.* In the Kellers it is *money against humanity.* In the Wingfields it is *social position against individuality.* In both families *everyone really loses,* because neither family is clearly enough committed to the ideas of humanity and individuality. Though the relevance of this theme to society at large has been only mentioned, the implication in both plays is that our society must make a commitment to human and individual values if it is to survive. If people do not make this commitment, *the destructive patterns in the Keller and Wingfield families will continue.*

There is another reason for the superiority of the theme on the right. In addition to sticking to the point, the writer in a number of spots suggests that the harmful influences of the parents are related to impractical or unjust economic values. At the end, the writer interprets his central idea by stating that society at large needs to commit itself to human values. In short, *the writer has made his idea grow.* He has not simply exemplified it but has tried to delve into some of its implications. You should be trying, always, to develop your central ideas in a similar way. Admittedly, in a short theme you will be able to move only a short distance with an idea, but you should never be satisfied to leave an idea exactly where you find it. Nurture it and make it grow. Constantly adhere to your topic and constantly develop it.

Whenever you write, keep this lesson in mind. Keep returning to the point you wish to make; regard the material of the work you have studied as material to prove your point, not as material to be described. Keep demonstrating that all exemplifying detail is relevant to your main point. Keep trying to develop your topic; make it bigger than it was when you began writing. If you observe these precepts, you should be well on the way toward handling any of the following theme assignments successfully.

The Summary Theme

1 The summary theme presents a number of important objectives for you as you begin writing themes about literature. First, you should show in the theme that you are able intelligently to follow and to understand the actions and dialogue in a literary work. Second, you should demonstrate your awareness that in literature, as in life, some actions and statements are more significant than others. Third, you should attempt to show that the events in the work do not occur haphazardly but take place as part of a pattern or form. If you can achieve the first objective in your theme, you have reached a plane, a platform, of understanding. If you can achieve the second and third objectives, you will demonstrate that you possess the insight and alertness needed for putting things together, for creating the new awarenesses that characterize the best thinking and writing.

The summary theme therefore represents a building block for the other kinds of themes to follow. Before you write a theme about the *structure* of a poem or a novel, for example, you must be sure that you understand the story and the main idea behind it and also that you can describe the relation of one part of the work to the others. If you cannot perform these basic tasks of the disciplined reader, everything you say about structure will be inaccurate or misleading. In short, the writing of a summary theme anticipates all the other writing about literature that you will do.

The first requirement for writing a summary theme is to read the assigned work carefully: be sure to take notes on the important events or ideas; be sure to look up all words that you do not know; be sure that you are able to understand the special context of the work. Without a knowledge of the context, you can get into difficulty. For example, a student once interpreted Wordsworth's poem "The Solitary Reaper" as

1

Wordsworth's celebration of the advent of the industrial age, since this student thought all the descriptions referred to the McCormick reaper! If he had provided himself with a wider context by reading even a few of Wordsworth's other poems, and also by checking the date of the invention of the reaper, he could have avoided this absurdity.

What Do You Summarize?

Once you have collected your notes on the work, you face the fundamental problem of exactly what to summarize. This problem may seem simple at first glance, but the experience of many students has shown otherwise. Most defects in summary themes result from an apparently imperfect idea of what is needed. You can solve the problem—and produce a good summary theme—if you keep the following in mind; in the literary work that you will be asked to summarize, there are two major elements that you should consider. The English novelist E. M. Forster has conveniently classified these elements.[1] The first is the *story*, or the main events, details, or happenings in the work as they appear in chronological order. The second is the *plot*, or the reasons or logic underlying the story and causing that story to take the *form* it does. The essence of plot is the existence of a *conflict* between opposing forces —either man against man singly or in groups, man against himself, or man against some natural or supernatural force. The conflict produces those actions and interactions that culminate in a *climax* or *dénouement*. In other words, attention to plot requires you to formulate some idea of the *why* and the *how* of the story, not just the *what*.

There is little question, of course, about what happens in the story, since all the events are before you and can easily be verified. But there is more room for interpretation and subjectivity about the plot, because the reasons why characters do things are not always clear, even to the characters themselves, and also because a particular work of literature may mean many things at once, all equally deducible from the story.

To show that the plot may be described in different ways, the short story summarized in the sample theme, F. Scott Fitzgerald's "Babylon Revisited," may be illuminating. The story relates the unsuccessful attempts of a man to regain custody of his nine-year-old daughter from his in-laws, who took the child when he was confined to a sanitarium for alcoholism. The plot, however, is not as easily described, and discussion of the story might bring out the following ideas about what the plot is: (1) the past constantly influences the present, (2) moral stability and strength can be acquired only at great cost, (3) wealth destroys human values and perspectives, (4) thoughtless or frivolous action produces un-

---

[1] *Aspects of the Novel* (New York: Harcourt, Brace & World, Inc., 1927), p. 130.

foreseeable consequences, and (5) men must answer for their actions even though they are driven by forces that they cannot control. Each one of these statements, taken singly or collectively, would serve as a satisfactory description of the plot. They do not cancel themselves out but complement and enrich each other.

Regardless of the work you have read, to write a good summary *theme* you must not only summarize the story but also must convey to your reader an explanation of why the story is as it is—in short, you must treat the plot as a part of your summary in order to convey an idea of the organization of the story. All these must be included in your summary theme.

Indeed, the principal danger in writing a summary theme is that you will neglect the plot and organization. It is entirely possible, for example, to summarize the main events without ever giving a hint of why those events take place. The objection to a simple summary of events is that it gives the impression of low understanding. However, if you assume that your reader has not read the work you are summarizing, you will realize that he wants to know not only the events (story), but also the reasons why the events happen together with at least a rudimentary explanation of the logic underlying the organization of the work.

You must therefore study your notes on the story or play carefully. Observe whether the events you noted fit into any sort of pattern. What seem to be the main points of the story? How do these events fit the main points? In *Oedipus Rex,* for example, you might determine that the events occur as part of a plan to illustrate Oedipus's pride; that is, you might say that all the events in the play are either caused by his pride or cause him to realize that he is proud; his realization may be regarded as the climax of the play. The plot may then be stated as an attempt to show that excessive pride causes destruction.

You may observe that there is usually disagreement and discussion about plot; indeed, some of your classroom discussions have shown that different persons may make entirely different interpretations. Such diversity is no problem, for instead of being a cause of uncertainty, it is a means of enrichment. Use your study to draw your own conclusions; decide what the main points are and what events are important in the making of these points. Above all, remember that events in works of fiction do not simply happen; they are always included by the author as part of a plan or idea. *Discover that plan or idea.*

Planning Your Theme

Once you have made your decision about the main idea of the story, you arrive at the recurrent problem of organization. Remember that you are writing a summary *theme,* and that a theme by definition must contain a dominating plan or idea. Remember also that your theme will be considerably shorter than the work you are summarizing, and that your theme is *not* that work but *your own*. All statements that you make must necessarily be your own, with the exception of short quotations from the text (which are desirable). Although what you say is *about* the original, it is your own work and must necessarily be *unlike* the original.

All these considerations will make you realize that when you write any theme you must be in charge and remain in charge. Therefore, you must decide what will be *your* central idea, which will be a statement describing what you consider to be the plot (e.g., "In this novel the main theme is the growth from childhood to adulthood," or "In this play the main character realizes the folly of trying to set himself above Fate," and so on). Without doubt it is difficult to make sure that your interpretation of the main point will coincide with that of your instructor, but remember that he will prefer any interpretation to none at all. You might realize that your interpretation is not necessarily the final and only answer to the question of plot. What you are trying to present here is an idea that will serve you as a basis for your *theme*. You should attempt an interpretation and use it as your central idea. Once you have done so, you are on the way to the development of your critical powers in using your central idea throughout your theme, and your instructor will honor your interpretation. Where you can go wrong is not in your interpretation, but in failing to maintain that interpretation as a central idea everywhere in your theme; in that event, it is your theme, not your interpretation, that is bad.

You should state your central idea in a thesis sentence, which will (a) state the plan of the work, and also (b) organize your own theme and enable you to bring out your central idea. A thesis sentence might be, "This growth is described by Mark Twain in an extensive trip on a raft down the Mississippi River, where numerous adventures cause the narrator, Huck, to grow to maturity despite the restrictive background from which he has come." Once you have decided on a central idea and thesis sentence, fill in the details of your theme and do the job of writing it.

Writing the Theme

In writing you need to follow through with your plan as outlined in your thesis sentence and to include enough detail to bring out your central idea. If you were summarizing *Huckleberry Finn*, for example, you would build on the thesis sentence by mentioning (a) the early events before the trip, and (b) the principal events on and off the river, in such a way that you would emphasize Huck's increasing maturity. Naturally you cannot summarize everything in the story; nor would everything be desirable, for your mythical reader could go to the novel itself if he wanted to know everything. Your use of topic sentences will help you here, for if you say that "The first part of the work describes the common sense of Huck when he is faced with Tom Sawyer's mental extravagances," you do not need to describe every detail but only the most significant ones. Similarly, after you have discussed the "first part," let us assume that there is a second, or third, or fourth part. Before you start summarizing each part, it is absolutely essential that you inform your reader of the new section. Then you need to include only as much detail as exemplifies your topic sentences. The object of your theme is to summarize, accurately, the work of literature assigned; the problem is to stay in control of the material, not merely to say "This happens" and "That happens," but instead to say "This happens as part of this pattern," and "That happens as part of that pattern." Control the material; do not let it control you.

How much detail should you include? You must give your reader as thorough but as brief a knowledge of the work as is possible within the limits of the assignment. If a man is murdered in your story, it is worth saying that "X shoots Y, who dies," or if a man steals a horse, it is interesting and perhaps important to say "Z steals Sheriff Q's horse." Unless details of this sort are essential, however, you should not lengthen your theme by including them. For example, in the ancient *Epic of Gilgamesh,* the hero Gilgamesh is reverent toward the gods and goddesses Anu, Shamash, Ishtar, and Ninsun, but in a summary theme there is no particular advantage in including these names; it is wise simply to say that the hero is pious or reverent. In this way the point is made without the inclusion of interesting but unnecessary details. The intelligence you show in selecting details—distinguishing the essential from the nonessential—will be extremely important in the quality of your finished summary theme.

The Organization of Your Theme

Usually there will be two parts in a summary theme.

PART I: INTRODUCTION

The introduction identifies the **work**, the most significant character or characters, and the general situation; it is the place for your *central idea* and *thesis sentence.* In the introduction you should also describe the most noticeable physical characteristics of the work summarized—that it is a play, story, essay, or novel; that the work is mainly in dialogue, or narration; that the narration of events is accompanied by descriptions of the hero's thoughts; that the story is told by the hero himself; that the description of present events is augmented by reminiscences of past events; that the reader must infer the relationships among the characters; that much of the story is in dialect, and so on.

PART II: THE SUMMARY

The summary itself grows out of your thesis sentence. The development of your theme should follow the form of the work that you are summarizing. That is, you should present the main events as they occur in the story, even if much of the story is related by a flashback method; you should try to re-create the actual movement of the story itself. Remember, however, that what characterizes your theme *as a theme* is your central idea—your general interpretation of the work—and your guiding topic sentences that give unity to each of your paragraphs. Remind yourself constantly as you write that (a) you should closely follow the work you summarize, (b) you should write accurately, precisely, and vividly, and (c) you should use an occasional word, phrase, or passage from the work in order to give your reader at least a taste of the original.

SAMPLE THEME

The Story of F. Scott Fitzgerald's "Babylon Revisited" 2

The short story "Babylon Revisited" is set in Paris shortly after the stock-market crash of 1929. The main character, Charles Wales (i.e., "wails") has experienced a crash too, a moral crash, and is attempting to reconstruct himself. In the indulgent days before the crash, he had become alcoholically neglgent of his family. When he was in a sanitarium to be cured of his alcoholism, his wife died and he relinquished legal control over his daughter Honoria to his sister and brother-in-law (i.e., his dissipations made him forsake his

---

2 In Maurice Baudin, Jr., ed., *Contemporary Short Stories, Volume II* (The American Heritage Series [Indianapolis and New York: Bobbs-Merrill Co., Inc., ca. 1954]), pp. 117-40. All parenthetical page numbers refer to this edition.

honor). Now, able to provide a home for her, he has returned to persuade his in-laws to give Honoria back. *Fitzgerald's theme is that such reconstruction can be effected only with great difficulty; past irresponsibility constantly endangers and frustrates healthy aims in the responsible present.* 〉 CENTRAL IDEA

In what here will be called the first section of the story, Fitzgerald concentrate on Charles's present moral worthiness; in the second he concentrates on the past and how it foils Charles's present plans for happiness; in the third Fitzgerald re-emphasizes Charles's strength of character and his anticipation of future triumph because of this strength. 〉 THESIS SENTENCE

The first part of the story comprises Fitzgerald's sections I and II, in which he emphasizes that Charles has successfully overcome his past, as far as his own character is involved. 〉 TOPIC SENTENCE: FIRST PART OF THESIS SENTENCE

Currently back on his feet and working prosperously in Prague, Charles returns to Paris to see his daughter and his in-laws. He visits the Ritz, a bar that he had frequented in former days, and discovers that everything there is hollow and empty. His one joy is his visit with his daughter Honoria, but his past returns to haunt him when he converses with her legal guardians, Lincoln and Marion Peters (Marion is a distrustful, vengeful, and nearly hysterical woman). Their conversation brings out Marion's belief that Charles's drinking had been a major cause in the death of his wife, Helen. After Charles leaves, he wanders through the Parisian scenes of his former extravagances, pondering his loss. His present moral worthiness is made clear by his refusal to go with a prostitute to her room.

Fitzgerald's second section continues the theme of Charles's moral reform that had concluded the first section, and hence these two sections form a coherent whole. 〉 TOPIC SENTENCE

Charles has lunch with his daughter, who declares her love for him and her dependence upon him. In the café he is met by two former companions in dissipation, Duncan Schaeffer and Lorraine Quarrles, whose frivolousness makes a discord in his present, harmonious sobriety. He and Honoria flee the two, even though they meet later at a variety show. It is as though Fitzgerald is showing that the past still encumbers Charles, no matter how strongly he tries to escape it.

The story's second part, composed of Fitzgerald's sections III and IV, demonstrates the hurtful effects of the past on the present. 〉 TOPIC SENTENCE: SECOND PART OF THESIS SENTENCE

In section III, the theme of Charles's determination to overcome the past is pursued to a temporarily successful climax. His manner and conversation convince Marion, the chief skeptic about his reformation, that he is now fit to care for Honoria, although Marion is not enthusiastic. Before she consents to release Honoria, the conversation discloses more details about the past, which Charles has worked so hard to conquer and which Marion so bitterly resents: Charles had begun drinking after stock-market successes had made him rich and idle. In a drunken rage one night, he had left Helen, gone home, and locked the door. When Helen came home with no key, and was unsuccessful in rousing Charles, she left and wandered hysterically in the snow for an hour before going to Marion's home. Subsequently the marriage became more unstable, and Helen became ill. Before dying, she arranged for Honoria's going to Marion; Charles consented because he was then in the sanitarium and did not have the self-confidence to resist.

Just as the previous section of the second part shows Charles victorious over his past, the next (section IV) shows the past victorious over him. } TOPIC SENTENCE
When he is speaking with Marion and Lincoln about details of taking Honoria back, Duncan and Lorraine burst in. They are drunk, and their behavior scandalizes Marion, who out of loyalty to the dead Helen had always distrusted Charles's attachment to Lorraine. It was with Lorraine, this section shows, that Charles had indulged in impossibly frivolous and childish pranks, though nothing more intimate is suggested. Charles brusquely ushers the drunken pair out, but all talk of his taking Honoria has now ended, and Marion is more adamant than ever against his attempt to establish a new life with his daughter.

The third, final, part of the story (section V) opens and closes with the idea that Charles is strong and resolute despite this reversal. } TOPIC SENTENCE: THIRD PART OF THESIS SENTENCE
Talking with Paul, the head bartender at the Ritz, he recalls that his own life had crashed because of the giddiness and unreality of the old bull market days. In other words, the real crash came because of easy wealth, not because of financial ruin. Although Charles sees Lincoln and learns that he must wait six months before talking again to Marion about Honoria, he is not discouraged. Under other circumstances, when he might have dissolved his disappointment in liquor, he is firm and steady: the story concludes on this note of stability:

He would come back some day; they couldn't make him pay forever. But he wanted his child, and nothing was much good now, beside that fact. He wasn't young anymore, with a lot of nice thoughts and dreams to have by himself. He was absolutely sure Helen wouldn't have wanted him to be so alone (p. 140).[3]

[3] Reprinted with the permission of Charles Scribner's Sons from "Babylon Revisited" (Copyright 1931 The Curtis Publishing Company; renewal copyright © 1959 Frances Scott Fitzgerald Lanahan) from TAPS AT REVEILLE by F. Scott Fitzgerald.

The Theme of
Character Analysis

2 An extremely popular theme subject, particularly in courses in drama and novel, is the analysis of character. Although writers in ancient times wrote character sketches and novel-like stories, and although many medieval and Renaissance writers, like Chaucer, were adept at the creation of character, real interest in particularized fictional characters did not develop until the seventeenth century. In the eighteenth century the novel emerged as an important literary form. With the advent of modern psychology, interest in patterns of human behavior has come of age. Of course drama, with its emphasis on a main character, has been popular since the time of the ancient Athenians. In our own times it is one of the more vital literary forms.

If you recollect some of the novels and dramas you have read or seen, you will realize that they are about characters, their reactions to an extended series of actions, and their attempts, both successful and unsuccessful, to shape those events. The novel and the drama are similar because they show the interactions of character and action in rather full detail. To these genres one might add epic and narrative poetry, which also center on character and action. Short stories and poems do not aim at the broadness and fullness of the larger forms but concentrate on only the essential high points of human experience.

What is Character?

Although sometimes we use the word *character* synonymously with "person," "human being," and "literary figure," more often we use it in reference to an individual's personal qualities and characteristics. Both senses should be retained (we can speak about the "character" of a character), but the second sense will be amplified here.

Other words used as either equivalents or modifications of character are *psyche, soul, ego, consciousness, moral fiber, being,* and many others. What is probably meant by all these terms, however, is the sum total of typical qualities and propensities in any given individual that are controlled by that individual's drives, aims, ideals, morals, and ideas of conscience. These qualities are manifested in his behavior under any set of circumstances, and we make observations about his character by drawing inferences from this behavior. Always, the character we are talking about is something that exists somewhere and somehow *within* that individual, or simultaneously *with* him. It is the uniqueness or typicality of that something that concerns us as we discuss the character of the individual. Most persons desire to get ahead in the world, but what makes our friends John and Tom unique is that John works ten hours a day to get ahead while Tom works five. In discussing John and Tom, we would note this behavior (assuming that it results from choice) and attempt to make inferences about their characters from it and from other behavior.

It is by such an inferential process that we learn about our fellow human beings, and if our inferences lead us to liking, this process (on both sides) leads us to form our friendships. We perceive the qualities of the person who is our friend by our contacts with him. We learn about his strengths and weaknesses by observing his speech and action and by listening to him as he communicates his thoughts and emotions to us. If we want to learn more about a particular quality, we ask him about it. With people who are not close to us, however, we are unable to acquire such information, and hence we have no very clear idea of their characters. This difficulty is even more pronounced when we, as voters, are asked to pass judgment on men who run for public office. These men therefore spend much time and energy, as do their campaign managers and aides, to project an "image" of themselves as men of fine, worthy character. The information we gain about them, however, must be supplemented with the comments of political analysts and opponents.

In studying character in literature, we approach a situation more like that of getting to know the public man than that of getting to know our friend. (Note this difference: the author usually attempts to describe every facet of the character, good and bad, not just those traits which create a one-sided view.) We can understand the qualities of a literary character only by interpreting what the author has written about him. All the character's actions, plus what he says and what is said about him, provide us with the only material from which we can make inferences, and we can expect no more than what the author has chosen to disclose.

For this reason, we may define *character* in literature as the author's creation, through the medium of words, of a personality who takes on actions, thoughts, expressions, and attitudes unique and appropriate to that personality and consistent with it. Character might be thought of as a reasonable facsimile of a human being, with all the qualities and vagaries of a human being.

How is Character Disclosed
in Literature?

Before you prepare to write your theme, you should know the four ways in which a writer usually indicates character to you:

1 By what the personage himself says (and thinks, from the author's third person omniscient point of view).
2 By what the character does.
3 By what other characters say about him.
4 By what the author says about him, speaking as either the storyteller or an observer of the action.

These four points require amplification.

1. What a particular character says about himself may frequently be accepted at face value for truth, but just as often it may be only a reflection of his intellectual and emotional state at a given moment. If a character in deep despair says that life is worthless, for example, you must balance that statement with what the same character says when he is happy. Then too, you must consider the situation in the literary work when a statement is made. If a character voices despair at the start, but is cheerful (or sad) at the end, there has been a development, or change, in that character's view of life. In *Crime and Punishment,* for example, Raskolnikov is convinced of his right to make judgments on the lives of other people, but at the end of the novel he doubts his right. A shift has taken place that any analysis of his qualities must consider. As you can see, you are free to interpret what a personage says in the light of the context in which it appears.

Most of the above applies to what a personage thinks as it is reported to us by the author acting as an omniscient narrator. If you detect differences between what the personage thinks and what he says, you may be sure that the author is demonstrating some quality of character, either (a) favorable, if the discrepancy is part of a worthwhile strategy, or (b) unfavorable, if the discrepancy is part of a worthless or ignoble one.

2. You have heard that what you do speaks louder than what you say. The same is true in literature, and sometimes actions illustrate important character traits. An author may create a character who professes honesty yet does dishonorable things. Uriah Heep in *David Copperfield*

and Tartuffe in Molière's play *Le Tartuffe* have such characteristics. Iago in *Othello* is another case in point: he professes to be Othello's friend, but secretly behaves like a devil. In analyzing what characters do, you must ask whether the character's actions are consistent with his words. If not, why not? What does the author communicate by showing inconsistencies? In the three examples just cited, the authors succeed in showing the diabolical nature of hypocrisy.

Exposing hypocrisy, however, might not be the reason for showing gaps between statement and action. This technique may illustrate ideas like "Human beings have a great capacity for self-deception," or "Human beings are weak." An author may show characters behaving consistently with what they say as a mark of favor to these characters (or also as a mark of credit to a rogue who is honest with himself, like Peachum in John Gay's play *The Beggar's Opera*).

3. In literature, as in life, people are always talking about other people. What they say of course raises the problem of *point of view*, because the character and motivation of a personage will condition whatever he says about someone else (see Chapter 3). You know, for example, that the word of a person's enemy is usually biased against that person. Therefore an author may frequently give you a favorable impression of a character by having a bad character say bad things about him. Similarly, the word of a close friend or political manager may be biased in favor of a particular character. In short, you must always consider the context and source of all dramatic remarks about a particular character. In Conrad's *Victory*, for example, an evil hotel manager named Schomberg always claims that the hero, Heyst, is a villain. The reader is to believe the opposite of what Schomberg says about Heyst, because Schomberg seems to be attributing his own evil motives to Heyst. By contrast, in *Macbeth*, when Macduff and Malcolm say that Macbeth and his rule in Scotland are bad, their statements should be accepted as truth because the two men are presented as honest, just, and good.

4. What the author says about a character is usually to be accepted as truth about that character. Naturally, the author must be accepted absolutely on matters of fact in the narrative or drama. But when in his own person he interprets the actions and characteristics of his characters, he himself assumes the role of critic, and his opinions are open to question. For this reason authors frequently avoid making overt interpretations, and devote their skill instead to arranging events in the drama or narrative so that their own conclusions are obvious to the reader. If the author chooses to present an analysis of character, however, he might resort to a personage in the work who will then be bound by his own limitations as an observer. In this case, the dramatic commentator is like the characters discussed in paragraph 3.

Character, Reality, Probability, and Decorum

We are entitled to expect that the characters in a novel or play will be true to life. That is, the actions, statements, and thoughts of a particular personage must all be what a human being is *likely* to do, say, and think under given circumstances. This is the standard of *probability*.

The phrases "true to life" and "given circumstances" need explanation, for they are vital to the concept of literary character as distinguished from real-life character. There are major differences between literature and life. First, literature presents a highly selective view of reality, even in the most "realistic" of works. That is, each action performed by a character within a work has organic significance; it may be interpreted either as a facet of character or sometimes as an example of an author's philosophy of life. Thus, those things in life that seem unpredictable, whimsical, and unaccountable are made to seem meaningful in literature. For example, the conversation of the soldiers on the watch at the opening of *Hamlet* is not there for just any reason at all, as it might be in real life when people sometimes simply "make conversation." Along with having a functional role in the exposition of the play, the talk shows the nervousness of the men, some of their characteristics, and their attitudes as midnight—the time the ghost walks—approaches. The speeches represent the way in which soldiers would likely talk under these circumstances; their speeches are not accidental, but are *probable* and relevant to the entire play.

In studying the characters in each work of literature, you may draw conclusions about the probability of the actions in this way. However, your judgment on this score requires a strong imaginative boost. You must not judge simply from your own point of view but must imagine what very different kinds of persons would do under exactly similar circumstances and with the same mental and philosophical outlooks. You must look carefully at the early parts of the work in order to see what tendencies the characters have exhibited. With these characteristics in mind, you must then ask yourself "Is the subsequent action a logical consequence of this man's qualities?" In the early scenes of *Macbeth*, for example, Shakespeare demonstrates that Macbeth is a loyal, strong, valiant, and almost foolhardy warrior, that he is ambitious, but that he is also kind and gentle. In view of Macbeth's later responsibility for a series of deaths and for a brutally oppressive regime as king, the question is how to square his characteristics with the subsequent action. If it is any consolation, keep in mind that you will probably not be able to please everyone by your answer to this question, or to most questions.

Ultimately, the best you can do is to make sure that your construction of the literary work is accurate and that your inferences are sound.

A second condition that you will meet in literature is that not all works are the same nor do they present probability or reality in the same way or in the same aspects. Fiction attempting to mirror life—the realistic or naturalistic or "slice-of-life" type of fiction—sets up conditions and raises expectations about the characters that fiction attempting to portray a romantic, fanciful world does not, and vice versa. A character might behave and speak "realistically" in the "realistic" setting, and these habits would be out of place in the romantic setting.

But the situation is more complex than this, for within the romantic setting, which is fanciful and dreamlike, a character might reasonably be *expected* to behave and speak in a fanciful, dreamlike way. Speech and action under both conditions are therefore *probable* as we understand the word, although different *aspects* of human character are presented in these two different types of works. In the Renaissance and eighteenth century, concern for adapting the notions of probability to fit the conditions of life as described in various types of works led literary critics to exalt the concept of *decorum,* or appropriateness. Authors of the period followed this principle in making their characters speak and act according to their class and circumstances and according to the type of literature in which they appeared. Thus, Shakespeare gave his noblemen elevated diction in poetic accents but gave his country bumpkins the slang of the Elizabethan streets.

Writers in the modern period have abandoned decorum as a practicing principle, but they still observe decorum to the extent that decorum coincides with common sense and also to the extent that their interest in various aspects of character leads naturally into certain types of literature. For example, modern psychology has had a far-reaching effect on this interest, and hence on the novel. Freud's metapsychology has led writers to explore means of delineating those aspects of character that in previous fiction were not expressed except as they appeared in behavior. James Joyce's *A Portrait of the Artist as a Young Man* relies heavily on an "interior monologue" that takes place within the mind of the young Stephen Dedalus; much of the earlier part of the novel is written as the expression of Stephen's conscious observations and reflections as they cause new thoughts and associations to develop within his mind. This technique would not have developed had it not been for psychology. Similarly, the sections entitled "The Camera Eye" in *U.S.A.* by John Dos Passos are written as the conscious musings of an enlightened observer on the American social scene of the 1930's. Joyce pursued his explorations into the mind to such an extent that in *Finnegans Wake* he attempted to describe the mental activity—the "stream of consciousness"—of a sleeping man.

The drama has also been heavily influenced by the altered and modified ideas of reality provided by modern psychology. Eugene O'Neill's massive drama *A Long Day's Journey Into Night,* for example, is not realistic by the standards of our ordinary acquaintance with life, but is realistic nevertheless because the members of the troubled family represent enlargements of human character; through these characters the anguish and disappointments of life are focused. Recent dramatists like Samuel Becket and Harold Pinter do not aim at everyday realism; instead, they focus on the abstract parts or aspects of human character and personify these parts through their stage figures. The resulting characters are still realistic, but realistic in the way that a microscopic view of the skin of a frog is realistic, particularly if the rest of the frog is not seen. The same criterion is applicable to most works of literature in which the literary form limits full character development, such as detective fiction, science fiction, and romantic comedy. Edgar Allan Poe's detective C. Auguste Dupin, for example (in *Murders in the Rue Morgue* and other stories), is realistic in the sense that his character is concentrated on the reasoning and deductive human powers; many other aspects of character are neglected by Poe because they are irrelevant to the detective-story form.

Judging the Completeness of Character Development

With all these considerations in mind, you can see the usefulness of the idea that literary characters should be "true to life under given circumstances," and to this phrase should be added another one, "within certain literary specifications." The key to your study of character should always be to discover if the character—whether intended by the author to be a full, complete, round, lifelike personage, a romantic hero, or an absurdist abstraction—is related to your concept of what human beings might reasonably be expected to do and say under the exact conditions presented by the author. Does the character ring true, or do the qualities of character presented in him ring true? In other words, does he come to life? Does he illustrate many qualities that add up to a really complete facsimile of a human being, or does he seem to be flat, one-sided, one-dimensional? Lola, a minor figure in Dreiser's *Sister Carrie,* is such a character; we see little in her beyond the fact that she is a worldly wise working girl in a chorus line. On the other hand, Stephen Dedalus in Joyce's *Portrait of the Artist* is totally realized, because his thoughts, words, responses, and actions are described fully from earliest consciousness to young adulthood. The degree to which an author can make a character come alive is a mark of his skill; if you think that your author is successful in this regard, you should say so in your theme.

The Organization of Your Theme

INTRODUCTION

As always, your theme should have a clearly stated central idea that runs throughout your entire character analysis. Your central idea here will be whatever general statement you make to describe the character you analyze. Your thesis sentence must be a brief statement of the main sections of the body of your theme.

BODY

Your organization is designed to illustrate and prove your central idea. You have much freedom in organizing your main points. Some possible methods are the following:

1. Organization around central characteristics, like "kindness, gentleness, generosity, firmness," or "resoluteness of will frustrated by inopportune moments for action, resulting in despondency, doubt, and melancholy." A body containing this sort of material would demonstrate how the literary work brings out each of these qualities.

2. Organization around central incidents that reveal primary characteristics (see, for example, the sample theme). Certain key incidents will stand out in a work, and you might create an effective body by using three or four of these as guides for your discussion, taking care to show in your topic sentences that your purpose in this arrangement is to illuminate the character you have selected, not the incidents. In other words, you would regard the incidents only as they bring out truths about character. In a discussion of the character of Stephen in *A Portrait of the Artist as a Young Man,* an effective arrangement might be to select the incidents of the pandybat, the prostitute, and the young girl standing in the water.

Naturally, with this arrangement, you would have to show how the incidents bring out the characteristics and also how they serve to explain other things the character might do.

3. Organization around various sections of the work. This arrangement is particularly effective if you are demonstrating that a character is undergoing changes and developments. In analyzing the character of Iago, for example, you might say that up to Act II, Scene iii of *Othello* he behaves in a reasonably motivated way, that from there to Act V he behaves like a devil, and that in Act V he becomes an enigma.

CONCLUSION

The conclusion should contain your statements about how the characteristics you have brought out are related to the work as a whole. If the personage was good but came to a bad end, does this discrepancy elevate him to tragic stature? If he was a nobody and came to a bad end, does this fact cause you to draw any conclusion about the class or type of which he was a part? Or does it illustrate the author's view of human life? Or both? Do the characteristics explain why the personage helps or hinders other characters in the literary work? Does your analysis help you to clear up any misunderstanding that your first reading of the work produced? Questions like these should be raised and answered in your conclusion.

A Warning About Diction

In view of the closeness between character analysis and psychology, you must realize that for a literary theme it is best to avoid technical terms from psychology. Even if you have acquired much skill in using these terms, your instructor will probably not receive them sympathetically if you substitute them for thoughtful analysis. Always explain yourself, and do not descend to jargon, as there is great danger of doing in this theme. Some words from psychology are admissible, however, without much amplification: words like *disturbed, frustrated, anxiety* are satisfactory because they are in common use, but if you start using words like *complex, neurosis,* and *psychosis,* you should explain the concepts, not just use the words. Be cautious, and use common sense. If you have any question about a word, ask your instructor.

SAMPLE THEME

The Character of Jim in Conrad's
Lord Jim

Jim is difficult to understand. He is seen mainly through the eyes of Marlow, who imparts his own values to much of the story. He is also the subject of much interpretation by other informants in the story, so that we receive many views of him. In addition, Jim is the principal figure in a richly symbolic tapestry, so that much of what he does and says is relevant to most people at most times. In this respect his individuality is sacrificed to his existence as a symbol. Despite these difficulties, however, Jim emerges as a fully developed individual, even though we do not hear of every detail that might ever have concerned him. *The key to understanding Jim's character is that he is a man capable of imagining the best in himself and in men generally—a man whose action at any given moment is controlled by an idea of the best.** He is, in Stein's word, a "romantic,"

* Central idea.

and I would add that he is an introspective dreamer. *His character is made clear by three incidents in the novel, all of which are connected with leaps, or jumps, that Jim either makes or does not make.*†

When Jim has his first opportunity to leap, he does not take it. This failure to jump is symbolic of Jim's preference for mental over physical heroism. It hurts his own high evaluation of himself. Imbued with the British ideals of manhood and adventure in the days of the naval empire, he has been dreaming of his own "devotion to duty" in a way "as unflinching as a hero in a book." [1] But when the opportunity comes to join in a rescue operation, he misses the boat. He does not jump. From this point Jim becomes a drifter, for this failure has given him a hint of the basic indecision (*cowardice* would be too strong a word at this point) which is worrying the bubble of his own self-esteem. This one incident, in short, explains the moral laziness which finally causes him to ship aboard the *Patna*.

The bubble of Jim's esteem is totally destroyed by his second jump—from the *Patna* when it is listing heavily and supposedly near sinking. This jump is the major incident in the novel, since it brings out the depths of Jim's being, that inner panic which destroys all his conscious dreams by causing a single cowardly act despite his good intentions. This jump brings out Jim's sense of shame, which must be overwhelming, since it causes him to wander all over the Indian Ocean, fleeing whenever anybody mentions the *Patna* episode. With his depths thus exposed, I believe that Jim feels morally naked, without the privacy that most of us have, since we know, or hope, that the depths of our own souls may never emerge to haunt us. Jim's emerges, and he runs from it, as run he must.

But the *Patna* jump also emphasizes Jim's good qualities. He has a high sense of justice, and before he runs he therefore faces trial, which can end in nothing but his dishonor and disgrace. His conscious dream of what is right has enabled him to face the consequences of his real guilt. Perhaps this facing of the trial when all the other deserters flee is the start of Jim's awareness, acted upon but never clearly stated by him, that life constantly demands expiation for guilt that is caused not entirely by our own choice.

Jim's final leap results from his own choice, however, and as such it enables him finally to live out his dream. It is a kind of triumph. Leaping over the fence enclosing Rajah Allang's courtyard, he allies himself with Doramin, and proceeds quickly to justify the title *Lord Jim* by acting wisely, in concert with Doramin, in

---

† Thesis sentence.
1 Joseph Conrad, *Lord Jim* (New York: The Modern Library, 1931), p. 6.

governing the forlorn outpost of Patusan. He is convinced of the value of his dream, and always behaves with justice, honor, and firmness, yet always with forgiveness. These are the conscious virtues, to which Jim adheres closely, since they are the embodiment of his character as a dreamer.

This adherence explains why he accepts the final responsibility for the death of Dain Waris. Beyond question, his third leap has enabled him to dedicate himself to the good life in Patusan as expiation for his guilt in the *Patna* episode. The personal quality of this dedication should be stressed, however, and contrasted with the quality of Jim's feelings after Gentleman Brown commits his treacherous act. In this affair Jim is responsible only for not having destroyed the Gentleman *before* the murder is committed. Yet, in Gentleman Brown, Jim apparently sees that the cowardly depths are common to all mankind, not just to himself. So Jim faces Doramin in expiation, just as he had earlier braved the court and the subsequent disgrace. But as Jim sacrifices himself, the best in him, his capacity to dream, triumphs over whatever it was that made him leap from the *Patna*. He is genuinely great at that moment of sacrifice, when he expiates for us all.

Admittedly, Jim is a puzzling character, since his characteristics show that human life is a mystery and since we never really get inside him. But Conrad uses him to demonstrate that, if life has its depths, it also has its high points. At the highest point, a human being willing to live out his dream, if this dream has value and ennobles mankind, can justify the claim that life is elevated and great. Jim, with all his frailty, is a truly great representation of a human being, since he has met and conquered life's greatest obstacle—the deflation of one's own high self-esteem.

The Theme About
Point of View
in a Literary Work

3 *Point of view* is the position from which action in a literary work is seen, heard, pondered, and described. The analysis of point of view is an analysis of that position and its effect on the work. Point of view is manifested in the person who tells the story—a person who may be either the author himself speaking in his own voice or a fictional voice created by the author. The analysis of point of view attempts to identify the voice, to determine by inference the qualities and characteristics of the speaker behind the voice, and also to determine the relationship between speaker and the narrative or argument. It is important to emphasize that point of view refers to the speaker telling the *entire* story, not to individual characters speaking in the dialogue that appears in the work.

Point of view may be determined by the way in which the action is narrated. If the story is told by an "I," you have a *first person* point of view, usually a fictional narrator. Nick Carraway in F. Scott Fitzgerald's *The Great Gatsby* is such a speaker, as is the speaker in many of Poe's stories and tales. If the narrator is not introduced as a character, you have a *third person* point of view. There are variants here. The third person point of view is called *omniscient* when the speaker seems to know everything that goes on in the minds of his characters, and *limited* when he confines himself only to reporting what can be seen, smelled, heard, tasted, and touched. James Joyce utilized the omniscient point of view frequently in *Ulysses,* but scrupulously observed the limited point of view in *The Dubliners.*

In short stories, poems, and novels, a writer is free to select any point of view he chooses. In drama, however, the point of view is, with rare exceptions (such as the traditional soliloquy), best regarded as third per-

21

son limited, because a dramatist presenting action and dialogue cannot show a character's mind except by what is spoken or acted.

Point of view has also been described as the way in which a writer *authenticates* his material. When we read something, we want to be convinced of its probability or authenticity. Therefore we want firsthand testimony rather than hearsay; we want to believe that we are witnessing events rather than having them described to us. Writers in the twentieth century have particularly attempted to create fiction that is, in point of view, realistic; they wish to give us the impression that we are observers, not listeners. In earlier times, writers devoted themselves similarly to the problem of authenticating their material, although they did not do so in quite the way of Conrad or Hemingway. Whereas modern writers approach point of view as a problem in storytelling, earlier writers approached it as a problem in rhetoric, following the Aristotelian idea that the speaker should pay great attention to the character he projects as his own *ethical proof* (see Aristotle, *Rhetoric,* I, 2, 1356[a]).

Point of View and Opinions

You must realize at the outset that point of view should be carefully distinguished from opinions or beliefs, although in popular usage point of view and opinions are frequently confused. Point of view refers to the position from which things are seen; in its broad sense, *position* comprises everything that affects the speaker as an observer, including opinions. Point of view conditions opinions. Suppose that a speaker is blind, or deaf; suppose that he is a child, or an old man; suppose that he has just been married, or that he has been disappointed in love. The opinions of these speakers about a painting, a piece of music, or love, would be necessarily limited by their conditions as observers of these matters. Remember, therefore, that opinions are only a function of point of view. You might say that studying opinions is to study *effects,* while studying point of view is to study *causes.*

Point of View, Character Analysis, and Tone

There are places at which point of view overlaps with *character analysis* (see Chapter 2) and *tone* (see Chapter 11). Thus any consideration of point of view must necessarily treat those character traits of the speaker that influence what he says. Similarly, point of view has the same relation to tone that it has to opinions: tone reveals the attitudes of the speaker toward his material and toward his audience, and these attitudes must inevitably be a product of the speaker's point of view. When you consider these similarities, however, you should realize that there are differences in emphasis: character study emphasizes everything connected with character; tone emphasizes the way language and structure are manipulated to convey attitudes; point of view emphasizes the total vantage point from which things are perceived.

The Purpose of a Theme About Point of View

The object of this theme is to cause you to observe the effect of point of view in a story or poem, with the implication that point of view is similarly influential in all literature. The basic questions you should answer are these: How have the speaker's attitude, knowledge, and limitations contributed to forming the literary work as it actually is? Has the point of view succeeded in making the work seem true, or authentic, or probable? Writing this theme should help increase your perceptions as a disciplined reader and, as always, should make you aware that literary study is a study of the creative process, an attempt to understand the artistic mind, and a way of appreciating literature.

Preparation for Your Theme

As you read the work assigned, you will perceive the point of view operating in the way in which certain actions are described. What words are used? Let us consider an example. A man walks into a room in which a party is taking place. How shall this act be described? A neutral observer might say, "The man came in and joined the party." An enemy might say, "The man intruded upon the company and dampened the spirits of the guests." The sweetheart of the man might say, "Even the artificial flowers bloomed when he walked in the room." You will quickly see that the words used to describe even this simple action will depend on the speaker's attitude and that the speaker will frequently employ highly connotative words in order to arouse a desired emotional response in his readers. The study of point of view should show how these effects have operated within an entire work in order to make the work seem true and authentic.

Your problem in reading, therefore, is to observe carefully not only the story, incidents, ideas, and commentary, but also the language used to convey these various elements. You must test the quality of the various words to see if you are expected to respond in any particular way. Then, when you have made your observations, you must develop them: What characteristics does the speaker have? How are these characteristics brought out? How do these characteristics determine the material in the story or poem? What details are selected for inclusion? How are they arranged in the work? What is the emotion or emotions in which the action and ideas are described, and do the emotions remain constant or do they shift? (Of these last two questions, one is structural and the other is concerned with tone. In determining the answer to either, however, you should always emphasize relationships with point of view.) How might the emotions have been different if a different speaker were telling the story? What can you learn about the present speaker from the contrast? The answer to questions like these, together with your consideration of the connotations of the diction, will be the subject of the theme.

The Organization of Your Theme

Specifically, you should have the following elements in your theme: (a) an analysis of the speaker and the situation to which he is responding, and (b) an analysis of the speaker's effect on the literary work, whether on the form of the narrative argument, the ideas, or the diction. Bear in mind that there is always interaction of the speaker and the situation to which he responds; just as the speaker influences events and ideas, there are ideas and events that influence him.

INTRODUCTION

Your introduction should describe the situation in the literary work. You might answer some or all of these questions in making your description. Who is the speaker? What is the character and background of the speaker? What is his relationship with the material he is presenting? What is his relationship with the person listening to him (if there is a listener)? Does he speak directly to the reader or does he speak in such a way that you become either a witness or an eavesdropper? How much knowledge does the speaker assume (i.e., does he write with the assumption that he knows what is going on in other people's minds, or does he confine himself to recording what he has heard, seen, smelled, tasted, felt)? Does the speaker ever rely on the information of others for his material? How reliable are these other witnesses? Is the speaker a participant in the action? Is he affected by the action? Is he the same at the end as he was at the beginning?

As you answer these questions you will arrive at a central idea about the speaker and his relation to the material. The sample theme builds to the idea that the speaker's attitudes change as the circumstances in the poem change. Similarly, you might be writing a story describing the effects of mass hypnosis, and you may discover that the speaker himself has been hypnotized (see Thomas Mann's "Mario and the Magician"). Whatever you discover in this way should be the point that you develop in the remainder of your theme.

BODY

In the body you should analyze the effect of the speaker on the situation and vice versa. Does the material proceed naturally or logically from the situation you describe in the introduction? How does the situation cause the speaker to respond? What evidence do you find of the speaker's emotional state? Is he emotionally involved in the situation or indifferent to it? Does he seem able or unable to judge it? What emotions are produced by the incidents, ideas, and language? Do you think that these emotions are appropriate to the speaker and to his reactions to the general situation in the work?

CONCLUSION

In your conclusion you should evaluate the success of the author's point of view: Was it consistent, effective, truthful? What did the writer gain (if anything) by his selection of point of view? What did he lose (if anything)? How might a less skillful writer have handled similar material? After answering questions like these, you may end your theme.

Problems in Writing Your Theme

1. In considering point of view, you will encounter the problem of whether to discuss the author or his speaker as the originator of the attitudes. It is probably best always to discuss the speaker, with the proviso, of course, that the author is always manipulating the speaker, even if the speaker is in truth a phase of the author's personality. An author and his speaker are not necessarily the same; the *persona* is just as much a creation as the literary work itself. Witness, for example, the cases of Swift and Gulliver, Marlow and Conrad. There will naturally be many ideas common to both the author and his speaker, but your statements about these must be inferential, not absolute.

2. You may have a tendency to wander away from point of view into a synopsis or a discussion of ideas. Emphasize the presentation of the events and ideas and the causes for this presentation. Do not emphasize the subject material itself, but use it only as it bears on your consideration of point of view. Your object is not just to interpret the work, but also to show how the point of view enables you to interpret the work.

Inevitably you must talk about the material in the work, but use it only to illustrate your assertions about point of view. You should avoid the following pattern of statement, which will always lead you astray: "The speaker says this, which means this." You must instead adhere to this pattern, which will keep your emphasis always upon your central idea: "The speaker says this, which shows this about him and his attitudes." If a particular idea is difficult, you might need to explain it, but do not do so unless it illustrates your central idea.

SAMPLE THEME

A Study of the Point of View in Donne's Poem "A Feaver"

In this seven-stanza poem the speaker is talking directly to a woman —his beloved—who is seriously ill, in the grips of a fever that becomes progressively worse as he speaks. The reader is therefore made witness to an intensely dramatic situation, since the issues in the poem are first, life and death, and second, the relationship of the speaker with his beloved. What might be expected from human beings under the circumstances of the poem? A bit of cheer? Some flowers? Some statements evading the central fact of death? A reaffirmation of love? The speaker's loss of emotional control? Depending on the seriousness of the illness, we might expect any or all of these from an ordinary person. But the speaker in this poem is not ordinary.

*He reveals himself as an enlightened, educated, witty man, well grounded in Christianity, whose love is both profound and lifelong.** When he speaks he preserves this character, and uses the language of his intellectuality to declare his love. He is losing his beloved, and his mood, at first reassuring and confident, accordingly sinks as this fact is impressed on him. But his final words are of love. *The poem therefore records realistically the emotional shift of the speaker in response to this dramatically moving situation.*†

In the opening stanza the speaker bravely faces the fact that his beloved might die, but his attitude is that she should not and will not. He is really trying to reassure his beloved, as anyone might do who is visiting and comforting a sick person:

> Oh doe not die, for I shall hate
>   All women so, when thou art gone,
>   That thee I shall not celebrate,
>   When I remember, thou wast one.[1]

* Central idea.
† Thesis sentence.
[1] *The Complete Poetry and Selected Prose of John Donne & The Complete Poetry of William Blake*, with an introduction by Robert Silliman Hillyer (New York: Random House, Inc., 1946), p. 13. All quotations are taken from this page.

Strong personalities these, that can joke this way in the face of death. After this initial jocularity, the speaker for the next two stanzas creates a complex and paradoxical mood of cheer, building on the initial directive that the beloved one should not die. Briefly, the speaker demonstrates his intellectuality by creating a logical argument claiming that the beloved not only should not, but cannot die, since the definition of death ("To leave this world behind, is death.") does not apply to her, for she *is* the world and cannot therefore leave herself behind. Or if she dies, then the remaining world—the earth we live on—will be nothing but a "carkasse" and "corrupt wormes" since the beloved will be gone. Certainly, the relationship of the speaker and the beloved must be an intellectual one. His estimation of her intelligence is high, at any rate, for he expects her to follow the argument, which is really the logical extreme of the lover's ordinary claim to his sweetheart, "You are all the world to me." Invalid as it is, this argument serves a higher kind of truth, since it establishes the closeness of the emotional ties between the speaker and his beloved in a mood of intellect against the backdrop of death.

At this point we may assume that the beloved one has been seized with a painful attack, for the speaker during the next two stanzas ceases to address her and instead makes an outcry to the "wrangling schooles" that have been asking the cataclysmic question about the fire that "shall burne this world" (this is the question about the final destruction of the universe). This question demonstrates the speaker's complex mind, for he is able to apply it to the problem of an individual death. His mind, with its power of analogy, is like lightning. First he pursues the image of stanzas two and three, to ask whether his beloved's fever might be the fire that will destroy the world. Then he moves in this frame of reference into a cosmic compliment to her. His logic is as follows: since his beloved is the world, and since she is being consumed by the fire or fever, she will not "long beare this torturing wrong," because fire needs much "corruption" as "fuell" on which to feed, and she is pure, and not corrupt (the speaker does not know the theory of oxidation, since the poem was written early in the seventeenth century). Therefore, concludes the speaker, she cannot sustain the fever, and will not suffer long because of it. Here, as he compliments her, the speaker is comforting himself—naturally, I think—since no one wants to see a beloved one suffer, even if death is the only release from pain. But the realization that death is near makes final words necessary in the next stanzas. The speaker is shown to be a person who can say the proper words.

Since death is near, the time for speech is short, and the speaker is forced to say everything to his beloved in two stanzas. He desires to comfort and to compliment her, and claims that her "burning fits" are like "meteors" that will burn out quickly, leaving her "unchangeable firmament." Here his erudition and background are again apparent, for he selects a Biblical word, *firmament,* which is rich with the connotations of the Creation, to show that his love is everlasting. We notice that his description of his beloved has moved from the "world" to the "firmament" as the entire poem moves toward death and the (hopefully) heavenly reunion, which is never specifically mentioned. We can see, however, that the speaker's attitudes toward death are contained within the limits of Christian orthodoxy.

In the concluding stanza the speaker asserts the power of his dream of love. Though his hold on the dying beloved one is tenuous, he says, he desperately clings to it:

> Yet 't was of my minde, seising thee,
>   Though it in thee cannot persever.
> For I had rather owner bee
>   Of thee one houre, than all else ever.

He knew that he could not possess her forever, in other words, but he dreamed that he could, because of his love for her. His deep despair and helplessness finish the logic, and his final word is "ever," suggesting the eternity in which the beloved one, and eventually the speaker, shall rest.

The poem, then, treats a difficult subject—the ultimate subject—delicately and truthfully, from a consistent point of view. The poem demonstrates how the human soul can react against the inevitable fact of death, which most of us avoid, and before which most of us are mute. The speaker's mind is therefore the real subject of the poem, and through his mind runs the continuous image of his beloved as first the world and finally the firmament. In lighter, happier moments, I believe, this image could furnish extravagant praise and elaborate compliments (as it does in other poems by Donne), but with the immediacy of death it defines, finally, the value of love in life. Within the subtle mind of the speaker—the point of view—the semiplayful logic reveals truthfully the state of the person in love: namely, the willingness to assert that deep love, possessed for just one hour, has more value than anything else the universe provides. The idea is not in the speaker's immediate thoughts at the start of the poem, but is verbalized only as the situation demands it. For this reason the poem portrays an intensely dramatic and genuinely true development of a vigorous, educated mind responding to sorrow and death.

The Theme on a
Specific Problem
in a Literary Work

4 The theme on a specific problem is a catch-all type frequently assigned in literature courses, just as the solution of problems is required in every course you will ever take. The question-and-answer discussion method, with which you have become familiar in your classes, is perhaps the best previous experience you have had with the general method of writing a specific-problem theme. In answering a question like "In *Heart of Darkness* why does Conrad state that Kurtz has made a lengthy study aimed at improving the lot of the natives?" you have been putting facts and conclusions together in the way you will follow in writing a theme on a specific problem. Only rarely can you answer such questions merely by summarizing subject matter or identifying characters in the work.

The idea behind the specific-problem theme is this: too frequently a person takes for granted everything that he reads, only to discover when challenged that he has not really understood or thought about the material. Therefore, if the material he reads can be seen as a problem, or as containing immediately unanswerable questions, he will search the material more deeply and develop more command over it. As he does so, he is also developing those skills and habits that characterize the educated person. Few people would dispute the assertion that education can aim at little better than putting students into the frame of mind of asking questions and seeing problems. To paraphrase Shelley, when problems are seen, can solutions be far behind?

The active reader, which you are trying to become, is always inquisitive. He constantly asks questions such as "What would this work be like without that?" and "What would this character do in other circumstances?" As he raises these questions, he learns about art and broadens his general ability to read and think. In attempting to find answers he must try out a number of provisional solutions; he must organize and structure his material convincingly and originally. He can solve some problems by simple exposition, whereas he can solve others only by presenting an argument or by making a certain major assertion seem valid or invalid.

How Assigned

The problems you deal with in this type of assignment may be assigned by your instructor (for both papers and tests), or they may arise in classroom discussion. Suppose that a particular question puzzles the members of your class. You might well find yourself with that problem as the subject of your next theme.

You might also be asked to make up your own problem for a theme assignment. In this event you must conceive of a problem and formulate it. Write down all questions that occur to you as you read. You might easily make one of these the problem you deal with in your theme. Here also you can use your classroom experience, which will help you eventually to develop feelings for the relevant sorts of questions that you should raise. Now, suppose that in class you have discussed a work in which the principal character is under a sentence of death. What questions arose? How were these questions answered? By contrast, suppose that the work which you have been assigned concerns people with an undetermined future (e.g., "they lived happily ever after"). Can you raise problems about this work similar to those that were raised in class? Or, suppose that in class you have discussed a comic work, and have answered questions about what makes it comic. If your assigned work is comic, you might bring some of the classroom discussion to bear on a problem of your own about the causes of laughter.

Your Problem in Writing This Theme

Your main job in this theme is to provide a convincing solution to the specific problem with which you are faced. You must perceive the most significant implications of the problem and decide on a suitable order in which to deal with them. Then you must judge the relevance of materials from your text. Choose only those that have an immediate bearing on the problem. Of course, both your sharpness as a reader and your close study of the text will bear fruit here, because much material seemingly irrelevant to a careless reader can be interpreted as vital by a keen, knowledgeable reader. As in all your assignments, your first objective is therefore to think carefully.

The Nature of Literary Problems

Problems may be of any kind, and in this respect all writing about literature may be fitted into the *problem* category. For convenience, the problems may be classified as *artistic* (concerning style, arrangement, and general content), *conceptual* (concerning ideas), and *historical* (concerning influences, background, and genre).

You should realize that a problem will often cause a fusion of these three classifications, because they are all interlocked in the literary work itself, and because the problem may certainly be relevant to any and all classifications. You should also realize that your method of handling the theme will depend on the way in which the problem is put. For example, the question "What is the influence of the pastoral machinery on Milton's 'Lycidas'?" would require an expository treatment of how the pastoral elements figure in the poem. The aim of a theme on this problem would be mainly expository. But a related problem might be "Does the pastoral convention spoil 'Lycidas' by making it seem too artificial?" You can see that writing a theme on this second topic would require argument rather than simple exposition. Naturally a certain amount of exposition would be necessary in the treatment of this problem, but the exposition would be used only as it related to the argument.

ARTISTIC PROBLEMS

Almost anything in a literary work can be dealt with in artistic terms, but you are here concerned with problems as they relate to matters of style, structure, and—by extension—motivation and character. Suppose, for example, you were asked the question, "What meaning does the name 'Joe Christmas' have in the novel *Light in August* (by William Faulkner)?" This question is directed toward the novel, and implies that you would answer it as it relates to the artistry of the novel, even though in doing this job you would need to answer the question of Faulkner's idea in the novel. If you interpret Christmas as a "reverse image of Jesus Christ" (as some critics have done), then it is necessary for him to be killed at the end, if your parallel is to be exact. Your consideration would therefore involve you in a discussion of *structure*.

As another case, suppose you ask why Browning, in "The Pied Piper of Hamelin," created "such a rhythmic verse and such happily jingling rhymes." To solve this problem, you would need to decide how true the assumption about the verse is, and then relate the quality of the verse to Browning's subject and intended audience (the subtitle "A Child's Story" suggests that the poet had a certain audience in mind). Your method, as you see, would not be simply to analyze and scan the verse, but to bring to bear the results of your analysis and scansion upon your conclusion.

Similarly, suppose you ask why the Polyphemus episode appears where it does in Odysseus's narrative in *The Odyssey*. Solving this problem really involves a discussion of *structure* in relation to your interpretation of the epic. Your solution might be something like this: "Since Polyphemus's curse is the cause of Odysseus's ten-year journey, it must come at the beginning of his wanderings, after his leaving Troy. Also, if *The Odyssey* is to some degree a story showing how Odysseus's ideas of personal responsibility grow, Odysseus must have time to recognize his guilt where Polyphemus is concerned and must also reconcile himself to what is essentially a tragic view of life."

You can see that dealing with a problem like this also involves a consideration of motivation and, necessarily, of character. If your problem, for example, is to answer the question of "How does Hurstwood change in Dreiser's *Sister Carrie?*" or "Why do the Schlegel sisters feel obligated to befriend Leonard Bast in E. M. Forster's *Howards End?*" and so on, you are dealing with causes, effects, and relationships among characters. All these problems are artistic.

CONCEPTUAL PROBLEMS

Problems of this sort are about ideas. Your intention in dealing with a problem about ideas, however, is not expository, but argumentative. For example, after reading Aldous Huxley's novel *Point Counter Point,* you might ask how valid his ideas are about the role of politics in modern life. This problem requires not only that you describe Huxley's ideas on the subject (perhaps as expressed through the character Mark Rampion), but also that you criticize these ideas, showing their validity and perhaps stating the degree of their applicability to modern society. And, if you conclude that they are not applicable, what other answers might be more applicable? You can see that solving a problem about ideas sometimes requires subjective responses; on many occasions you might dispute with your author, at other times you might agree with him. How, for example, would you solve the problems implied in "Wordsworth's ideas on 'The Old Cumberland Beggar' and modern welfare"? Or try "Did the ideas of Dos Passos on politics really change from *U.S.A.* to *Mid-Century?*"

HISTORICAL PROBLEMS

Most problems of this sort require a certain amount of research. Suppose that you are dealing with a problem of influences (you should know that many instructors object strongly to the assumptions underlying the word *influence,* and would probably not give you such an assignment). You are given the problem of Virgil's influence on Chaucer.

You probably could not solve this problem yourself and so would have to consult a secondary source or sources in your libarary. If this problem were put in a different way, however—let us say "The similarity of ideas in certain works by Virgil and certain works by Chaucer"—you could probably solve the problem yourself by recourse to a comparison-contrast method, though you would certainly not claim that one poet influenced the other. Even in this inquiry, however, you would probably help yourself by using a secondary source. (A *secondary source* is a book *about* the works or authors you are reading; a *primary source* is usually the work itself.)

Problems of *background* and *milieu* also require varying degrees of research. Background information about the position of the Jewish people in medieval history would assist you in solving a problem like "How did Chaucer's audience interpret *The Prioress's Tale?*" *Milieu* refers to the intellectual and artistic currents prevailing at the time of a particular writer. If you were asked to solve the problem: "What was the milieu of Shaw's *Mrs. Warren's Profession?*" you would need research in secondary sources to help you with your answer.

A similar need to do research would occur in problems of *genre* or *type*. As with *influences,* the study of genre has fallen into some critical disrepute. But if you determine the genre of a work, you will know what to expect from it and can thereby make a reasoned evaluation. It would be folly for you to read a Greek tragedy and compare it unfavorably with *Hamlet* because "*Hamlet* has more action than the Greek tragedy, and besides, the Greek choruses are dull." You must understand that the conventions of Greek tragedies were different from those in Shakespeare's plays. A consideration of genre would permit you to understand the differences and lead to a better appreciation of both kinds of plays. As another example, you may fail to appreciate certain works of poets who wrote during the neoclassic period of English literary history. A realization that these writers wrote according to rules of genre would make you able to recognize the requirements which they set for themselves (i.e., epic satire, Horatian satire, mock-epic satire, pastoral poetry, discursive poetry, heroic drama). Once you recognized the limits of their achievements, you would be better able to recognize their merits. In this way, the study of genre brings a wider range of appreciation than you could gain without it. Remember one thing, however: when genre leads to unwarranted conclusions (for example, pleading that because Housman was a great poet within the limits he set for himself he is to be regarded as Milton's equal), it has defeated its own purpose—reasonable appreciation.

In dealing with a problem of genre, then, you will need to learn the special conditions under which the work was composed, and the type that the work was supposed to be. Some problems of genre would be: "*Hamlet* as a revenge play," "*Gulliver's Travels* as a travel book," "Dryden's *Annus*

Mirabilis as a 'historical' poem," *"An American Tragedy* as a realistic novel," *"The Nun's Priest's Tale* as a beast epic," *"The Rape of the Lock* as a mock-heroic poem," and "Virginia Woolf's *Mrs. Dalloway* as a stream-of-consciousness novel." Your problem would be to set up an idea of what to expect from the work that you have considered and then to show how it successfully lived up to these expectations.

Problems of genre can also require a treatment employing argument. For instance, "To what extent is *Gulliver's Travels* more than just a parody of contemporary travel books?" or "Did the revenge motif in *Hamlet* limit Shakespeare in treating Hamlet's responses to Claudius?" Questions like these can be multiplied indefinitely. In dealing with one of them you would (a) examine the truth of the assumption about genre, and (b) deal with the relation of the genre to the problem at hand.

Your Approach in Writing

As you may conclude from the types of problems discussed, it is impossible to predict all the various problems that will occur not only in your classes but also in your mind as you read literature. For your theme, however, remember the following: Your job is to convince your reader that your solution to the problem is valid. Your theme will therefore most often require an argument designed to support your central idea (which is in fact a short statement of your solution to the problem). The various parts of your theme will be subpoints supported by evidence.

As you read your literary work, take notes on relevant details. Study your notes carefully after you have finished reading. From your notes you should arrive at a major conclusion, which you will make the central idea of your theme. The material in your notes may then be arranged in an order suitable to the logical steps of your argument. When you begin to write, you may suddenly realize the importance of other material that you did not include in your original notes. Work in this new material, but take care to illustrate its relevance to your central idea.

Depending on the degree of argument required by your topic, you will find a need to examine closely the key words in the statement of your problem. It is always wise to study these words carefully. If your instructor has phrased the problem for you, his phrase may contain words having implications with which you do not agree. That is, some of his words may "beg the question." You will also find it necessary to determine the limits within which you wish a certain word to operate. Or, if you object to the way a problem is phrased, you may wish to rephrase it. What would you do, for example, with problems phrased like these: "How much misanthropy does Swift show in *Gulliver's Travels?*" or "Show why Faulkner is the great American novelist." You can quickly see that these are "loaded" questions. To answer the first you would need to determine the meaning of *misanthropy* and if you admitted the word at all, you would need to limit its use to Swift's meaning. For the second question you would need to spend time on the meaning and admissibility of the phrase *is the great* before you could write a good theme. The sample theme considers the meaning of the term *successful* when applied to Robert Frost's poem "Desert Places." This theme sets up reasonable conditions for determining whether or not the poem is successful and proceeds to argue and demonstrate that the conditions are met. It thereby develops from the discussion of one of the major terms presented in the original statement of the problem. You might profit from employing a similar method whenever you are confronted with a similar literary problem.

As with all themes except the summary, you may assume that your reader has knowledge of the literary work you have read. Your job is to arrange your materials convincingly around your main point. You should not use anything from the work that is not relevant to your central idea. You do not need to discuss things in their order of appearance in the work. You are in control and must make your decisions about order so that your solution to the problem may be brought out most effectively.

The Organization of Your Theme

INTRODUCTION

If your problem requires an examination of any of its key words, the introduction is the proper place for this examination. Once that is done, your introduction should describe the problem in terms of either its importance in the work you have read or its general importance in life and literature. Thus, say you have the problem: "Is Moll Flanders's bad life justified by her economic circumstances?" You might wish to look first at the phrase "bad life" and may conclude that it is properly descriptive. Then you might wish to deal with the issue of justification in either or both of two ways: (a) whether, and to what degree, the immediate circumstances justify the sins of which Moll is guilty; (b) whether environment is generally a justification for human conduct. Ultimately, you might find yourself raising other perplexing moral and artistic questions that develop from these; for once you have raised the original problem, more problems usually follow, and they should be used to strengthen your argument. Although the original problem is particular, it raises general implications that should also be dealt with if a solution is really to be found.

Your introduction should also describe your solution to the problem in a brief statement, which will be your central idea. Your thesis sentence should include the introduction.

BODY

The body should contain the main points of your argument. Another way to look at the body is to think of it as stating the main reasons for which you have arrived at your solution. Generally, you will state a point (topic sentence) and then show how a certain amount of representative material from the work supports that point, and so on throughout the body. Always keep emphasizing how the material supports your point. Just to present the material is to write a synopsis, and this theme is not to be a synopsis.

CONCLUSION

Your conclusion should affirm your belief in the validity of your solution in view of the supporting evidence. You must recognize that in nonscientific subjects like literature there are rarely absolute proofs, so that your conclusions will not actually be proved. But your conclusions, along with the evidence, should be *convincing,* and you should always give the impression that you have not been grinding an axe. The conclusion of your theme should therefore build conviction in your reader. If you think your reader may have doubts, you should satisfy these doubts in your conclusion. It is a good rhetorical method to answer any objections or contrary claims that might be raised against your solution. Whether you state the objections fully or only make them implicit, you ought to answer them. In this way you convince your reader that your solution has been reasoned wisely and that you have omitted nothing in seeking out evidence and in thinking of solutions.

SAMPLE THEME

In the Poem "Desert Places" (1936), is Frost Successful in Shifting the Meaning of the Term "Desert Places"?

This question is another way of asking whether the poem itself is successful, for Frost's shift of meaning is both the emotional climax and the physical end of the poem. If the shift does not work, the poem does not present its major point successfully. Frost first uses the term in his title to refer to "places that are deserted." In the first lines of the poem he applies this meaning specifically to the field on which snow is falling, and in lines 13 and 14 he applies it to interstellar spaces. In the last line of the poem he uses the term both metaphorically and pejoratively to suggest that the speaker's soul is a desert place. Presumably, the shift from a natural to a human application would not be successful if it were totally unrelated to everything before it, but it would be successful if the contrary were true. One might also claim failure if the term did not acquire the clarity necessary for full effectiveness, since nothing at all comes after it as explanation and development. It seems clear, however, that Frost's shifting of the meaning is accomplished successfully and hence that the poem itself is successful. Both the general metaphor of the poem and Frost's reliance on a well-acknowledged tradition of the humbling of the self answer any objections that might be made to his semantic shift.

The primary cause of Frost's success is the generally metaphoric quality of the first three stanzas. To the reader who is accustomed to finding more than one level of meaning in a natural description, the introduction of the field suggests a comparison with the human soul: the field is a broad expanse enclosed by a woods; weeds and grain or hay both grow there; sometimes the summer sun shines on the field and at other times the night of winter reigns. Now, only weeds and stubble show through the accumulating snow, which covers the hibernating animals. All these details suggest a state in which life is being overgrown, cut off, buried, and enveloped in darkness.

When Frost connects this "lonely" scene with the "absent-spirited" speaker, the invitation to read the details metaphorically has been made clearly. The darkness, the surrounding woods, the weeds, the stubble, the smothered animals, the cold, the loneliness—all these metaphorically suggest that not only snow, but men themselves, are benighted. Along this avenue of suggestion, one might take the date of the poem, 1936, to make a reading of lines 9 and 10: the prediction in these lines of a dark future suggests the despairing state of mind of a sensitive person during those ominous years preceding World War II—certainly an episode that sprang from the uncultivated wilderness of the human soul. In other words, even before the final lines, the reader has been readied for the suddenness of Frost's metaphoric shift of meaning—a climax that may thus be seen as integral to the poem.

All the above details are pulled together and focused by the shift of meaning at the end. The final words crystallize the poem, providing the reader with a second view of it and putting everything into a meaningful pattern. Although nothing follows, the placement of the words makes it seem as though something indeed has followed. The term "desert places" thus achieves clarity. It can be construed as a reference to something like spiritual isolation, human indifference, lack of human warmth, or what is sometimes called the "emptiness" of human existence. The meaning is not exact, but it is sufficiently clear in view of human experience; and the condition referred to is real enough to "scare" the speaker (line 16). Frost thus emphasizes the speaker's self-realization as much as the meaning of the metaphor.

By this means Frost limits the metaphor and in effect answers the potential charge that he is generalizing. Specifically, if some mythical reader were to object by saying that not everyone possesses "desert places" (an unlikely claim), the phrase "my own" in line 16 has confined the desert places only to the speaker, and to the speaker's self-awareness. The meaning is thereby limited and for this reason is not an issue for dispute. Because of the metaphor, however, it can reach a wide application, for there are many readers willing to assent to it.

Frost is actually relying on such assent, for the poem is in a long tradition of self-analysis and self-abasement. The proper Christian attitude of the prayerful person is to declare his unworthiness before God and to state his fears of being alone without God's kindness and protection. Although the speaker does not mention God, Frost is touching this habit of self-study and criticism. Uriah Heep to the contrary, we tend to trust someone who expresses fear at his own limitations and shortcomings. Such is the building block of human progress; all of Frost's poem fashions this block, which is given final shape in the concluding metaphor. Prompted by the discoveries of the galaxies and intergalactic distances in the 1920's and 1930's, the poem is seen as an expression of the human idea that men should solve human problems before they ponder outer space (or enter it). Therefore, nothing about the final metaphoric shift is unusual; the meaning is both a logical turn within the poem and a natural turn of mind in our own culture.

Despite these arguments, the shift of meaning may still be open to the charge that Frost has been too brief in his development of the idea; he simply states it and leaves it. Of course, a long psychological study about all the worst aspects of human personality would tell more than Frost does. His aim, however, is to employ his material briefly in order to produce the reader's assent in a flash of insight. A poetic wholeness is Frost's goal here; his wish is to use the idea in a poetic structure, not to explicate it. A better charge might be in fact that the final meaning of "desert places" is trite and therefore that the poem is unsuccessful. If one were to lift the term out of its context, this charge might be maintained. But the phrase must be kept in context, and there it offers freshness and surprise. Frost has used it to connote the cold, the distant, the blank, the emotionless aspects of human beings—the ice of human neglect, not the fire of human passion. This connotation of the term is particularly meaningful as world population increases and as men develop callousness toward the plight of others. Frost's term is carefully wrought and skillfully presented, an element of success in a successful poem.

The Theme on the Setting of a Literary Work

5 *Setting* refers to the natural and artificial scenery or environment in which characters in literature live, move, and have their being. Setting also includes what in the theatre would be called props or properties—the implements and manufactured goods employed by the characters in various activities. Such things as the time of day and the consequent amount of light at which an event occurs, the flora and fauna, the sounds described, the smells, and the weather are all part of the setting. Paint brushes, apples, pitchforks, rafts, six-shooters, watches, automobiles, horses and buggies, and innumerable other items belong to the setting. References to clothing, descriptions of physical appearance, and spatial relationships among the characters are also part of setting. In short, the setting of a work is the sum total of references to physical and temporal objects and artifacts.

The setting in a story or novel is very much like the sets and properties of the stage. Dramatists, however, are physically limited by what can be placed and carried. A typical play today takes place in a single area, with differences in time of day or season suggested by lighting and movable properties. In Shakespeare's day the stage was a bare platform with almost no movable scenery, and scenes were necessarily independent of place with focus on action, language, and imagery. Except for the use of various appurtenances of the stage, the effects of setting on Shakespeare's characterizations are negligible. By contrast to dramatic works, the nondramatic writer is limited only by his imagination. It is possible for him to include details of many places without the slightest external restraint. Therefore, for purposes of the present theme, the references to setting will be to stories, novels, and those poems that establish a setting either in nature or in man-made things.

It goes virtually without saying that the action of a story may occur in more than one place. In a novel, the locale may shift constantly. Although there may be several settings in a work, the term *setting* refers generally to all the places mentioned. If a story is short, the scenes may all be in one city or countryside, so that a theme about setting could include a discussion of all the locations within the story. If your assignment is on a novel, your discussion could best be devoted to the setting of only one major scene; otherwise you would necessarily be forced beyond the limits of a single theme.

Types of Settings

Usually writers who describe a primitive, wild, natural setting emphasize both the beautiful and dangerous aspects of nature. Frequently, in fact, the wilderness will represent a constant threat to the characters. Literature dating from superstitious times emphasizes the fabulous, the remote, the supernatural; hence the labyrinth of ancient myths—Olympus, Valhalla, the cave of Polyphemus, or the treacherous cliffs of Carthage. Medieval writers wrote of fairy worlds, which included dark, brooding forests and fire-breathing dragons. In more recent times nature is usually not dangerous; rather literature about pioneer life has presented the land as a slow, debilitating force acting against the men who tried to cultivate it. Writers of today, when much of nature has been tamed, create a natural setting that is more friendly, and often nature serves as a backdrop for religious meditation. Where there is wilderness, however, there is usually awe and grandeur and also danger.

Artificial scenery always refers to the societies that created it. Hence a building, or a room, bespeaks the character of those who build and inhabit it, and ultimately it reveals the social and political orders that maintain the condition. A sumptuous artificial setting emphasizes the sumptuous and refined taste of the characters living in it, and also their financial and political resources. With a few cracks in the plaster and some chips in the paint or wallpaper, the same setting may well reflect persons of the same taste undergoing a decline in fortune and power. More recently the development of the idea that environment has a vital influence on human character has produced a number of stories that emphasize the deleterious effect of dirty, cold, ill-lit cities and drab rooms. D. H. Lawrence, who wrote many works in which environment is shown to have a shaping influence on character, wrote vehemently that ugliness hurts human beings —an idea that underlies much *realistic,* or *naturalistic,* fiction:

> Now though perhaps nobody knew it, it was ugliness which really betrayed the spirit of man, in the nineteenth century. The great crime which the moneyed classes and promoters of industry committed in the palmy

> Victorian days was the condemning of the workers to ugliness, ugliness, ugliness: meanness and formless and ugly surroundings, ugly ideals, ugly religion, ugly hope, ugly love, ugly clothes, ugly furniture, ugly houses, ugly relationship between workers and employers.[1]

This is not to say that an author cannot describe slovenly conditions to show that his characters are also slovenly, but it is to say that he may often include such descriptions to show that an ugly environment has contributed to the weariness, insensitivity, negligence, or even hostility in his characters.

Setting refers not only to place but also to time and everything that time implies. Morning, for example, is a time of beginning, and perhaps of optimism, whereas twilight is close to evening and hence a less optimistic time. The spirits of the hero Werther in Goethe's novel *The Sorrows of Young Werther* are directly related to spring, summer, autumn, and winter; as the seasons change Werther becomes more depressed until the winter of his soul overwhelms him. A happier mood is established by Wordsworth in "Lines Written in Early Spring," where the title and the first two lines lead into a meditation on the discrepancy between the joyful season and the mismanagement of human beings by one another.

Studying the Uses of Setting

On the very primary level setting has served as a means of creating a semblance of realism in literature. Realism of course depends on the beholder, but men will always assent to the description of observable phenomena. Realism in a broad sense may be extended to include what is described from philosophical or religious points of view; psychological and political viewpoints will also color what is seen and described yet still determine what is called "realistic."

As a writer wishes to stress character, plot, or action, he may emphasize or minimize setting. At times a setting will serve as a mere location for events, as in Henry James's short story "The Tree of Knowledge." In this story the setting is minimal, and all the emphasis is on conversation and analysis of character. In other stories, however, the setting may become so significant that it virtually becomes an active participant in the action. A noteworthy example is the setting of Thomas Hardy's novel *The Return of the Native*. The desolate area known as Egdon Heath directly influences the characters who live there; it governs their lives and most of their activities. Although the Heath occasionally serves to bring characters together, more often it acts as a barrier, and it is even the active cause of the death of Mrs. Yeobright and Eustacia Vie.

[1] *The Portable D. H. Lawrence,* ed. Diana Trilling (New York: The Viking Press, 1947, reprinted 1950), p. 620.

In studying the setting of any particular work, your first concern should be to discover all details that conceivably form a part of setting and then to determine how the author has used these details. This concern is artistic. You might observe, for example, that the manipulation of setting may be a kind of direct language, a means by which the author makes statements that he may or may not interpret. In the concluding scene of E. M. Forster's *Passage to India,* a large rock divides the path along which the two major characters are riding. This rock is a direct barrier between them, and Forster is at pains to point out this fact.

Another way to use setting as a kind of statement is to describe a setting in lieu of describing events, in this sense placing the setting on the level of metaphor (this technique has become common in motion pictures). The language used by the author to describe the setting is an important clue for you to follow in interpreting his story. Allan Seager's "This Town and Salamanca" provides such an example: the narrator describes the adventures of a childhood friend who spent his early manhood as a world traveler. The narrator dwells longingly and lovingly on the places visited by the friend, using language that gives them a romantic, heroic glow. At the same time, he describes his home town in matter-of-fact, flat language. As a result of this technique, Seager makes the assumptions and ideals of his narrator clear.

An author might also manipulate setting as a means of organizing his story structurally. It is often comic, for example, to move a character from one environment to another (provided that no harm is done in the process). Thus, Stephen Crane provokes smiles, if not laughter, in the first part of "The Bride Comes to Yellow Sky" by shifting a provincial town marshal into the plush setting of a Pullman car. Crane's description of the awkwardness of the marshal and the patronizing airs of the other characters, who are accustomed to the setting, is humorous. The same shifting of environment causes a bitterly comic and finally tragic effect in Aldous Huxley's *Brave New World,* in which the main character, John, leaves a primitive world for a hyper-modern, super-urbanized one.

Another structural manipulation of setting is the "framing" method: an author "frames" his story by opening with a description of the setting and then returns to the description at the end. Like a picture frame, the setting constantly influences the story. An outstanding example of the framing method is found in Hemingway's story "In Another Country," which is set in Milan in World War I. The opening picture is one of windy, autumnal chill, with dusky light illuminating dead poultry and dead animals hanging in a butcher's shop; the twilight casts a pall over a hospital courtyard, from which many funeral processions begin. At the story's end, one of the principal characters, a major, receives news that his wife has died of pneumonia (caught, presumably, because of the chill). He has been wounded in action and is at the hospital undergoing physical therapy by machine, and the news of his wife's death leaves him despondently looking out the windows. What he sees is obviously the same gloomy scene described at the opening of the story. By concluding in this way, Hemingway has framed the events in a setting of dusk, depression, and death.

A more full use of setting is the "enclosing" setting—a setting that serves as the place of the entire action and that is constant and prominent throughout the story. A notable example is the Usher mansion in Poe's "The Fall of the House of Usher." The house is approached, entered, and left by the narrator after a short lapse of time, which comprises the entire action; all attention in the story is focussed on the house and its owners, Roderick Usher and his sister. Details of the house itself are vital to the action, and the condition of the house is symbolic of the condition of its occupants. Few stories have had setting, character, action, and mood so skillfully integrated as does this one.

To the degree that a setting can add metaphoric energy to its purely mechanical functions, the discussion of setting fuses with that of *imagery* (see Chapter 10). Setting is often a form of imagery, for the qualities of a setting, like anything else, can be abstracted; if these qualities are generally true, then the setting is metaphorical and may become symbolic. The ease with which the language itself becomes metaphoric assists this process. Thus, when Poe writes that the stones of the Usher mansion possess a "still perfect adaptation of parts and the crumbling condition of the individual stones," it is obvious that he speaks not only of the house but also of the deteriorating psyche of Roderick Usher. Robert Frost's poem "Mending Wall" describes the scene of two men mending a stone wall in the springtime. Frost makes it clear that the wall refers metaphorically to those barriers that prevent close relationships between human beings, those protections of silence and indifference that allow a person to refuse understanding and compassion to others. Once this metaphorical significance is established, it is possible to carry the meaning of the wall still further; it can refer to political or social boundaries or more generally to any barrier between individuals or groups. Another wall that is symbolic is that in Jean Paul Sartre's story "The Wall," in this case a wall against which prisoners are lined up and shot. The wall serves as a symbol of Sartre's idea that the termination of life is arbitrary and ridiculous and that the activities of life itself are similarly arbitrary and ridiculous. So well known is this use of setting that Sartre's wall has been claimed as a symbol of modern Existentialist philosophy, of which Sartre is a leading advocate.

The fact that setting merges into metaphor and symbol should make you constantly on the alert to determine when the two become one. You might note that the description of an action requires only a functional description of setting. An action set in a forest needs no more description than that the forest is there. But if a writer describes the trees, the colors, the shapes, the light, the animal inhabitants, or the topography, you should try to determine his purpose. That is, descriptions of setting may vary from the purely functional and appropriate to the evocative and to the outrightly symbolic; but they are almost never purely accidental or gratuitous. A full, colorful description may be designed as an appropriate setting for a happy action; but it might just as easily be interpreted as an ironic backdrop for an unhappy one. You can make your determinations as you read the story carefully, and you can see when the setting becomes evocative and symbolic. In Dickens's *Bleak House,* for example, Dickens describes a district called "Tom All Alone's" as a shadowy, dark, unhealthy, hopeless place. The district is symbolic of the bleak fate of all those human creatures doomed to live there. By contrast, Dickens creates a cheerful symbol in his constant references to the bubbling fountain toward the end of *David Copperfield.* The fountain suggests the upsurging fortunes of David and his growing love for Agnes.

Just as setting performs a vital functional role and also contributes to overall meaning because of metaphoric significance, it also affects the *atmosphere* or *mood* of stories and poems. The styles and shapes of things described, their colors, the language used to describe them—all have their own connotative life that an author may utilize to fulfill his aims. A description of happy colors (like reds, oranges, yellows, and greens) may contribute to a mood of gaiety, whereas one of sombre colors (like blacks and greys) may suggest sobriety or gloom. The introduction of references to smells and sounds brings the setting even more to life by asking more responses from the reader than those merely to sight. The setting of a story on a farm, or in a suburban split-level home, or in a large apartment, may evoke a response to these habitats that may contribute to a story's atmosphere.

The style with which things are described may have an effect on atmosphere, for a writer may make his scene static or still with many linking and passive words for one mood, but evoke another mood in a lively scene through the use of active verbs. Sometimes a setting may speak for itself, without authorial comment, but often the author will introduce comments designed to connect the setting with the characters or else to suggest the proper response to the reader. Here is a fragment from a lengthy description of a setting in Sir Walter Scott's *Kenilworth.* This description performs both functions, skillfully linking description to reader and character:

> . . . Formal walks and avenues, which, at different points, crossed this principal approach, were, in like manner, choked up and interrupted by piles of brushwood and billets, and in other places by underwood and brambles. Besides the general effect of desolation which is so strongly impressed, whenever we behold the contrivances of man wasted and ob-

literated by neglect, and witness the marks of social life effaced gradually by the influence of vegetation, the size of the trees, and the outspreading extent of their boughs, diffused a gloom over the scene, even when the sun was at the highest, and made a proportional impression on the mind of those who visited it. This was felt even by Michael Lambourne, however alien his habits were to receiving any impressions, excepting from things which addressed themselves immediately to his passions.[2]

Although the description of a setting may thus contribute to atmosphere in a number of ways, it is important to remember that atmosphere is a large concept and is affected by everything in the story, not just the setting. Action, character, dialogue, idea, allusion, and style are all elements that contribute to atmosphere.

The Organization of Your Theme

The object of this theme should be to relate the setting to some aspect of the work being studied. You should not simply describe the setting and be satisfied. You should make your description a part of a point such as "The author's description of setting reveals an eye for detail, spatial relationships, and color," and so on. Then, your discussion would take the shape required by your central idea; your own detail would be functional. Your theme should move from a discussion of setting toward a discussion of its effects.

INTRODUCTION

Here you should limit that aspect of the setting you wish to discuss and relate it to your central idea and thesis sentence. Any special problems and qualifications should be mentioned here.

BODY

Here are some ideas about what to include in the body of your theme. You may concentrate on one of these, or two or three, depending on the story or poem that you are analyzing. Your principal aim should be to say as much as possible about the setting within the assigned length.

1. The relationship of physical characteristics of the setting to some general observation about these characteristics. If the author has been particularly careful to mention many details of the setting, you could fruitfully discuss these details in an attempt to re-create what you think the author envisaged and to make observations about the qualities of the setting. The settings of Shirley Jackson's "The Lottery" or Franz

2 *Kenilworth* (London: Everyman's Library, 1906), p. 25.

Kafka's "In the Penal Colony" could be treated in this way. Among the questions you might attempt to answer are these: Can the setting be re-created and imagined by the reader? Are the details about the setting specific, or are they vague? How great a bearing do the details have on the action of the story? Are they constantly used, or are they put aside once the action has begun? What details are neglected that the author might possibly have mentioned? On the basis of your study, what conclusions can you draw about the author's ability to paint a verbal picture (does the author describe shapes and distances better than colors, or vice versa)? Is he perceptive to smells and sounds? Does he introduce new details as the need seems to arise, or does he rely on his first descriptions?

2. The relationship of the setting to character. In many instances the author emphasizes the effect of environment on character, as in O. E. Rölvaag's novel *Giants in the Earth,* Melville's story "Bartleby the Scrivener," or Theodore Roethke's poem "Dolor." Your aim in a theme on this subject is not, as in the first type, to describe the details of setting, but to select those details with the most bearing on character and to speak about their effects. Questions that would lead you into the topic might be the following: What tasks do the characters perform that involve them in the setting? What particular physical and moral strengths do these tasks require? What weaknesses do they bring out? What traits enable a person to adjust to these conditions and to prevail against them? What outlooks toward God, life, and Nature do the characters have that may be traced specifically to their environment? That is, does the world seem difficult, easy? Does God seem benevolent, all-powerful, harsh, or nonexistent? Does Nature seem to be an enemy or a friend? Are the views justified in terms of the life envisaged in the story, or do some characters receive false impressions? Do they ignore aspects of their environment? What other character traits may be traced to the way of life on the soil or before the mast or within the sweatshop or behind the desk? Emphasize constantly the interaction of setting and character.

3. The relationship of setting and (a) atmosphere (b) structure and action and (c) ideas. This theme attempts to deal with artistic relationships and effects. A theme on atmosphere and setting should establish the prevailing atmosphere or mood of the work and then attempt to fit the setting into this whole. Colors, shapes, time of year (or day) and the effects that these things generally produce are relevant here. If the atmosphere of the setting is at variance with the general effect of the story, you should emphasize this variance and attempt to determine why it exists.

A theme about the relation of setting to structure and action should attempt to show how significant the setting is in the form and principal actions of the story. Is the setting a frame, an enclosure? Is it mentioned at various divisions or shifts in the action? Is it brought in as a natural place for the characters, or does it become significant accidentally? That is, does a character move naturally from, say, a park to a pastry shop to home, or does he move from the park and then accidentally walk down a street he never walks down, where the main action takes place? How important a role does the setting play in the action? Do the characteristics of a room seem appropriate for a private conversation, for private grief, or for personal isolation? Do the characteristics of a natural scene enter directly into the action as land that is to be plowed, trees to be cleared, or great nautical distances to be traversed? Does the setting afford any natural pleasures of which the characters take advantage? Does it afford natural dangers that the characters either avoid or to which they fall prey?

A theme about setting and ideas should emphasize the setting as statement and metaphor. A writer, for example, may establish that a ship, where the action occurs, is similar to the world at large and, therefore, that his ideas about life aboard ship are also true of life in general. A natural setting that is crisp, clear, and bright, with precisely defined relationships, might be created by an author as a way of saying that truth in the universe can be readily grasped; yet a setting that emphasizes haziness, difficulty of determining things at a distance, or vastness might be construed to mean that truth is not easily found and that much of life is mysterious. Similarly, the conditions of buildings, rooms, and tools might be interpreted as statements about the conditions of life generally. When settings become symbolic, as discussed earlier in this chapter, then the value of the symbols should be described. In this theme you should stress not only the ideas represented by the setting but also the means by which the setting lends itself to statement. Before attempting a theme about setting and symbol, you would do well to read the chapter on imagery (Chapter 10).

SAMPLE THEME

The Setting of Conrad's Story "The Secret Sharer"

If the setting of Conrad's "The Secret Sharer" were not as descriptive and detailed as it is, the story would not be effective. The setting aboard ship in the Gulf of Siam, described in the Captain's words, leads to the relevant action in the first part of the story, namely the Captain's decision to conceal Leggatt both from his own crew and from the Captain and crew of the *Sephora,* the ship aboard which Leggatt "committed" his crime. By law, the Captain does wrong in aiding and abetting Legatt, and a great deal of explaining and describing on Conrad's part is necessary to justify this baffling of courtroom justice. The concealment itself, to be plausible, requires detailed description of the Captain's cabin and the adjacent parts of the ship. Conrad's picturesque and detailed description of the setting therefore serves first to persuade the reader to see things as the Captain sees them—to focus attention on his human, personal considerations—and second to act as a passive agent in the sometimes melodramatic action of the story.

Although the only essential actions in the first quarter of the story are the Captain's conversations with Leggatt and the decision to shelter him, the section contains much description both of the seascape and of the ship. Because the Captain is the observer and narrator, the setting reveals his broad, full perspective. He is an inquisitive, understanding man who sees and notices much. His perceptions take in shapes, distances, and colors:

> . . . when I turned my head to take a parting glance at the tug which had just left us anchored outside the bar, I saw the straight line of the flat shore joined to the stable sea, edge to edge, with a perfect and unmarked closeness, in one leveled floor half brown, half blue under the enormous dome of the sky.[3]

Because of this eye for detail, the reader is inclined to accept the Captain's generalization, which concludes the opening descriptions:

> In this breathless pause at the threshold of a long passage we seemed to be measuring our fitness for a long and arduous enterprise, the appointed task of both our existences [i.e., the ship's and the captain's] to be carried out, far from all human eyes, with only sky and sea for spectators and for judges (p. 649).

Indeed, Conrad's main reason for the opening detail is to establish confidence in the Captain. If the reader can accept the Captain's sensitivity toward the natural world, it will be possible then to accept his judgment and protection of Leggatt, for Leggatt is portrayed with characteristics so similar to those of the Captain that he is constantly referred to as the Captain's "double." The two characters have much in common; the sea links them in the brotherhood of naval life, and the sea itself is the means by which they meet. It is also the Captain's observations of the effects of the sea on Leggatt's appearance that emphasize their kinship. Leggatt comes to the ship at night through the dark water, cast in a "ghastly, silvery, fishlike" and "greenish cadaverous glow" (pp. 655, 654). The setting itself underscores the Captain's unspoken but

---

[3] Morton Dauwen Zabel, ed., *The Portable Conrad* (New York: The Viking Press, 1950), p. 648. All parenthetical page numbers refer to this edition.

clearly felt awareness, personified in Leggatt, that within each human being is the potentiality of trouble and that this danger stems from our very origins, symbolized by the darkness (of the soul) and the water (from which life comes). Some are lucky enough to avoid trouble, but when it emerges, we must protect ourselves from it. Something like this reasoning makes understandable the Captain's decision to protect Leggatt, whose claims of innocence are not necessary to the Captain's feeling of kinship with him. By using the setting to show the Captain's sensitivity, Conrad makes his actions acceptable.

To make the events acceptable to the reader is also the purpose of Conrad's attention to detail throughout the story, particularly to those details of the ship and the coast of Cambodia that permit the successful concealment of Leggatt. It is vital to the story's credibility that the details of the Captain's cabin be presented. The *L* shape of the cabin is mentioned as providing a number of hiding places—the hanging coats, the bathroom, the curtained bunk. The tension resulting from the near-discoveries by the steward all depend on details about the cabin being known. Similarly, touring the ship itself becomes a means by which the Captain preserves his composure when the *Sephora's* captain comes aboard searching for Leggatt. The noise made by sailors walking on the deck above the Captain's cabin permits the Captain and Leggatt to speak together without fear of being overheard. The sail locker is the place of concealment for Leggatt as he prepares to leave the ship.

Many details of this sort could be mentioned, for it would be difficult to refer to any action in "The Secret Sharer" that is not closely related to the setting of the ship. The section of the story in which details about the setting become most important, however, is the conclusion, when the ship itself is in danger of foundering on the Cambodian shore. With the "black mass of Koh-ring" hovering over the ship, the Captain steers dangerously close to land, in an action symbolic of the decision he has made to save Leggatt. The closeness of Koh-ring to the ship and the consequent danger to the Captain's future suggest the difficulty and danger men generally must face if they are to carry on in life. Symbolically, even though the tug boat at the story's beginning leaves the Captain's ship and thus emphasizes man's independence of action, Koh-ring emphasizes the threat hanging over man as he exercises this independence.

The setting of the story thus verges between the real on the one hand and the symbolic on the other. Without the realistic details about the ship and navigational methods, the story would not be as believable or as exciting as it is. The setting permits the reader to accept the story on the easiest level, that of the action, without becoming involved in the aura of symbolism that surrounds the action.

If one chooses to savor the incidents, however, the details support conclusion after conclusion. The setting of the tale within the tale—Leggatt's narration of how he strangled the sailor—might be construed to mean that men are sometimes faced with circumstances in which by doing right (putting up a sail to rescue a ship in a severe storm) they also inadvertently do wrong. Judgment in such cases, if possible in view of the facts, must be tempered with understanding. The Captain shows such understanding, for clearly he can see himself behaving the same way under the same conditions. Such possible interpretations enable one to conclude that Conrad's use of setting provides a dynamic image of the world that men must face. This world is vast and mysterious, and the consequences of action in it are not predictable. If a good action produces a bad effect, this action should be judged fully, in view of the resultant good and character of the actor, and should never be considered apart from all its effects.

The Theme About a Literary Work as it Embodies Ideas

6 The word *idea* is closely related to the actions of seeing and knowing. It is variously defined as a mental image, picture, or perception and also as a concept, thought, opinion, or belief. This second meaning is the more widely held and the one that will be used in this chapter. You may have expressed the idea that men are punished for their sins or that they are not punished. This idea fits the definition of belief. Or you may have attempted to think of the idea of *freedom,* which is a concept about a desirable political and personal condition. These ideas are simple in the sense that they do not call forth reasoning. But the word *idea* may also refer to plans and schemes that are products of the thinking or reasoning process. Thus the idea of *democracy* is a complex one that involves a certain analysis and belief in human nature; it is a plan, based on this analysis and belief, about proper political organization and operation to utilize the best in human nature and to control the worst. In studying literature you will encounter both simple and complex ideas.

You have spent much of your reading time in discovering and profiting from ideas, just as much classroom time on literature is devoted to the discussion of ideas. But bear in mind that although ideas are important, they are not all. Try to find a "message" in Keats's "To Autumn," and you will realize that looking for ideas and *only* for ideas has limitations (e.g., searching only for ideas might make a reader oblivious to literary pleasures derivable from such things as the artist's diction, manipulation of sound, comic techniques, and control over structure). Within these limitations, however, the study of ideas is valuable. If you have been asked to write about ideas, your purpose should be to analyze the literary work in order to name, discuss, and evaluate the ideas contained within it. Usually it is best for you to concentrate on one major idea rather than several.

The Place of Ideas

In expository literature there are few special obstacles to understanding the principal idea or ideas, because a major purpose of exposition is to present ideas. Except for the special kind of exposition known as dialogue, exposition offers only the ordinary difficulty of understanding the ideas as they are presented—a difficulty that every college student encounters when he listens to a lecture or reads a textbook.

In imaginative literature, however, which tells stories and presents attitudes, the perception of ideas is more difficult, since the ideas are usually presented indirectly and are therefore subject to interpretation. Although ideas are subordinate to the story and although the story could be enjoyed without reference to them, the ideas are important reasons for which the writer has written the story. Sometimes they will have dictated both the shape that the story takes and also the various characterizations. Suppose a writer may have an idea that a particular custom or institution of society is wrong, or he may have an idea that human beings should be free or should not be. He may then write a story or novel to make these ideas apparent. Hence, many works exemplify or dramatize political, psychological, or social ideas. Sometimes a writer may introduce the same idea into different works, perhaps to test the idea by varying it and seeing how far it can be pursued. Ideas, in short, are vital in the content and form of literature, and an analysis of ideas necessarily implies a consideration of their artistic effect.

How to Find Ideas

You should therefore know the ways, direct and indirect, by which authors express ideas. The following descriptions are for convenient analysis only, because in a literary work the methods described may all occur simultaneously.

DIRECT STATEMENTS BY THE AUTHOR   Often an author makes direct statements of ideas in order to guide or deepen your understanding of his story. George Eliot, for example, is noted for the many discussions about human character and motivation interspersed throughout her novels. Also, an author manipulates literary devices such as metaphors, similes, settings, and physical descriptions in such a way that these may be interpreted as statements of his own ideas. In the stories of J. D.

Salinger the introduction of a bright, intuitive child has the importance of a symbol, for the child always suggests Salinger's idea that the insights of children, who are close to God in time, serve as evidence of God's being and for this reason are spiritual and emotional stimuli to jaded adults.

When an author states ideas in his own person or through literary devices, you should consider these at face value. It is reasonable, when you discuss these ideas, to attribute them to the author. Remember, however, that your attribution should not have the weight of absolute biographical fact. You are reading an author's work, not his mind, and an author may well exercise his right to express ideas of the moment or ideas with which he does not agree. When in writing a theme you say "George Eliot believes" or "It is Faulkner's idea that," you must always realize the limitations of your statements: you are really not talking absolutely about the *authors* but instead are talking about their *works*. With this reservation your remarks about an author's ideas should usually be acceptable.

DIRECT STATEMENTS BY THE AUTHOR'S PERSONA   Frequently, instead of narrating in their own persons, authors will write from the point of view of a character in the work (for example, Frederick Henry in *A Farewell to Arms* and Gulliver in *Gulliver's Travels*). Such a character is called a *persona*, with life and independence of his own and with the freedom to state ideas peculiar to himself. Whereas the author unquestionably might agree with the ideas of his *persona*, you can never know exactly when this agreement takes place. Although the statements of a *persona* may be direct, you must use your ingenuity and intuition in deciding how closely the *persona's* ideas correspond with the author's.

DRAMATIC STATEMENTS MADE BY THE CHARACTERS IN THE WORK   In any dramatic work, and in most novels, stories, and poems, the characters will state ideas. What the characters say will often be in conflict, for an author may sometimes present thirteen ways of looking at a blackbird and leave the choice up to you. He may provide you with guides for your choice, however. For instance, he may create an admirable character whose ideas presumably coincide with his own. The reverse would be true for a bad character, and so forth.

CHARACTERS WHO STAND FOR IDEAS   The characters themselves often represent ideas. In this case, interactions of the characters may represent the interweaving of ideas, and the conflicts between characters may represent conflicts between ideas. For example, in allegories like *The Faerie Queene* and *Pilgrim's Progress,* the characters stand for ideas in conflict. Aldous Huxley, in his novels, has evolved a form called *the novel of ideas,* where the various characters in the story are made to represent ideas that in Huxley's opinion give his novels intellectual life.

THE WORK ITSELF AS IT IMPLIES IDEAS   Perhaps the most important method by which authors embody ideas in a literary work is to manage carefully the total impression of the work. All the events and characters may add up to an idea that is made particularly powerful by the emotional impact of the story itself. Thus, although an idea may never be stated in the work, it will be apparent after you have finished reading it. In the novel *A Passage to India,* E. M. Forster shows that political institutions and racial and national barriers prevent men from realizing that they are brothers. He does not use these words, but this idea is clearly embodied in the novel: the separation of the Indian and Anglo-Indian communities even after the charges against Dr. Aziz are dropped and the differences in customs between the English and the Indians, and even between the Hindus and the Moslems among the Indians themselves, all point toward this idea. Your reading would be incomplete if you did not see this implication. Similarly, Shakespeare's *Hamlet* might be interpreted as an illustration of the idea that evil breeds evil upon evil, sweeping both the innocent and guilty before it. You will recognize that this act of interpreting the basic idea in a work of fiction is the same that you have been performing whenever you form a central idea for any theme you write.

It should be apparent that your easiest task in determining ideas will occur when the author speaks directly. In all the other cases you must interpret indirect and dramatic statements and be alert to the implications of each work that you read. You must be certain that there is adequate justification *in the literary work* for the points that you are making about it.

Two Critical Problems

Two critical problems are raised by the analysis of literature for ideas. The first is whether or not literature should be purely "instructive" or purely "pleasing" or both. The classical or "Horatian" view is that it should be both. Some writers have denied one or the other of these two aims (e.g., Poe, who said that the writer should aim only at giving pleasure, and Shaw, who said that the only justification for writing was to instruct). The issue is not only how pleasing are ideas themselves but also how relevant are they to literature. You are free to decide this issue for yourself, but you should realize that the Horatian view has been the most influential, historically, and that therefore many writers have written with both an instructive and a pleasure-giving intention.

The word *intention* brings up the second problem, for it is often difficult and sometimes almost impossible to claim that an author *intended* that you derive a certain idea from his work. For example, there has been a long controversy over Shakespeare's idea about Shylock in *The Merchant of Venice:* did Shakespeare present Shylock as a farcical outsider in a Christian society or as a sympathetic outcast and a victim of religious prejudice? Similarly, in reference to Shakespeare's *Henry V,* many critics have thought that Henry is engaged in a righteous war that brings out the valor and strength of the English people and that he is one of England's great kings. But other critics have thought that Henry cynically embarks on a war of aggression and is responsible for many needless deaths. These differences of interpretation bring up the question of whether the writer's intention is even relevant, because the author seldom states his intention explicitly.[1] Many critics have asserted that great works have new meanings for each succeeding generation, in spite of the writer's intention. There is some validity to this claim, and one must assent to it to the degree that the ideas in every work are to be taken as having value for the present, unless their irrelevance can be proved. Still other critics, as a result of research into the intellectual milieus of the various literary periods, have claimed that an author's probable intentions can be discovered and that his work is an important piece of evidence in the determination of his intentions. This kind of research is essential in the historical study of literature. As with the first problem, of course, you are free to weigh the relative merits of these views and to decide what your position will be.

Your Theme

There are two major steps in analyzing imaginative literature for ideas. The first is to "translate" the concrete story into the usual language of ideas—namely, expository prose. You must be sure that the statement of your own central idea is couched in this way. For example, Jane Austen's novel *Northanger Abbey* (completed in 1803) is commonly recognized as a satire on the supernatural, Gothic novels popular at the end of the eighteenth century. If you are to write a theme about a major idea in the novel, however, you should not attempt to develop the statement that the novel is a satire. Instead, you should take some aspect of the satire that can be analyzed and discussed *as an idea.* Possibly your thesis might become "Jane Austen's idea is that human nature and human drama are best found in incidents of everyday life, not in imaginative fantasies." Another theme idea might be, "Jane Austen's

---

[1] See W. K. Wimsatt, Jr., "The Intentional Fallacy," *The Verbal Icon* (New York: The Noonday Press, 1960), pp. 3-18.

idea is that the true qualities of heroism are stability and common sense." Both these ideas can be derived from the satire of *Northanger Abbey* and could be treated readily within theme limits. Satire itself is not readily dealt with because it is a literary mode, not an idea. The decision by an author to employ such a mode stems from an idea like the two just cited. The important point you must remember is that in dealing with ideas you must use the language of ideas; it is easy to go wrong if you do not.

The second major step in writing on ideas is to determine the form of your own theme by pursuing the idea and its ramifications within the work being studied. An idea itself usually does not require many words to express, but in order to write a good theme about it you must, in addition to naming and describing it, show how and where it is exemplified; you must demonstrate its importance in the work as a whole. A theme on the second idea about *Northanger Abbey*, for example, might demonstrate that the development of the heroine's character takes the pattern of increasing awareness of the truth that heroism is stability and common sense. Everything that happens to her in the novel may be seen as demonstrative of this truth.

In forming your own theme, you might help yourself by answering questions like the following about the idea you are discussing: What is the best statement of the idea that you can make? What has the author done with the idea? How can the actions of the major character or characters be related to the idea? Can the organization of the story be seen as a function of the idea? Does the setting have any relationship to the idea? Is there imagery or symbolism that develops or illustrates the idea? Does this imagery or symbolism recur? Are there any characters, or actions, who may be measured according to how they fail to live up to the idea? In short, develop your theme by interpreting the work in light of the major idea you have chosen for discussion.

You can easily see that your discussion will lead you into statements with which someone else might take issue. Remember, however, that your interpretation will usually be respected so long as you base your statements accurately on the story itself. If for some reason you happen to make errors, either because of faulty understanding or because of your own prejudgments, you will of course be subject to correction. Be sure that your reading is accurate and that your interpretation can be defended at each point by material within the work.

The Organization of Your Theme

In your themes your instructor will look for the intelligence, skill, and accuracy with which you make use of the story materials as a base for your discussion of ideas. The general form of your theme will probably be (a) statement of the idea, and (b) discussion of the relevance and place of the idea in the work.

INTRODUCTION

In the introduction your naming of the idea will in fact be the central idea of your theme. You should state that the idea has interest and importance in order to arouse your reader's curiosity about your paper. You might also show how you arrived at your decision to write about that particular idea. Conclude your introduction with a thesis sentence.

BODY

The body of your paper should show the ways in which the writer has brought out the idea in his work. Your discussion might touch everything in the work, but in a short theme you cannot discuss everything fully. Therefore you must, as always, be selective in what you choose to discuss. Use only those details that are essential and clearly relevant.

It is easy, when you illustrate your point, to let the detail become an end in itself rather than a means toward asserting the truth of your central idea. Once you start describing the story and move away from your point, you actually have started to summarize. Remember, *your central idea must always be foremost in your reader's mind*. The unifying element in your theme is this idea, and you must keep mentioning it. As you are writing, stop at various times and ask yourself: "Is this material relevant to my point so that my reader could immediately see its relevance, or is it just synopsis?" It is advisable to keep restating the original idea, in order to remind your reader of your purpose in writing. Everything you say should be relevant, and you must remember that your reader is not likely to be as aware of your point as you are. How can he know unless you tell him? Don't force him to do too much guessing, or he may stop reading your paper.

CONCLUSION

In your conclusion you ought to evaluate the idea and its function in the text. The evaluation of the idea is sometimes external to the text, because it may include individual attitudes (e.g., a student considering Bunyan's idea of Christian salvation in *Pilgrim's Progress* would probably discuss his own ideas too). However, the consideration of the idea's function is artistic. How forcefully is the idea presented? How convincing is it in the story? With answers to these questions you may conclude.

SAMPLE THEME

The Idea in D. H. Lawrence's
"The Horse Dealer's Daughter"
that Man's Destiny is to Love

Lawrence demonstrates so many ideas about the love between man and woman in this story that I cannot possibly discuss them all here. A few separate ideas are: that love is a part of the uncontrollable side of man's life—the emotions; that love starts with the body, and that no satisfactory relationship between man and woman can be achieved without this basis; that love transforms life into something new; that love gives security since it fills an otherwise un-fillable void in one's life; that only love gives meaning to life; that love is not only something to live for but something to be feared. Perhaps the one idea that takes in all these is that loving is an essential part of man's nature—that it is man's destiny to love. Lawrence's story seems to be one grand embodiment of this basic idea. It controls the form of his story, and all characters seem to be judged on the basis of how successfully they live up to this idea. I will therefore discuss the idea as it appears in what I consider to be the two main divisions of the story.

In the first part Lawrence shows us characters who are without love and whose lives are therefore incomplete. Thereby he illustrates the idea that men who are not living according to their destiny will be frustrated, cantankerous, and sullen, and that they will try to find fulfillment in some other way (which will not, however, make them happy). Their lives are virtually like those of the great draft horses, which Lawrence describes as moving with "a massive, slumbrous strength, and a stupidity which held them in subjection." [2] Time, Lawrence implies, is running out on people in this condition, and unless they do something they are doomed to misery. But, according to the main idea, an evasion of the destiny to love will not avert this doom. Joe, the oldest of the Pervin brothers, has arranged for an apparently loveless marriage to achieve economic security. With deliberate finality, Lawrence disposes of Joe, who thereby becomes an example of the main idea: "He would marry and go into harness. His life was over, he would be a subject animal" (p. 115).

---

[2] "The Horse Dealer's Daughter," in Cleanth Brooks, John T. Purser, and Robert Penn Warren, eds., *An Approach to Literature,* Alternate 4th ed. (New York: Appleton-Century-Crofts, 1967), p. 115. All page numbers refer to this edition.

This idea that life virtually ends without love is finally brought to bear on Mabel, the lone girl in the Pervin family, and the figure for whom the story is named. Just as the death of her father has precipitated the breakup of the family (who melt away at this point), the breakup is precipitating some drastic action on her part. Here the operation of Lawrence's idea is brought out clearly: since it is man's destiny to love and since life without love is a kind of death and since Mabel has no love on earth to anticipate but only the love for her dead father to remember, she stolidly and deliberately chooses real death with dead love, which she prefers to a life on earth without any love at all. The first section of the story closes as Mabel attempts to drown herself. She walks "toward the centre of the pond, very slowly, gradually moving deeper into the motionless water, and still moving forward as the water got up to her breast" (p. 119).

But this pond—symbolic of death as Mabel walks into it—is also a symbol of life and regeneration (for example, infant baptism employs water, and the major symbol for life in Freudian psychology is water). This generative symbolic value is dominant in the second part of Lawrence's story and also puts into operation the second part of his idea (which has frequently been described by the old saying "Love finds a way"). Rescuing Mabel from the death to which she has consigned herself is Dr. Fergusson, who has previously been introduced as a person leading a life of quiet desperation, even though he also has derived a power from his closeness to the lives of his patients (is he living a vicarious life, or is he simply sublimating his desires?). Perhaps the good doctor's common cold, mentioned when we first meet him, is to be interpreted as a symbol of the sickness of the soul without love, and therefore the need to be well would become a strong support for Lawrence's basic idea. Whether this interpretation is right or not, however, it is important to note that Dr. Fergusson's rescue of Mabel is therapeutic not only for Mabel, but also for himself.

For the rescue follows the pattern of Lawrence's idea and is actually a symbol of the attainment of this idea: that love rescues the life without love. But love is complex, suggests Lawrence (and in this case, it is mildly comic), and it creates new problems once it has been realized. Therefore, Lawrence builds the idea that love is something to be desired but also something to be feared. It brings out emotions that are new and strange; it violates man's naturally conservative nature; it upsets previously established equilibrium; it changes life so fundamentally that no life will ever be the same after having been touched by love. Is it any wonder that Lawrence concludes his story in the following words:

"No, I want you, I want you," was all he answered, blindly, with that terrible intonation which frightened her almost more than the horror lest he should *not* want her.

—p. 123

This complexity of emotions raises Lawrence's treatment of his idea above the level of the popular, romantic, "Hollywooden" conception of love, and answers all potential objections that love between Mabel and the doctor happens too rapidly (incidentally, Lawrence carefully demonstrates that there were emotional contacts between the two lovers before the outpouring of their love in the deserted room of the Pervin house). Lawrence's idea is mature and profound. Clearly, he suggests, love itself creates problems as great as those it solves, but it also builds a solid platform of emotional strength from which these new problems can be attacked and solved. The idea is that this strength can be achieved only when a man and woman know love, because only then are they living life as it was designed. The problems facing them then, Lawrence suggests, are the real problems that man and woman should face, since the problems are a natural result of their destiny. By contrast, the men and women without love, like those at the beginning of the story, have never reached fulfillment and consequently they face problems that, though certainly severe and immediate, are really peripheral to life as it should be lived. The entire story of Mabel and Jack is an extensive example of Lawrence's dominating idea that it is the destiny of man and woman to love.

The Theme on a Close Reading
of a Passage or Work:
The Analytical-Reading Theme

7 One of your main tasks as a reader is to understand and appreciate the page before you. Beyond the words, phrases, clauses, and sentences are implications, shades of meaning, and beauty. For a full understanding and appreciation you should, theoretically, spend as much time reading a work as the author spent writing it; that is, you should spend this much time, using all your alertness and skill, if you really want to grasp everything. Unfortunately, time is prohibitive, and therefore you must settle for something less. With good reading skills, however, you can perceive and appreciate a great deal of the expressed and implied meaning.

To assist you in developing good reading techniques, your instructor will probably spend much classroom time in explicating and discussing with you various poems, novels, plays, and stories. As you experience this classroom guidance, you should develop the ability to read well without guidance. The theme asking you to perform a close reading of a passage is an important means by which your instructor can verify your progress as a reader.

The close-reading theme can be either very general or very technical, depending on the skills you have acquired when you undertake to write it. Mainly, however, the aim of the assignment is to give you a chance to exercise your general perceptions and knowledge as a reader. The theme can take the form of your abilities and interests. You may, for example, be concerned with the character of the principal male in Willa Cather's novel *The Lost Lady,* for most of the story's action is presented more or less as he sees it. You might therefore wish to concentrate on what a particular paragraph reveals about him. Or you may have acquired some interest and knowledge of political science and may wish to concentrate on the political implications of a passage in Shakespeare's *Richard II,* and so on. In short, the close-reading assignment can change as you change. It might be interesting to write such a theme early in your college days and then to write another one later, perhaps even about the same passage, after you have acquired more experience as a reader.

The assumptions behind the close-reading theme are these: if you can read a page, you can read the entire book of which the page is a part; if you can read a speech, you can read the entire play; if you can read one poem by a poet, you can read other poems by the same poet. Underlying these assumptions are others: in a good literary work, each part is absolutely essential; nothing could be eliminated without damage to the work. In the same way, all the writings of each author form a homogeneous unit, with each work contributing something to that unity. A close reading of an individual passage, therefore, or of an entire work, should indicate essential truths about the work or about the author being studied. Your reading of a passage or of a poem should indicate your ability to handle entire works. This is not to say that the writing of an analytical-reading theme automatically qualifies you to read every work by the same author. Few people would maintain that the reading of passages from Joyce's *The Dubliners* makes it possible to read passages from *Finnegans Wake* immediately. What you are showing instead is a skill, an ability to bring your knowledge and understanding to bear on a specific passage and to develop a thematically conceived response and interpretation.

A close reading of a passage requires a certain awareness of *style* and *prosody* (see Chapters 13 and 12), but your focus in this theme will only touch on these elements indirectly. Instead, you are to focus attention on everything in the passage or work assigned. If the work is particularly rich in meaning, you will need to select from the super-abundance; if the work seems thin, you can cover everything. Works by good writers, however, generally offer God's plenty for your study.

Various Assignments

A close-reading theme will frequently be assigned in courses in drama or the interpretation of poetry, although it can be assigned in any course, including courses in novels and short stories. Your instructor might give you the assignment as "Write a paper on this passage" or "Write an analysis of this poem." When you have received this assignment, you have the job of writing a theme based on close reading.

Although you are concerned here with writing a theme, you might be given the assignment as part of a classroom impromptu or examination (see Appendix A, on tests). Either you might be required to analyze a poem or passage, or you might be given a number of passages as identification-and-comment questions. If you have a passage to identify, concentrate on its subject matter and position in the work and in the philosophy of the writer.

Preparing to Write

Your first job is to read the entire work in order to make sure that you understand the relation of the passage to the whole. If you do not read the entire work first, you are likely to make inexcusable blunders in your reading of the specific passage. Read carefully. Then study the passage you are to write about. First, be sure to use the dictionary for all words that are even slightly obscure. Sometimes you may not be getting the sense of a passage at first or even second reading. Remember that even the simplest looking words may offer difficulties. Therefore, you must look up *all* the words in the passage that is giving you trouble, and frequently you will discover that your trouble resulted from attaching the incorrect meaning to a word. Use the dictionary whenever you have the slightest question. In Shakespeare's Sonnet No. 73, for example, this famous line appears:

> Bare ruined choirs, where late the sweet birds sang.

If you regard *choirs* as an organized group of singers (as you are likely to do at first), you simply will not understand the line. The dictionary will tell you that *choirs* may be an architectural term referring to the part of a church in which the singers usually are placed. Let us take another line, this time from John Donne's first Holy Sonnet:

> And thou like Adamant draw mine iron heart.

Unless you look up *Adamant* and realize that Donne uses it to mean a magnet, you are likely not to know the sense of *draw,* and you will thus miss the meaning of the entire line.

You also ought to use your imagination to find whether the words in the poem or passage convey any consistent patterns, as a pattern of references to flowers, to water, to high finance, or to political life. In your preparation for writing, do not hesitate to pick out such references in each line. Try to classify them into categories, for you can frequently achieve an extremely good reading by making drawings and schemes.

Once you have understood the words, pay some attention to the sentence structures, particularly in poetry. If you read the line "Thy merit hath my duty strongly knit," be sure that you figure out the proper subject and object of the verb ("Thy merit hath strongly knit my duty"). Or, look at these lines:

> Let such teach others who themselves excell,
> And censure freely who have written well.

> —Pope, *Essay on Criticism,* lines 15-16

On first reading, these lines are difficult. A person might even conclude that Pope is asking the critic to censure (For an assignment, look up *censure* in the O.E.D.) those writers who have written well, until the lines are unraveled thus:

> Let such who themselves excell teach others,
> And let such who have written well censure freely.

There is quite a difference here between the correct reading and the misreading. What you must keep in mind is that your failure to understand a sentence structure that no longer exists in everyday English can prevent your full understanding of a passage. Therefore you must be absolutely sure, in your preparation, that you have untied all the syntactic knots.

With this preparation done, you may go on to plan and write your theme.

The Organization of Your Theme

INTRODUCTION

Your introduction should describe the particular circumstances of the passage or work. Who is talking? To whom is he talking? Under what circumstances is he talking? Why? What is the general subject matter of the passage or work? These questions are relevant to whole poems as well as to fragments from a drama or story.

When you have answered these questions, you should make plain your central idea. Never begin to write until you have developed a general reaction to the passage or work assigned; your description of this reaction, or consideration, will be your central idea. The sample theme argues that in the passage analyzed Hamlet is speaking about himself— giving a self-revelation, as it were. The remainder of the theme develops this idea. In a theme showing a close reading it is sometimes difficult to arrive at a central idea, but if your theme is to be good, you must produce some guiding point that makes sense out of your reading.

BODY

Your plan in the body of the theme is to combine the results of your close reading with the central idea you have asserted. You might be guided by the following:

SPECIAL CIRCUMSTANCES Observe the special circumstances of the passage or work to see how they influence the language, and therefore how they illustrate your point (e.g., suppose that the speaker is in a plane crashing to the ground or suppose that he is on his way to meet his sweetheart; either of these circumstances must be mentioned and kept in mind throughout your discussion). The sample theme analyzes Hamlet's disturbed state of mind when he is addressing the ghost, who has just left the stage. The presence of the ghost is a special circumstance that accounts for Hamlet's shock and confusion.

DICTION Discuss the meaning of the words as related to the speaker's background and state of mind. In Browning's "Soliloquy of the Spanish Cloister," for example, the speaker is a jealous, worldly monk. His language is the kind a monk might use, but his interjections and schemes all show that he is a spiteful, petty person, certainly not a saintly, holy one. The language in Keats's "Ode to a Nightingale" indicates that the speaker is in despair, disappointment, and uncertainty, but it also shows his joy in life's fullness and in the beauty provided by the imagination. The sample theme demonstrates that Hamlet's diction is that of a student; therefore it is natural for him to use the references to *tables* in the academic sense.

When you discuss diction it is also proper to make observations on both the direct statements in the work and the implications and suggestions. Also, if there are any special problems with words, describe these problems and show how their solution (by aid of the dictionary) has assisted you in your reading.

OTHER ELEMENTS Discuss all other things that are relevant to your point. Here you might include either or both of the following:

1. Any noteworthy ideas. Your emphasis, however, should not be on the ideas *as ideas*, but on the way they are related to the central idea of your theme. For example, the sample theme briefly discusses the Renaissance theory of faculty psychology but is less concerned with explicating this theory than with relating it to the central idea of Hamlet's self-revelation.

2. The sentence patterns and rhythms of your passage. Because this analysis is fairly technical, it anticipates the prosodic analysis of poetry and the stylistic analysis of prose. In the present theme, however, you need to show only those qualities of style and versification that are relevant to your point. The sample theme demonstrates that at the end of the passage there are falling, trochaic rhythms that are sympathetic to the spirit and mood of Hamlet's speech. By emphasizing relationships of this sort, you can make your discussion of technique contribute to the thematic unity of your paper.

CONCLUSION

If the passage you have analyzed is a paragraph in a story or a portion of a play, as in the sample theme, you should conclude by making statements about the relationship of the fragment to the rest of the work. You are in effect pointing out the organic nature of the entire work, because you are emphasizing that your passage is essential to the whole (for more detail on this topic see Chapter 9, on *Structure*). The sample theme asserts that the passage being analyzed is the climax of the first act of *Hamlet* and that it anticipates much of what Hamlet does later.

It is also possible that the passage you have analyzed has meaning that is worthy of discussion independent of its context. You might then conclude by discussing the implications of this meaning. If you have been analyzing an entire poem, you might then conclude by discussing the relationship of the poem to other works by the same poet, or by other poets, on the same theme. Such a conclusion might involve you briefly in *comparison and contrast* (see Chapter 8). Whatever you write about in your conclusion, be sure that you touch once more on your central idea before you end your paper.

A Note on Mechanics

For quick, easy reference, you should include a copy of the passage you are analyzing. If the passage is not numbered, number it, by lines or sentences, beginning with *1*. If you are quoting a passage that is already numbered, you should use these numbers in your duplication. (The following fragment from *Hamlet*, for example, is numbered according to the Neilson and Hill edition of Shakespeare.) Whenever you quote from your passage, indicate in parentheses the line number or numbers of your quotation, as follows: (21), (26-28), (24, 43, 38), and so on.

SAMPLE THEME

Hamlet's Self-Revelation: A Reading
of Hamlet (I, v, 95–109 [1])

Remember thee!	95
Ay, thou poor ghost, while memory holds a seat	96
In this distracted globe. Remember thee!	97

[1] *The Complete Plays and Poems of William Shakespeare,* William Allan Neilson and Charles Jarvis Hill, eds. (Cambridge, Mass.: Houghton Mifflin Company, 1942), p. 1056.

Yea, from the table of my memory	98
I'll wipe away all trivial fond records,	99
All saws of books, all forms, all pressures past,	100
That youth and observation copied there,	101
And thy commandment all alone shall live	102
Within the book and volume of my brain,	103
Unmix'd with baser matters. Yes, yes, by heaven!	104
O most pernicious woman!	105
O villain, villain, smiling, damned villain!	106
My tables, my tables—Meet it is I set it down	107
That one may smile, and smile, and be a villain!	108
At least I'm sure it may be so in Denmark.	109

In this passage from Act I of *Hamlet,* Hamlet is alone on stage immediately after the ghost has left, and so the character addressed is the ghost, at least at first. Actually, the speech is a soliloquy, because Hamlet almost immediately seems to be talking to himself or to the open air. Although Hamlet speaks about the ghost, his mother ("O most pernicious woman"), and his uncle (the "villain"), the real subject of the speech is himself. His words describe his state of mind; his selection of words indicates his background as a student, his awareness of what is happening to him, and his own highly agitated mental condition at the moment.

For Hamlet has clearly been disturbed by the ghost's message that Claudius is a murderer. Whereas previously the young prince has been melancholy and ill at ease, feeling the need to do something but without any reason for action, he has now realized that definite action will be necessary in the future. His desire for revenge here reaches the fury that he will later feel in the "rogue and peasant slave" soliloquy. His passionate dedication to vengeance is sworn "by heaven!" His disturbance, which he himself recognizes in line 97, is demonstrated first by his decision to wipe away "all trivial fond records" from the "table" of his memory (99, 98), and then by his writing down (or so we presume) in his "tables" (i.e., his commonplace book, his notebook) that "one may smile, and smile, and be a villain" (108). Can this distinction between his declaration and his action do anything but indicate his mental confusion?

Regardless of this confusion, Hamlet's selection of words related to *tables* indicates that his existence as a character has been completely visualized and perfected by the dramatist, Shakespeare, who has created a diction that is in perfect accord with Hamlet's background as a student. Hamlet's speech is therefore the most telling indication that his subject is really himself. *Table, records, saws of books, copied, book and volume of my brain, baser matter, tables, set it down*—all these smack of the classroom, where Hamlet has so recently been occupied. And in lines 96 through 104 there is a complicated but brief description of Renaissance psychology, a subject that Hamlet has just been learning, presumably, at Wittenberg. Briefly, he states that his mind, or his memory, is like a writing tablet, from which he can erase previous experience and literature (the "pressures past" of line 100), and which he can then fill with the message that the ghost of his father has just transmitted to him. In short, his mind will never be quite the same, since the new message will occupy it entirely.

Once Hamlet has decided to erase all previous impressions, it is as though he has killed his past, and once he has made his resolution, his future project will be to murder Claudius. It seems deliberate, then, that the last lines of this passage are characterized by many trochaic rhythms, which would have been described in Shakespeare's day as having a *dying fall*. There are falling rhythms on *yes, by heaven,* and *O villain, villain, smiling, damned villain!* The last two lines end with trochees (*villain, Denmark*). This rhythm is unlike most of what went before, but will be like most of what follows, particularly the interjections in the "To be or not to be" soliloquy and the conclusion in that soliloquy (on the word *action*).

Since this passage reveals Hamlet's character so clearly, it is startlingly relevant to the rest of the play. From this point onward Hamlet will constantly be spurred by this promise to the ghost, that the ghost's "commandment all alone shall live / Within the book and volume of . . . [his] brain" (102, 103) and Hamlet will feel guilty and will be overwhelmed with self-doubt and the urge for self-destruction because he does not act on this promise. His attitude toward Claudius, which previously was scornful, will now be vengeful. His budding love for Ophelia will be blighted by his obsession with vengeance, and as a result Ophelia, a tender plant, will die. Truly, this passage can be regarded as the climax of the first act, and the prediction of the remainder of the play.

The
Comparison-Contrast
Theme

8 A popular theme subject is the comparison of different authors, of two or more works by the same author, of different drafts of the same work, or of different characters, incidents, and ideas within the same work or in different works. Your instructor may assign this theme in many ways, such as "Compare *X* and *Y*" or "Discuss the idea of *Z* in such-and-such works." No matter how the assignment is made, your job is to write a comparison-contrast theme. This assignment requires a detailed study and a thorough consideration of a much wider range of material than is needed to write a theme about a single work, idea, character, or author.

Comparison-Contrast as a Way to Knowledge

Comparison and contrast are important means to the gaining of understanding. If you have ever looked at your hands together, for example, you probably just saw two hands, but if you put your hands next to someone else's, you quickly were able to see salient characteristics of your own simply because of the contrast. You realized that hands are hands, with all their identical qualities, but you also perceived differences between yours and the other person's. In short, similarities between things are brought out by *comparison,* and differences are brought out by *contrast.* The essences of objects and artistic works can be quickly illustrated by use of the comparison-contrast method.

You will quickly perceive that the comparison-contrast method is closely related to the study of *definition,* because definition aims at the description of a particular thing by identifying its properties while also isolating it from everything else. Comparison-contrast is also closely allied with Plato's idea that we learn a thing best by reference to its opposite; that is, one way of finding out what a thing *is* is to find out what it is *not*.

As you study literature, your use of comparison-contrast will enable you to define and describe the particular characteristics of a particular writer or work by showing the general category to which your subject belongs and also by differentiating it from all other members of the category. Another way of thinking of a comparison-contrast assignment is to regard it in the same way that a jeweler regards a fine jewel, which can be made more beautiful if put into a fine setting. To a great degree, the method of comparison-contrast can be used to set off a great literary work by comparison with inferior works. In these senses, this type of theme is an integral part of literary classification, literary history (because it takes time differences into account), and literary evaluation (it implies that along with separation goes the cause for separation, including the rating of works and authors into orders of superiority and inferiority). When your instructor asks you to "Compare Pope and Tennyson" or to "Compare and contrast Chaucer with Edgar Guest," you should realize that he is asking you to bring out some of the important points that make the study of literature a true discipline.

Intention

Do not begin to write this, or any theme, without a plan or intention. Your first problem is to decide your objective. You ought to relate the material of the assignment to the purposes of the course, for the comparison-contrast method can be focused on a number of points. One focal point may simply be the equal and mutual illumination of both (or more) subjects of comparison; thus, in a survey course, where your purpose is to gain a general understanding of all the writers in the course, a theme about Milton and Pope would serve to describe the methods of both poets without throwing primary attention on either. But suppose you are taking a course in Milton—then your comparison-contrast theme could use Pope's methods as a means of highlighting Milton's; your theme would finally be about Milton, and your discussion of Pope would be relevant only as it related to this purpose. Conversely, if you were taking a course in eighteenth-century literature, you might use a discussion of Milton only as it illuminated Pope, and your theme would ultimately be about Pope. Your first task is therefore to decide where to place your emphasis, because comparison-contrast may be used for both purposes described in this paragraph. In the sample theme, the writer has compared two poems by Donne and Wordsworth, and his rhetorical purpose is to demonstrate Donne's superiority. Thus the sample theme is actually about Donne.

The Need to Find Common Grounds for Comparison

Your second problem is to select the proper material —the grounds of your discussion. It is useless to compare essentially dissimilar things, for then your basic conclusions will be of limited value. Therefore your task is to put the works or writers you are comparing onto common ground. Compare like with like; that is, style with style, subject with subject, idea with idea, structure with structure, characterization with characterization, prosody with prosody, milieu with milieu, evaluation with evaluation, and so on. Putting your subjects on common ground makes you arrive at a reasonable basis of comparison and therefore a legitimate occasion for contrast. Nothing can be learned, for example, from a comparison of "Pope's style and Milton's philosophy." But much can be learned from a comparison of "the influence of philosophy on style in Milton and Pope." The first promises little, whereas the second suggests common ground, with points of both comparison and divergence and with further implications about the ages in which the two poets lived.

In attempting to find common ground, seek possible similarities as you prepare yourself by reading and taking notes for the assignment. Here your generalizing powers will assist you, for apparently dissimilar materials may meet—if you are able to perceive the meeting place. Thus a comparison of *The House of Mirth* by Edith Wharton and *The Catcher in the Rye* by J. D. Salinger might put the works on the common ground of "The Treatment of the 'Outsider'" or "Corrosive Influences of an Affluent Society on the Individual" or "The Basis of Social Criticism," even though the works are about different characters living in different ages. As you can see, what appears at first dissimilar can often be put into a frame of reference that permits analytical comparison and contrast. Much of your success in writing will depend on your ingenuity in finding a suitable basis for comparison.

Methods of Comparison

Let us assume that you have decided on your rhetorical purpose and on the basis or bases of your comparison: you have done your reading, taken your notes, and know what you want to say. The remaining problem is the treatment of your material. Here are two acceptable ways.

A common, but inferior, way is to make your points first about one work and then to do the same for the other. This method makes your paper seem like two big lumps, and it also involves much repetition because you must repeat the same points as you treat your second subject. This first method, in other words, is only satisfactory—it is no better than a *C* method.

The superior method is to treat your main idea in its major aspects and to make references to the two (or more) writers as the reference illustrates and illuminates your main idea. Thus you would be constantly referring to both writers, sometimes within the same sentence, and would be reminding your reader of the point of your discussion. There are reasons for the superiority of the second method: (a) you do not need to repeat your points unnecessarily, for you can document them as you raise them; (b) by referring to the two writers in relatively close juxtaposition in relation to a clearly stated basis of comparison, you can avoid making a reader with a poor memory reread previous sections. Frequently such readers do not bother to reread, and as a result they are never really clear about what you have said. As a good example, however, here is a paragraph from a student theme on "Nature as a basis of comparison in William Wordsworth's 'The World Is Too Much with Us' and Gerard Manley Hopkins's 'God's Grandeur.' " The virtue of the paragraph is that it uses material from both poets as a means of development; the material is synthesized by the student:

> 1 Hopkins's ideas are Christian, though not genuinely other-worldly.
> 2 God is a God of the world for Hopkins, and "broods with warm breast and with ah! bright wings" (1.14); Hopkins is convinced that God is here and everywhere, for his first line triumphantly proclaims this. 3 Wordsworth, by contrast, is able to perceive the beauty of Nature, but feels that God in the Christian sense has deserted him. 4 Wordsworth is to be defended here, though, because his wish to see Proteus or to hear Triton is not pagan. 5 He wants, instead, to have faith, to have the conviction that Hopkins so confidently claims. 6 Even if the faith is pagan, Wordsworth would like it just so he could have firm, unshakable faith. 7 As a matter of fact, however, Wordsworth's perception of Nature gives the contradiction to the lack of faith he claims. 8 His God is really Nature itself. 9 Hopkins's more abstract views of Nature make me feel that the Catholic believes that Nature is only a means to the worship of God. 10 For Hopkins, God is supreme; for Wordsworth, Nature is.

If *H* and *W* are allowed to stand for ideas about Hopkins and Wordsworth, the paragraph may be schematized as follows:

> (Each number stands for a sentence number.)
> 1 = H.   2 = H.   3 = W.   4 = W.   5 = W, H.   6 = W.
> 7 = W.   8 = W.   9 = H.   10 = H, W.

This interweaving of subject material (two of the sentences contain references to both poets) gives the impression that the student has learned both poems so well that he is able to think of them together. Mental "diges-tion" has taken place. When the student discusses Hopkins's idea of Na-ture, he is able to think of it immediately in relation to Wordsworth's, and brings out references to both poets as he writes. You can profit from his example. If you can develop your comparison-contrast theme in this interlocking way, you will write it more economically and clearly than you would by the first method (this statement is true of tests as well as themes). Beyond that, if you have actually digested the material as suc-cessfully as the interlocking method shows, you will be demonstrating that you have fulfilled one of the primary goals of education—the assimila-tion and *use* of material.

Avoid the "Tennis-Ball Method"

As you make your comparison, do not confuse an interlocking method with a "tennis-ball method," in which you bounce your subject back and forth constantly and repetitively. The tennis-ball method is shown in the following example from a comparison of A. E. Housman's "On Wenlock Edge" and Theodore Roethke's "Dolor":

> Housman talks about the eternal nature of men's troubles whereas Roethke talks about the "dolor" of modern business life. Housman uses details of woods, gales, snow, leaves, and hills, whereas Roethke selects details of pencils, boxes, paper-weights, mucilage, and lavatories. Hous-man's focus is therefore on the torments of man close to Nature; Roethke's on civilized, ordered, duplicated, grey-flanneled man. Housman states that the significance of human problems fades in the perspective of eternity; Roethke does not mention eternity but makes men's problems seem even smaller by showing that business life has virtually erased human emotion.

Imagine the effect of reading an entire theme presented in this fashion. Aside from its power to bore, the tennis-ball method is bad because it does not give you the chance to develop your points. You should not feel so cramped that you cannot take several sentences to develop a point about one writer or subject before you bring in comparison with another. If you remember to interlock the two points of comparison, however, as in the example comparing Hopkins and Wordsworth, your method will be satisfactory.

The Organization of Your Theme

First you must narrow your subject into a topic you can handle conveniently within the limits of the assignment. For exam-ple, if you have been assigned a comparison of Tennyson and Pope, pick out one or two poems of each poet and write your theme about them.

You must be wary, however, of the limitations of this selection: generalizations made from one or two works may not apply to the broad subject originally proposed. If you state this qualification somewhere in your theme, your comparison will have much value, and your instructor will probably be pleased with the wisdom of your selection.

INTRODUCTION

State what works, authors, characters, and ideas are under consideration, then show how you have narrowed the basis of your comparison. Your central idea will be a brief statement of what can be learned from your paper: the general similarities and differences that you have observed from your comparison and/or the superiority of one work or author over another. Your thesis sentence should anticipate the body of your theme.

BODY

The body of your theme depends on the points you have chosen for comparison. You might be comparing two works on the basis of *structure, tone, style,* two authors on *ideas,* or two characters on *character traits.* In your discussion you would necessarily use the same methods that you would use in writing a theme about these terms in a single work, except that here (a) you are exemplifying your points by reference to more subjects than one, and (b) your ultimate rhetorical purpose is the illumination of the subjects on which your comparison is based. In this sense, the methods you use in talking about *structure* or *style* are not "pure" but are instead subordinate to your aims of comparison-contrast. Let us say that you are comparing the ideas in two different works. The first part of your theme might be devoted to the analysis and description of the similarities and dissimilarities of the ideas *as* ideas. Your interest here is not so much to explicate the ideas of either work separately as to explicate the ideas of both works in order to show points of agreement and disagreement. A second part might be given over to the influences of the ideas on the *structure* and *style* of the particular works, that is, how the ideas help make the works similar or dissimilar. Or, let us say that your subjects of comparison are two or more characters. Your points might be to show similarities and dissimilarities of mental and spiritual qualities and of activities in which the characters engage.

CONCLUSION

In this section you should bring out the conclusions that have emerged from your study. If your writers were part of a "school" or "period," you might show how your findings relate to these larger movements. You also should illustrate the limitations and implications of your treatment; you might show that more could be done along the same lines, and what might be the effects of pursuing the method further.

SAMPLE THEME

The Use of Westward *In Wordsworth's "Stepping Westward" and in Donne's "Good Friday, 1613, Riding Westward"* [1]

The reason for comparing these two poems is obvious from the titles, and the similarities become more obvious as a person reads the poems. Both employ "westward" as the direction in which the speakers move. As they move, they become aware of death, since the west—where the sun sets and the day dies—is the traditional direction symbolizing death. The reality of this situation causes the speakers to meditate on religion and philosophy. There is a difference in the ways in which the speakers move. Wordsworth's speaker is *stepping* westward, while Donne's is *riding* (i.e., being carried). If these actions can be interpreted symbolically, Wordsworth may be suggesting that his speaker's will is governing him, whereas Donne may be suggesting that his speaker's will is subordinate to something external. The poems tend to bear out this distinction. My feeling is that the differences in these poems are more noteworthy than the similarities and that Donne's poem emerges as better, more forceful, and more realistic than Wordsworth's. This superiority can be seen clearly in the ideas that both poets have about the forces that govern life.

The idea of moving westward prompts both poets to be concerned with the nature of life once the fact of death has been taken into account. Death is, in other words, the one unavoidable fact that causes everyone to pause and think. On the nature of life, Wordsworth seems to be raising a question that Donne has already answered. Wordsworth's poem asks whether we are governed by chance—the *"wildish* destiny"—or whether we are controlled by

---

[1] Quotations from "Good Friday, 1613" are taken from *The Complete Poetry and Selected Prose of John Donne & The Complete Poetry of William Blake,* with an introduction by Robert Silliman Hillyer (New York: Random House, 1946), pp. 247-48. Quotations from "Stepping Westward" are taken from *The Complete Poetical Works of Wordsworth,* Andrew J. George, ed. (Cambridge, Mass.: Houghton Mifflin Co., 1932), p. 298.

"*heavenly*" forces. Naturally, he opts for the "heavenly" destiny to guide him on his "endless way." Donne does not raise this question, however, for there is no doubt in his mind that the heavenly destiny exists; his idea, instead, is that his speaker is riding *away* from his destiny, since God is in the East, and "Pleasure" and "businesse" are whirling his "Soule," like a "Spheare" westward away from God. On a nonparadoxical level, Donne uses this opposition of East and West to bring out a conflict between faith and human frailty—a conflict that is far different from the relative calm in Wordsworth's poem.

Donne's poem is not only more agitated than Wordsworth's, but it contains images demonstrating that Donne is out after bigger game than Wordsworth. The first image is described by the sentence "Let mans Soule be a Spheare." The individual soul, from this image, is a world in itself over which the forces of good and evil contend, and the loss of any individual is of cosmic significance to God. I have sought unsuccessfully for anything of comparable imaginative force in Wordsworth's poem. Donne's other image is that of Christ on the Cross, a symbol at once of both death and life, who, in Donne's paradoxical expression, by dying made death an entry way into life. The westward direction of travel therefore becomes not only the direction of death but also of life—heavenly life—since it ultimately is the direction in which one must travel in order to see God:

> Hence is't, that I am carryed towards the West
> This day, when my Soules forme bends towards the East.
> There I should see a Sunne, by rising set,
> And by that setting endlesse day beget;
> But that Christ on this Crosse, did rise and fall,
> Sinne had eternally benighted all.
>
> —lines 9-14

This short passage, ending with the word *all,* demonstrates that man's soul is in the balance. The conflict is thus not just personal, it is typical of all men. On the one hand they see the good, but on the other they do not follow it, and so the conflict is cosmic. But as they avoid God, they move toward death, which is another and more permanent way to God.

Donne's world, in short, is much more complex and difficult than Wordsworth's. I do not imply that Wordsworth interprets life as easy, for "In a strange Land and far from home" his speaker feels that "The dewy ground was dark and cold; / Behind, all gloomy to behold"; (4, 9, 10). But Wordsworth is simply not as forceful as Donne. As a result, after Wordsworth's speaker decides that his destiny is "heavenly," the dark, dewy ground is transformed into a "region bright" (16). This change seems a little too simple, a little too pat. By contrast, Donne's world (the soul) is constantly "Subject to forraigne motions," which drive it away from its heavenly destiny, corroding it and deforming it. His speaker therefore ends the poem in anguished prayer, asking God to purify his life so that he can withstand death:

> O thinke mee worth thine anger, punish mee,
> Burne off my rusts, and my deformity,
> Restore thine Image, so much, by thy grace,
> That thou may'st know mee, and I'll turne my face.

—lines 39-42

Thus, for Donne, the only salvation in this difficult life is God's love, which enabled endurance upon the Cross, where His flesh was "rag'd and torne" (28). Paradoxically again, God dying on the Cross is a sight on which the speaker "durst not looke"; consequently his ride westward is an almost inevitable result of his own weakness, for which God is the only remedy. These are contorted, tortuous ideas, which are sharply in contrast with Wordsworth's emphasis on "human sweetness" and "The very sound of courtesy." Both ideas are in accord so far as they account for the individual's dependency for support on something external, but Donne's thought is full of pain, uncertainty, anguish, and paradox, whereas Wordsworth's is characterized by calm, certainty, and simplicity.

The principal difference between the two poems is that Donne's view of life is fuller, rounder than Wordsworth's. Wordsworth's problem ends where Donne's begins. This difference is perhaps the same one that exists between a fairy tale ending on the note that "They lived happily ever after" and a modern novel that treats the problems and anguish that frequently appear in adult life. This difference applies only to these two poems, for Wordsworth brings out personal conflicts elsewhere: poems like *The Prelude,* the "Ode to Duty," and the "Immortality" ode illustrate that life, to him, was not pure unruffled calm. Nor does he, presumably, have in his poem the idea of the Crucifixion before him, as Donne of course did on Good Friday. But even in these poems one does not find a view of life comparable in forcefulness to what Donne shows in his poem about the errant soul's westward departure from God hanging "upon the tree" (36).

The Theme Analyzing
the Structure of
a Literary Work

9 *Structure* in literary study may be defined as the organization of a literary work as influenced by its plot (in fictional works) or main idea (in expository works). The work is also sometimes defined as the pattern of emotions in the literary work. Although these two definitions are distinct, they are closely connected and under most circumstances are virtually inseparable. The word *structure* is in fact a metaphor implying that a work of literature, both topically and emotionally, is as connected and unified as a building—a structure.

In imaginative works, structure refers to the chronological position of parts, scenes, episodes, chapters, and acts; it also refers to the logical or associational relationships among stanzas, ideas, images, or other divisions. In expository works, the word necessarily refers to the arrangement and development of ideas. Structure is a matter of the relationships among parts that are usually described in terms of cause and effect, position in time, association, symmetry, and balance and proportion (the last two are usually concerned with evaluation, whereas the first three are more closely involved with description).

Literary artists universally aim at a unified impression in their works, and because literature is a time art (it cannot be comprehended as a whole in one moment, as can a painting or a work of sculpture), the study of structure attempts to demonstrate that the idea and the resulting arrangement of parts produces a total impression. You can see, therefore, that a study of structure is one avenue to the evaluation of literature, because such a study would bring out any lack of unity in a work and make that work subject to adverse criticism.

The Importance of Structure

In a very real sense, all studies of literature are either directly or indirectly concerned with structure. If you talk about the happy or unhappy ending of a short story, for example, you in fact consider the conclusion in relation to what went before it; inevitably you mention whether the earlier parts of the story demonstrated that the characters earned or deserved what happened to them. This consideration must touch on the logic of the story's action, and hence it is a subject of structure. Similarly, in considering Shakespeare's Sonnet No. 73 (quoted below, pp. 82-83), you may observe that the first quatrain compares the speaker to dead trees, the second to twilight, and the third to a dying and self-extinguishing fire. Whether or not you determine that there is a logical or topical relationship among these quatrains, you are discussing structure.

Since structure is so closely tied to all phases of literary study, you might ask in what way structure is unique. How, for example, does a theme about ideas, or a summary theme, differ from a theme about structure? The difference is one of emphasis: in studying structure you emphasize the logic, or the causes, underlying the major divisions in the work being analyzed; in a summary theme you emphasize the events or ideas that you have cast in a reasonable plan of organization; in a theme about ideas you emphasize the ideas and their importance as they are made apparent in the work. In fact, no matter what topic you are writing about, your finished theme is usually related to the structure of the work; for the major parts of your theme can be conveniently dictated by the organization of that work. Always, however, in studying structure, the organization of the work and the causes for it are your primary concern. Ideas, events, and other things such as tone, point of view, and imagery are relevant only as substance for your discussion of structure.

In a good work of literature, the parts are not introduced accidentally. One part demands another, sometimes by logical requirement. Elder Olsen's study of Pope's poem *Epistle to Dr. Arbuthnot*,[1] shows that in the first sixty-eight lines Pope illustrates a comic idea that constitutes a minor logical premise, namely that a number of bad poets and other people have been waving ass's ears in his face. Then in the next ten lines Pope illustrates a major premise, namely that when people have ass's ears, you have to tell them about it. Finally, in four following lines, Pope draws a logical conclusion (which is also a defense of himself as a satirist), namely that he had written a lengthy poem, *The Dunciad*, to tell the world that the people mentioned in the first sixty-eight lines had

[1] "Rhetoric and the Appreciation of Pope," *Modern Philology* XXXVII (1939), 13-55.

ass's ears. In short, the first eighty-two lines of the poem form a syllogism, not necessarily valid logically, but certainly valid comically and rhetorically.

Some works may have similar logical coherence, and in others the guiding plan may be chronology. It is never enough simply to assert that events happen in time; time is important only as it permits human reactions to take place, and hence chronology in literature is primarily a convenient classification for the logic of human motivation. For example, in Frost's poem "The Road Not Taken," the first three stanzas describe the speaker's taking one road at a fork in the road he was already traveling. As the stanzas progress it becomes clear that the road taken was actually the way of life chosen by the speaker. In the final, fourth stanza, the speaker observes that his choice was a major landmark in his life, affecting his present and future and making him different from what he would have been had he taken the road not taken. The structure of the poem is such that the stanzas move naturally from a brief account of events to their human effects and implications. The last stanza stems inevitably and necessarily from the first three; it could not be transposed and still make the same sense.

Aids in Studying Structure

In studying structure, be sure to take whatever assistance the author has given you. Has he made divisions in the work, such as stanzas, parts, chapters, cantos, or spaces between groups of paragraphs? Try to relate the subjects of these various divisions, and develop a rationale for the divisions. Is there a geographical location (or several locations) that lends its own mood and color to the various parts of the story? How can these be related to the events? Does the time of the day— or time of year—shift as the work progresses? Can the events be shown to have a relationship to these various times? Does one event grow inevitably out of another; that is, do the events have logical as well as chronological causation? Is a new topic introduced because it is similar to another topic (see, for example, Joyce's *Portrait of the Artist as a Young Man*)? All these and like questions should assist you in your study.

You might also help yourself by following a suggestion made by Aristotle in his *Poetics:*

> . . . the plot (of any work), being an imitation of an action, must imitate one action and that a whole, the structural union of the parts being such that, if any one of them is displaced or removed, the whole will be disjointed and disturbed. For a thing whose presence or absence make no visible difference, is not an organic part of the whole.[2]

2 Ch. VIII. 4, in S. H. Butcher, *Aristotle's Theory of Poetry and Fine Art*, 4th ed. (New York: Dover Publications, Inc., 1951), p. 35.

As an exercise, you might imagine that a certain part of the work you are studying has been taken away. You might then ask what is wrong with the work remaining. Does it make sense? Does it seem truncated? Why should the missing part be returned? As you answer these questions, you are really dealing with the logical necessity of structural wholeness. For example, let us suppose that the second stanza of Frost's "The Road Not Taken" is missing. The poem immediately becomes illogical because it omits the chronological event leading to the conclusion, and it also omits the logic of the speaker's choice of the road he selected. If you attempt similar imaginative exercises with other works, you can help yourself in determining whether these works are organic wholes.

You might also aid yourself by drawing a scheme or plan to explain, graphically, the structure of the work you are analyzing. The story "Miss Brill," by Katherine Mansfield, for example, may be conveniently compared with a person running happily along a narrow path deep within a dark forest and making a turn only to plunge suddenly and unexpectedly off a steep cliff. You might graph this comparison like this:

In writing a theme about the story, you could employ this scheme as a guide for your discussion. This is not to say that the structure of the story could not be profitably analyzed in another way but that the scheme would help to give your own study penetration, meaning, and form.

Sometimes the use of an illustration can create an insight or series of insights that might at first not have been clear to you. For example, Shakespeare's Sonnet No. 73, already mentioned, has three quatrains and a concluding rhymed couplet:

Stanza I	That time of year thou mayst in me behold,
	When yellow leaves, or none, or few do hang
	Upon those boughs which shake against the cold,
	Bare ruined choirs, where late the sweet birds sang.

Stanza II	In me thou seest the twilight of such day,
	As after sunset fadeth in the West,
	Which by and by black night doth take away,
	Death's second self that seals up all in rest.

Stanza III

In me thou seest the glowing of such fire,
That on the ashes of his youth doth lie,
As the death bed, whereon it must expire,
Consumed with that which it was nourished by.
This thou perceiv'st, which makes thy love more strong.
To love that well, which thou must leave ere long.

Let us assume, without proof, that the poem is an organic whole (this is an assumption that you should make at first about every work you read, and you should maintain it until or unless your experience disproves it). The quatrains, then, are connected in some way, and the couplet is similarly connected with everything going on before it. Allowing for the fact that each part must be unique as well as connected, an ideal plan of this distinctness and connection might be graphed with the use of four overlapping triangles, with the areas of overlap representing the subject matter common to the three quatrains and also to the concluding couplet:

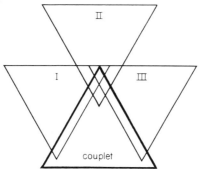

As yet, no connection has been demonstrated, but in attempting to justify the drawing, you will discover many connecting elements. In each quatrain the phrase "in me" appears with the phrases "thou mayest behold," "thou seest," and "thou seest" again. In the couplet the phrase "thou perceiv'st" and the word "that" as a pronoun referring to the speaker appear, so that each major unit contains references to the speaker and his listener. In addition, a common subject of the three quatrains might be various stages of light or conditions affecting light; in quatrain one, referring to late autumn, the sun would be low in the sky, just as in quatrain two the sun has set and in the third the coals retain only a dull glow. Similarly, in quatrains two and three, death is mentioned specifically, and quatrain one refers to barren branches from which dead leaves have fallen. All three quatrains either imply or refer to something that has passed, namely summer (I), daylight (II), and a bright fire (III), and all these are analogous to the speaker, so that the statement "To love that well, which thou must leave ere long" in the concluding couplet is a fitting resumé of the poem. With all these connecting links supplied, the drawing may be filled in, with the list of common elements placed next to it as a "key":

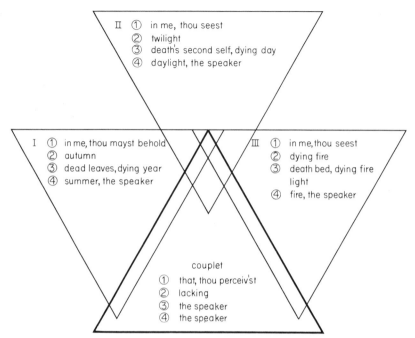

II ① in me, thou seest
② twilight
③ death's second self, dying day
④ daylight, the speaker

I ① in me, thou mayst behold
② autumn
③ dead leaves, dying year
④ summer, the speaker

III ① in me, thou seest
② dying fire
③ death bed, dying fire light
④ fire, the speaker

couplet
① that, thou perceiv'st
② lacking
③ the speaker
④ the speaker

CONNECTING LINKS

1. (a) in me   (b) thou . . . st
2. time of low or absent light
3. Death or something dead
4. things that have passed or will pass.

In the above sketch, triangles work successfully to show the structure and the connecting links, but in analyzing a work you might try circles, lines, planes, or other geometric figures. If you wish, you might make a list, or you might do nothing more than study and take notes carefully. What is important is that you attempt to look at the work you are studying as a *structure* of some sort and that you write a theme about this structure. Making a drawing or a graph has the virtue of giving you a visual grasp of the fact that the parts of a unified work are distinct and connected—important discoveries both for your understanding of the work and your writing a theme.

The Structure of Emotions

In keeping with the second definition of structure, it is important to realize that structure may refer to the emotional pattern of a particular work. This element is so important that it is included as a part of the first sample theme and is the subject of the second. One should always keep in mind that authors arrange their material in order to build interest and emotional involvement and that without such involvement, very few people would do much reading. Each work of literature is a complex emotional structure. Shakespeare's Sonnet No. 73, for example, builds feelings of regret, sadness, and resignation but concludes on a note of affirmation (although in a minor key). Any account of the poem's structure should attempt to deal with how the causes for these emotions are locked into the arrangement of the various parts.

Similarly, the aim of detective fiction is to create suspense by the introduction of doubt and consequent anxiety; such fiction arouses related emotions, such as sympathy and fear. It also creates both properly and improperly directed hostility; finally, it produces satisfaction when the solution of the mystery ends all doubt and anxiety.

The creation of a certain degree of anxiety is perhaps the principal means by which authors maintain interest. The author of a story about a pioneering trip across the American plains, for example, creates anxiety about whether the forces of nature will permit the successful outcome of the journey. If human agents such as outlaws are introduced as antagonists, then this anxiety can be related to hostility and fear, and if the principal characters are virtuous, they usually become objects of admiration. Many western stories and detective stories build strongly on the indignation that is usually aroused by an outlaw committing some outrageous crime or taking advantage of the momentarily helpless hero. The hero's eventual triumph over the outlaw is therefore made much more satisfying.

Such emotions are also coextensive with the structure of drama. Each play develops a major *conflict,* which is structured in such a way that maximum tension is produced. In the nineteenth century, a German novelist and critic, Gustav Freytag, suggested that the rising and falling actions and tensions in the typical five-act drama resemble a pyramid: emotions are incited with the exposition of the drama and are heightened as the plot complications develop until a climax is reached in the third act; after this point, the falling action begins until the final catastrophe, or dénouement, is reached (compare this description with the sketch for the action of "Miss Brill," above, p. 82). The emotions preceding the climax are those that spring from uncertainty; those afterwards spring from inevitability. One major idea in the Aristotelian idea of tragedy is that tragedy aims at the purgation—catharsis—of pity and fear. In the Freytag pyramid, you might observe that fear is touched most heavily before the climax, whereas pity becomes predominant after it, although the two are intermingled throughout a tragedy. The point here is that Aristotle's description of the aims of tragedy presupposed a proper arrangement of incidents and that this concern, like his other commentaries on plot in *The Poetics* (VI-XIV), was mainly structural.

If a literary work is an emotional structure, it should reach a satisfactory emotional conclusion—a relaxation of tension. In Greek tragedy, the concluding action, the *exodos,* consists of choral speeches that ponder the meaning of the action: this relatively intellectual section provides the opportunity to relax after the emotional peak of the play. In Milton's "Lycidas," although anger and indignation are strongly brought out in Milton's famous "digressions" (which are integral in the poem), the conclusion permits relaxation and satisfaction. Indeed, one major distinction between art and propaganda is that propaganda is deliberately designed to create dissatisfaction. Art is complete emotionally, whereas a political speech is as emotionally unfinished as the political work remaining to be done. This is not to say that art cannot be propagandistic nor propaganda artistic but that this distinction can help you to analyze and judge works of literature.

Examples could be multiplied. The important point, however, is that the study of structure is not confined exclusively to the physical placement of scenes, acts, episodes, and so on, in the work under consideration. Structure is equally concerned with the logic and unity of a work, and the patterning of emotions is a significant element in literary logic and unity.

It is most important that in discussing the structure of a work with emphasis on emotions, you should focus your efforts on the work itself, on the way in which the physical, lexical structure is also an emotional structure. Many persons respond individually and often unpredictably to what they read. But if you emphasize your observations about the work you can rule out this possible avenue into complete subjectivity (another name for complete subjectivity is the "affective fallacy").[3] In writing on such a topic, concentrate on the author's skill in the creation of suspense, interest, resignation, happiness, sympathy, pity, satisfaction, and whatever other emotional states are brought out in the work.

Problems

You will of course encounter problems in your theme about structure. You must interpret the idea of the work properly; and you must also arrive at a sound conclusion about the work's effect. This problem is extremely subjective, but your interpretation will always be respected so long as it is reasonable.

3 See W. K. Wimsatt, Jr., *The Verbal Icon,* 2nd ed. (New York: Noonday Press, 1960), pp. 21-39.

Even more difficulty will be encountered when you attempt to relate your analysis and description of the parts in the work to your interpretation of the work's idea and effect. It is here that you must be especially careful. If your first judgment is that one part is not relevant, be sure that you have not missed some essential idea that would make it relevant. Make sure that your central idea is accurately comprehensive. One well-known writer, for example, stated that the last section of *Huckleberry Finn* is "just cheating." It seems apparent that his judgment resulted from an inadequate idea about the meaning of the novel. If he had considered that the novel contrasts common sense (Huck's idea of freeing Jim) with quixotism or faulty judgment (Tom's idea of freeing Jim with "style"), he would have modified his statement in keeping with this consideration.

You also have the usual problem of selectivity. What you choose to discuss will be made on the basis of your initial analysis of the idea and the effect of the work you analyze. A mere description of what happens in the work and where it happens is nothing more than a synopsis. Your instructor is of course interested in your ability to describe the organization of the work, but he is much more interested in what you *make* out of your description. You must employ summary in your paper, but the summary must always be relevant to the point you are making about idea and effect. As always, your point is of primary importance and should be kept foremost.

The Organization of Your Theme

INTRODUCTION

You should consider what you think is the most important idea in the work that you have analyzed, and you should also consider the principal emotional pattern in the work; make an attempt to relate these two. The problem here is finding the lowest common denominator that will take in all the principal events or statements in the work; you must make a general statement that is true for the work and that therefore makes purposive all the events or statements in the work. Thus, a principal idea governing Milton's "Lycidas" is that life and effort have a final purpose (that life has meaning); a discussion of this idea would take into account the structure of the poem. Similarly, the main idea in Hemingway's *Farewell to Arms* is that happiness is not to be found on earth. Once you have arrived at an idea in this way, you should make it the central idea of your theme. Conclude your introduction with a thesis sentence.

BODY

Work from your introduction into a discussion of the way in which the idea influences the form of the work. In this section you must describe the main parts of the work, showing the relationships among the parts. Use the central idea to show how all the various parts are dependent on all the others (if the work is actually so well unified).

CONCLUSION

You should conclude your theme with an evaluation of the author's success so far as structure is concerned. Are all the parts of the work equally necessary? Do they occur in the best order? Would the work be damaged if any parts were left out, or if any parts were transposed? Are the parts successful in creating a total impression? If your answer to any of these questions is no, you have grounds for saying that the structure of the work is faulty. If your answer is always yes, you should probably conclude your theme with praise for the author, for you have been analyzing a perfectly unified work.

FIRST SAMPLE THEME

An Analysis of the Structure
of "The Three Strangers"
by Thomas Hardy

Hardy's principal aim in "The Three Strangers" is to show the warm, kind, human qualities of the Wessex natives who are so prominent in the story. To bring out this human kindness, Hardy demonstrates the reactions of the natives to a series of incidents that clearly present a conflict between (1) duty toward law, and (2) duty toward a human being under condemnation of the law, whose crime has, in their eyes, been extenuated. In order to create a favorable impression that justice has been done and the eternal laws of humanity obeyed, Hardy utilizes the device of suspense: he thereby shows how the sympathies of the natives are favorably disposed toward humanity and the first stranger and unfavorably disposed toward a punitive law and the second stranger. As he controls the attitudes of the natives, he controls the emotions of his readers in the same way. To make his case credible Hardy extensively describes not only the natives but also the characteristics of the first two strangers. These are ambitious aims, which Hardy successfully achieves.

The opening one-fifth of the story is an introduction to the human kindness of the natives. The section moves from the big to the little—from the natural scenery surrounding Higher Crowstairs, to the general scene of humanity within the house, to the specific scene represented by Shepherd Fennel and his wife. Hardy is at great pains to show the perpetually human ways of the folk, not only in 182–, but by implication during all periods of human history. He makes the scene universal in his description of the dancing, which he describes in the words *apogee* and *perigee*. In other words, the dancing has been going on as long as the planets have been moving in their orbits. The incident the natives celebrate is the age-old one of birth and initiation into life (in this specific case, a Christening). These people, Hardy suggests, are human beings uncontaminated by anything modern, for they have an "absolute confidence" in each other which begets "perfect ease," and which makes them immune to the modern poison of allowing business interests to interfere with friendship.[4] In short, this first section establishes contact with the folk and with their basic humanity— so strong a contact that it will not be lost during the remainder of the story. Clearly, Hardy is going to make use of these human characteristics later on. This first section is therefore an effective introduction.

Against this backdrop, the second section builds suspense and offers the possibility of a false resolution. Covering slightly more than half of the story, this section introduces suspense in the persons of the three strangers and the actions in which they are engaged. Although throughout the section a person might lose focus on the natives, it must be emphasized that Hardy's real purpose in bringing in the strangers is to illustrate his main idea that the natives are kind and human. Each of the strangers is mysterious, although Hardy resolves the mystery of the second stranger almost immediately. Of the three strangers, the first is characterized by his likeableness, his desire to remain anonymous, his lack of tobacco, and his taking a weapon when the second knock on the door is heard. The second stranger is of course the hangman, upon whom Hardy focusses dislike. The third stranger is not developed at all, except that the section closes with the idea that he is the escaped criminal. Momentarily, therefore, attention is drawn away from the mystery surrounding the first stranger, since the third is actually a red herring. The second section therefore concludes on a note of suspense.

[4] *Short Stories for Study,* 3rd ed., Raymond W. Short and Richard B. Sewall, eds. (New York: Holt, Rinehart & Winston, Inc., 1956), p. 108. All page numbers refer to this edition.

The third section, the last part of the story, brings out the events leading up to the resolution of the suspense caused by curiosity about the identities of the first and third strangers. In a comic scene the natives search for and capture the third stranger, who then informs his captors that the first stranger, and not himself, is the escaped criminal. At this point Hardy demonstrates that his story all along has been building up to the reaction of the natives when they learn this fact. The knowledge forces them into a decision, which they tacitly make "on the side of the fugitive," since they feel that "the intended punishment was cruelly disproportioned to the transgression" (p. 131). After this climax—the human decision of the natives—the story quickly ends.

The total effect of Hardy's structure, therefore, belies the expectations aroused by the title, and a casual reader might feel that Hardy has cluttered his story with too much detail about the natives. But more consideration shows that the action concerning the three strangers exists in order to bring out the warm humanity of the natives, and that the story, just like all stories, is finally about the entire society in which it occurs. In this case, Hardy suggests, or implies, that the story is as old as the race.

His use of suspense supports my claim. He deliberately avoids saying until the very end that the first stranger is the escaped sheep-stealer, although his hints about this fact, at second reading, are obvious. In this way, he builds up sympathy for the stranger, and avoids an early, purely legal reaction against him until all the facts are in. Because of this delay in our knowledge, Hardy successfully molds opinion about the stranger *as a human being* and *not* as a criminal. And, since the reader's opinion is formed along with that of the natives, he becomes sympathetic toward their decision to neglect the strict letter of the law in favor of the more compelling human obligation, particularly in view of the obnoxious and severe character of the law as personified by the hangman. Hardy wants no enduring suspense about the harshness and injustice represented by this second, horrid figure who delights in his ghoulish work.

Hardy therefore ends his story just as he began it, on the notes of (a) the overwhelming need for human kindness and (b) the permanence of life, in which birth and death are cycles. Thereby, he has created a unified structure with a total impression similar to the one occasioned by his statement about the life of the folk, the natives, in his poem "In Time of 'The Breaking of Nations' ":

> Yet this will go onward the same
> Though Dynasties pass.

SECOND SAMPLE THEME

The Emotional Undulations of
Steinbeck's Story "The Snake"

John Steinbeck's story "The Snake" is a mystery story, not in the detective sense but in the sense that it creates perplexity, bafflement, mild thrills, and final satisfaction. Before the end, the story provides a series of shocks plus a few touches of wry amusement. The principal character Dr. Phillips, the marine biologist, seems at first worthy of admiration, but then he becomes offensive; finally, however, he becomes worthy of deep commitment. At the same moments that Steinbeck redeems the doctor, he builds up repulsion and perplexity through his second major character, for the story, in keeping with its name, moves from extremes of emotion like the undulations of the rattlesnake who figures so prominently in the action.

The first section of the story, characterized by flat description, creates only mild interest concluded by mild shock. The opening two pages follow Dr. Phillips with the proper detachment from the tide pool to his commercial laboratory. His execution of the cat, however, because it is described in the same flat manner, is shocking. No matter how intellectually one can be convinced of the need for killing animals for experiments, the description of an actual killing causes shock. Steinbeck creates a hostile response to Dr. Phillips when the cat to be killed is removed from the cage:

> Dr. Phillips lifted down the milk and walked to the cat cage, but before he filled the containers he reached in the cage and gently picked out a big rangy alley tabby. He stroked her for a moment and then dropped her in a small black painted box, closed the lid and bolted it and then turned on a petcock which admitted gas into the killing chamber. While the short soft struggle went on in the black box he filled the saucers with milk. One of the cats arched against his hand and he smiled and petted her neck.[5]

This quiet description is devoid of any pity or repulsion, and thus produces a vacuum of emotion that the reader must, temporarily at least, fill. The emotional response is also accompanied by shock and resentment against the doctor, whose smile, and whose immediate preparation of a can of beans, seems cold and unfeeling.

Having established this mood of mild repulsion, Steinbeck in the next section of the story introduces a new character, a

[5] John Steinbeck, "The Snake," in T. Y. Greet, Charles E. Edge, and John M. Munro, eds., *The Worlds of Fiction: Stories in Context* (Boston: Houghton Mifflin Co., 1964), p. 362. Parenthetical page numbers refer to this edition.

woman who replaces the doctor as an alienated figure. Steinbeck presents wryly amusing details about her to show that she has snakelike features: her forehead is "flat"; her eyes glitter; she is exceptionally silent and patient, like the snake waiting for his prey; and her chin, between her "lower lip and point," is short (p. 364). Because Steinbeck does not explicitly make the comparison but presents the details so that the reader must make the comparison for himself, the amusement of the portrait is accompanied by the thrill of discovery.

Mildly comic as the discovery is, however, the woman does not sustain amusement but becomes an object of repulsion. Steinbeck brings out this reaction against her at the same time that he elicits admiration for the doctor. He polarizes emotions between the two characters by showing the doctor as increasingly more human while the woman evinces no warm human qualities at all. He uses the omniscient point of view for the doctor but the limited for the woman in order to define the doctor's shock at the lady's desire to buy the rattlesnake. The story's emotional undulations reach their widest curve as Steinbeck describes the doctor's feelings about the lady's request:

> He hated people who make sport of natural processes. He was not a sportsman but a biologist. He could kill a thousand animals for knowledge, but not an insect for pleasure. He'd been over this in his mind before (p. 366).

Admiration for the doctor's humanitarian role is reinforced when he saves the woman from being bitten when she puts her hand into the rattlesnake's cage.

Simultaneously with admiration for the doctor, the woman's responses to the death and eating of the rat elicit disgust. It is as though the S shape taken by the snake in approaching the rat is descriptive of the responses Steinbeck wishes to effect. Although the snake's desire for the rat is natural, the woman's seems unnatural, ghoulish: Steinbeck's repeated descriptions comparing her with the snake no longer amuse; they repel. Again, however, the style influences one's responses. The flatness, the almost clinical narration, prevents repulsion from hardening into hate. Steinbeck's scene is a medical laboratory, where scientific detachment produces the attitude that people should be rescued, not condemned.

Because the doctor never sees the woman again and is therefore prevented from helping her, and also because her strange desire to see the snake eat the rat is never explained, the dominant emotion produced in the final page of the story is perplexity. Although the reader's curiosity and the wish to see things through is thus frustrated, the story's conclusion is by no means frustrating. That the woman never returns to see another rat eaten, even though she promised to do so, suggests that her desires were satisfied by the incident. There is a "Lady or the Tiger" mystery about what gave rise to her need, but at least this one episode is completed.

The emotional pattern of the story is therefore a gentle weaving from emotion to emotion, from shock to wry amusement, from sympathy to disgust, from bafflement to satisfaction. None of these states is extreme, for the flat, straightforward descriptions prevent extremes. Steinbeck so structures his development of Dr. Phillips' character to evoke the maximum sympathy; from a distant figure externally described, the doctor develops as an acquaintance and then almost as a friend, with understandable human doubts and perplexities. The woman, on the other hand, receives no such favorable treatment; her external appearance and manner reflect some internal torment that the reader is not privileged to understand. In the absence of any mitigating detail, the reader must either be repelled by her or at best must reserve judgment. In other words, although the story itself comes to an end, the subject matter touches an unknown part of human life that has not yet yielded to the researches of science. The doctor nevertheless continues to search for an answer, and this, his most admirable trait, is sufficient to produce a conclusion that satisfies emotionally.

The Theme on Imagery in a Literary Work

10 *Imagery* is a broad term referring to the verbal comparison of one or many objects, ideas, or emotional states with something else. The use of imagery is a means by which an author relates something he wishes to express to something you yourself either have experienced or can easily imagine as your own experience. He accomplishes this end through *analogy;* thus, at the heart of communication through imagery is this assumption: "I cannot describe this idea for you, nor can I tell you how this character felt, but I can provide you with an analogy—an image—which by its similarity to your own experience or by its ability to touch your imagination will make you understand the idea or re-create his emotional state." Thus, a writer wishing to express a character's joy may say not simply "He was happy" but might write a sentence like "He felt as though he had just received a million-dollar check." It is unlikely that any of the author's readers have had such an experience themselves, but they can easily *imagine* how elated such an experience would make them feel, and therefore they can re-create the joy experienced by the literary character. The author has illustrated one thing— joy—in terms of another—the receipt of a large sum of money.

KEATS'S SONNET ON CHAPMAN'S HOMER

As a literary parallel to the million-dollar check image, let us examine Keats's poem "On First Looking Into Chapman's Homer." Keats wrote the poem after he first read Chapman's translation of Homer, and his main idea is that Chapman not only translated Homer's words but also transmitted his greatness. A fair expository restatement of the poem might be the following:

I have read much European literature and have been told that Homer is the best writer of all, but not knowing Greek, I couldn't appreciate his works until I read them in Chapman's translation. To me, this experience was an exciting and awe-inspiring discovery with extensive implications that I only dimly realized.

It is also fair to say that this paraphrase destroys Keats's poetry. Contrast the second sentence of the paraphrase with the last six lines of the sonnet as Keats wrote them:

> Then felt I like some watcher of the skies
>   When a new planet swims into his ken;
> Or like stout Cortez when with eagle eyes
>   He stared at the Pacific—and all his men
> Looked at each other with a wild surmise—
>   Silent, upon a peak in Darien.

Notice that Keats did not say, as did the paraphrase, that he felt the excitement of a great discovery; instead he used imagery to show and to objectivize his feelings, so that the reader might re-experience feelings similar to his own. The prose paraphrase does not demonstrate the feelings sufficiently, but the use of imagery allows the reader to experience and visualize exciting moments of great discovery and thereby to share the poet's attitudes. Most of us have difficulty in seeing things as others see them, and therefore we are often indifferent when someone tells us of his emotions. If Keats had said only "I felt excited," his poem would probably not cause anything but skepticism or boredom in us, because we would find no descriptions of objects from which we could reconstruct the precise degree of his emotion. But we certainly can respond to the situation that Keats's imagery causes us to visualize. Imagery, in other words, conveys a close approximation of experience itself, and it calls forth the most strenuous imaginative responses from the reader. In fact, a person cannot regard himself as a good reader until he can re-experience what the writer shows through his imagery.

A Summary and Some Definitions

The word *image* refers to single literary comparisons. Keats's reference to the "watcher of the skies," for example, is an image. *Imagery* is a broader term referring to all the images within a passage ("the imagery of line 5, or of stanza 6"), an entire work ("the imagery of Eliot's 'Prufrock'"), a group of works ("the imagery of Shakespeare's Roman plays"), or an entire body of works ("the development of Shakespeare's imagery").

To describe the relationship between a writer's ideas and the images, particularly the metaphors, which he chooses to objectivize them, two useful terms have been coined by I. A. Richards (in *The Philosophy of Rhetoric*). First is the *tenor,* which is the sum total of ideas and attitudes not only of the literary speaker but also of the author. Thus, the *tenor* of the million-dollar check image is joy or elation. Second is the *vehicle,* or the details that carry the tenor; the vehicle of the check image is the description of the receipt of the check. Similarly, the tenor of the sestet of Keats's sonnet on Chapman's Homer is awe and wonder; the vehicle is the reference to astronomical and geographical discovery.

Characteristics of Literary Imagery

Imagery is important in both expository and imaginative writing. In fact, it would be difficult to find any good piece of writing that does not employ imagery to at least some extent. But imagery is most vital in imaginative writing, where it promotes immediate understanding and makes suggestions and implications—nonlogical processes that are not central to expository writing.

Usually, imagery is embodied in words or descriptions that denote sense experience that leads to many associations. A single word naming a flower, say *rose,* evokes a definite response in most readers: a person might visualize a rose, recall its smell, associate it with the summer sun and pleasant days, and recall the love and respect that a bouquet of roses represents as a gift. But the word *rose* is not an image until its associations are called into play by a writer, as in these famous lines by Robert Burns:

O, my luve's like a red, red rose
That's newly sprung in June: . . .

Once the comparison has been drawn, all the pleasant connotations of the word *rose* are evoked; these connotations become the *tenor* of the image. That a rose may have unpleasant associations, however, perhaps because of its thorns, should probably not be considered. Such an extension of meaning, although truthful, would likely represent a misreading of the lines.

It would, that is, unless the writer deliberately calls some of these less happy ideas to mind. In one of the most famous poems about a rose, by Edmund Waller ("Go Lovely Rose," in which the speaker addresses a rose that he is about to send to his reluctant sweetheart), the speaker draws attention to the fact that roses, when cut, die:

Then die—that she
The common fate of all things rare

> May read in thee:
> How small a part of time they share
> That are so wondrous sweet and fair.

Here the poet is directing the reader's responses to the speaker's original comparison of the rose with his sweetheart, and the structure of the poem is coextensive with the development of the image. In this poem, the tenor is an awareness that life is both lovely and fragile.

Imagery may of course become complex, and it may be found everywhere. Aristotle, in describing methods of argumentation in his *Rhetoric,* mentions that writers often will use *inductions* or *examples* in order to advance their ideas (Book II, Ch. 20). An induction is actually an image that advances the argument—it is a part of argument. The ancient Aesop composed *fables,* which were little pointed stories to which later editors have attached *morals,* or explanations of Aesop's arguments. Jesus Christ spoke constantly in *parables,* which are little narratives embodying profound religious insights. These parables, like those of the Good Samaritan and the Prodigal Son, are being interpreted today in sermons and church-school classes throughout the world. Medieval preachers utilized the *exemplum,* a little story that served as the springboard for a sermon. The medieval Englishman *Orm* wrote the *Ormulum* as a long collection of such *exempla* for use in the churches. All these types of stories today may properly be discussed as imagery.

Imagery and Language

Not only is imagery essential in all types of literature, but it is at the heart of language itself; it is ingrained in our very habits of thought and expression. As only one example out of tens of thousands, the word *channel,* with its allied word *canal,* referred originally to a large trench, ditch, or canal. Because it is a vivid term, it has been used as an image in reference to "directing or forwarding, placing within confines"; anyone familiar with bureaucratic procedures knows what it means to go through "channels." When the wide commercialization of television required the creation of new terminology, *channel* was applied to the frequencies used by the various stations. Quickly the term was applied to the stations themselves, and thus we speak of "Channel 2" and "Channel 4" without thinking about the way in which the word was fashioned in this sense. When an image loses its power to stimulate, as in this instance, we speak of it as a "dead image," or "dead metaphor." Despite the many dead metaphors in our language, the process of image-making continues, as it has in the past, to add to our word stock. New needs and situations call forth the utilization of existing words and concepts, which are usually applied as images.

Imagery and Rhetorical "Devices"

The vehicles of imagery have been classified rhetorically; the fable and the parable, for example, are distinctive enough to be classified as rhetorical types. The most important types you can look for are these:

SIMILE A simile is a comparison using "like" or "as." The second line in these two lines is a simile:

> It glows and glitters in my cloudy breast
> Like stars upon some gloomy grove.

In the six lines from Keats (above, p. 95) there are two similes, each conveying the excitement of discovery. In imitation of Homer and Virgil, Milton wrote "epic similes," that is, fairly extensive similes that attempted to elevate his subject matter.

METAPHOR A metaphor is a comparison that does not use "like" or "as." The tenor is *implied* in the vehicle and is not introduced by a preposition or a clause marker. A metaphor may consist of a single word, as in Keats's poem "To My Brothers."

> Small, busy flames *play* through the fresh-laid coals.

It may also be more extensive, as in Shakespeare's Sonnet No. 146, when the speaker compares his body to a house and his soul to a tenant in the house:

> Why so large cost, having so short a lease,
> Dost thou upon thy fading mansion spend?

CONCEIT A conceit, specifically a "Metaphysical conceit," is a fairly long simile or metaphor that introduces an especially unusual or witty image. Frequently the development of the conceit controls the structure of the poem. Perhaps the most famous metaphysical conceit is Donne's comparison of lovers and compasses in "A Valediction: Forbidding Mourning."

SYNECDOCHE In a synecdoche, which is a special kind of metaphor, a small part stands for a large part, as in the nautical phrase "All hands aboard," where the word *hands* signifies all the sailors, presumably because their hands are so vital in the management of the ship.

METONYMY A metonymy, also a metaphor, is a term that stands for something with which it is closely associated. The President, for example, is closely associated with the White House, so that "news from the White House" is in effect news of actions and policies of the President.

Similar to this are "the Pentagon," "Madison Avenue," "Broadway," and so on.

SYMBOL A symbol—a most important term—is the second half of a metaphor or simile with the first part left out. The vehicle in a symbol has its own objective reality, but it also stands for something else. Thus, the flag symbolizes the aims and aspirations of the nation. In George Herbert's poem "The Collar," the collar is, first of all, the collar of a clergyman, but second it stands for the Christian religion with all that Christianity signifies. Many objects are commonly understood as symbols; some of these are mistletoe, rings, the laurel bough, water or the sea, and many others. References to these objects as symbols usually require little emphasis or explication by the author.[1] Quite often, however, a writer may develop his own symbols within a work or series of works. In Swift's poem "Description of the Morning," the reference to wheel ruts in the street symbolizes Swift's general idea that London life of the time was worn and grooved. Sometimes a character may become symbolic, like Figaro in Beaumarchais's plays *The Barber of Seville* and *The Marriage of Figaro*. Figaro, the barber, was taken as a symbol of the good, able man who was kept servile by the aristocratic social and political system of eighteenth-century France.

The use of symbolism has characterized a great deal of modern literature. William Butler Yeats, for example, worked constantly with symbols like the *gyre* and the city of Byzantium. James Joyce, in his fiction, developed a theory of symbolism that he employed in his works—the idea of "epiphany" or radiance. Joyce thought that certain objects, statements, actions, and details crystallized or summarized everything he wanted to say about a character or group of characters. Thus, in the story "Counterparts" from *The Dubliners,* a man beats his young son after a day during which he himself has been browbeaten. His action symbolizes the human tendency to take frustrations out on others.

Closely connected with symbol is the term *controlling image,* which is an image developed so thoroughly throughout a work or which is so vital and pervasive that one may interpret the work in the light of the image. In the sample theme, attention is drawn to Shakespeare's controlling image of the prophet, or prophetic voice, which runs throughout John of Gaunt's speech.

Also merging with symbol and metaphor is intensely vivid descriptive writing. Such writing, of course, is every author's goal, and it is usually not regarded as imagery. To the degree that an accurate and vivid description can evoke an impression that the author wishes to control, however, the effect of vivid writing is the same as that of imagery

[1] See J. E. Cirlot, *A Dictionary of Symbols,* trans. Jack Sage (New York: Philosophical Library, 1962).

and specifically symbolism. John Masefield's poem "Cargoes" is a three-stanza poem describing three ships from three periods of history. Although Masefield does not make any comparisons, his views of the different periods are made explicitly clear by his descriptions. Similarly, a description of a natural setting that refers to colors, shapes, conditions of light, and so on, will suggest responses that are sympathetic to the author's story, and for this reason such descriptions in truth are like symbolism and metaphor.

ALLEGORY   Allegory has been often defined as extended metaphor, or as moving symbols. An allegory is an entire story that is self-sufficient but that also signifies another series of events or a condition of life as expressed in a religion or philosophy. The most widely read allegory in our language has been Bunyan's *Pilgrim's Progress,* which at one time was almost as important as the Bible. Spenser's *Faerie Queene* is a series of allegorical narrative poems, each one referring to separate concepts of Christian goodness. The parable and the fable without the moral attached are in effect short allegories. Ancient *myths* were also allegorical in nature.

PERSONIFICATION   In personification, something abstract, like a season of the year, is given human attributes, as in this famous example from Tennyson's "In Memoriam":

> . . . Nature, red in tooth and claw,
> With ravine, shriek'd against his creeds.

Imagery and Attitudes

In considering the tenor of any given imagery, you ought to recognize that imagery is effective in rendering attitudes. It can elevate the subject matter or reduce it in size or ridicule it. Further, it can also produce these same effects on the speaker, if the author so wishes. To see some of these effects operating in a short space, the following passage from Shakespeare's *Antony and Cleopatra* is instructive:

> The hearts
> That [spaniel'd] me at heels, to whom I gave
> Their wishes, do discandy, melt their sweets
> On blossoming Caesar; and this pine is bark'd,
> That overtopp'd them all.
>
> —IV.xii.20-24

The word *hearts* in the first line is a synecdoche, by which hearts refers to Antony's followers. The image implies (a) that his followers seemed to be fully committed to him ("with all their hearts"), and (b) that they stayed with him through emotion and not principle, and therefore they found it easy to leave him when their emotions had shifted.[2] The images of *discandying* and *blossoming* both connote a strong attitude of disparagement on Antony's part, particularly when they are compared with the final metaphor, which is drawn from the experience of woodsmen. Antony is tall and firm as a pine, and like a pine he "overtopp'd" everyone and everything around him. But now his strength is gone, as is the strength of a tree when its bark is removed; even though he has not yet crashed to the ground and is as tall as ever, he will inevitably die. His imagery indicates that he knows the political fate of a leader without followers, and it also suggests his belief that he still is superior to those who will replace him in power and prestige. As you can see, these images convey a completeness of statement and implication that literal language could approximate only with many more words and then not as well.

Imagery can also serve as a comic device, usually by diminishing the thing being compared. The question, "Are you a man or a mouse?" suggests a metaphor of diminution if the response is the second alternative. A more extensive image of diminution is this mock-epic simile that Henry Fielding wrote in *Tom Jones* just before his description of a family battle between Mr. and Mrs. Partridge:

> As fair Grimalkin, who, though the youngest of the feline, degenerates not in ferocity from the elder branches of her house, and though inferior in strength, is equal in fierceness to the noble tiger himself, when a little mouse, whom it hath long tormented in sport, escapes from her clutches for a while, frets, scolds, growls, swears; but if the trunk, or box, behind which the mouse lay hid, be again removed, she flies like lightning on her prey, and, with envenomed wrath, bites, scratches, mumbles, and tears the little animal.
>
> —Book II, Chapter 4

Imagery and Allusions

Fielding's image becomes more meaningful when one recognizes its dependence on epic similes as they were used by Homer and Milton and also when one identifies "Grimalkin" as a witch in cat form that is referred to by the witches in *Macbeth*. In other words, a certain amount of literary knowledge is required for full understanding and appreciation. Imagery is often complicated in this way by the *allusion* to other works, such as the classics or the Bible. The image in the original source, having been used in this way, then becomes a vital part of the

---

[2] The word *spaniel'd* in line 21 is a conjectural emendation by one of Shakespeare's editors, but it is a powerful comparison of dogs and Antony's followers that would be worthy of Shakespeare's imaginative genius, and it is very likely the word that Shakespeare used.

writer's context. In Donne's sonnet "I Am a Little World Made Cun-
ningly," for example, the concluding lines are:

> . . . burn me, O Lord, with a fiery zeal
> Of Thee and Thy house, which doth in eating heal.

The problem raised by the paradox in the last line is partially solved
when you realize that the image in the metaphor is from Psalms 69, 9:
"For the zeal of thine house hath eaten me up." Until the Biblical image
is known, however, the line will be difficult to visualize and understand
completely.

This example brings up the problem of the amount of definition
necessary for the comprehension of imagery. For the most part your
attempt to visualize, smell, taste, touch, and hear the experience described or suggested will suffice to convey the meaning of the imagery
to you. In these cases a dictionary is superfluous. But an allusive image,
like the Biblical one in Donne's poem, or an archaic image may require
a dictionary in addition to any explanatory notes supplied by the editor
of the work you are reading. As an example, let us look briefly at these
lines from Pope's *Essay on Criticism:*

> Some, to whom Heav'n in Wit has been profuse,
> Want as much more, to turn it to its use;
> For *Wit* and *Judgment* often are at strife,
> Tho' meant each other's Aid, like *Man* and *Wife.*
> 'Tis more to *guide* than *spur* the Muse's Steed;
> Restrain his Fury, than provoke his Speed;
> The winged Courser, like a gen'rous Horse,
> Shows most true Mettle when you *check* his Course.

> —lines 80-87

Pope has sometimes been dispraised by the assertion that he was not an
imaginative poet, but instead was ratiocinative or "discursive." A close
look at a passage like this one renders this assertion absurd. Pope is
talking about the relationship of reason to imagination, and is stating,
briefly, that judgment (the perceptive, critical, discriminating faculty)
must always be in control of imagination (or *fancy,* the other common
word for the faculty, which is related to the words *fanciful* and *fantastic*).
Pope compares judgment to a rider on a race horse. All the strength and
speed of a thoroughbred ("gen'rous Horse") are of no value, he says,
unless a good jockey rides and paces it well. In line 86 Pope mentions
"The winged Courser" (a flying horse) and opens the door to allusion.
By referring to a classical dictionary, you can learn that the flying horse
of antiquity was Pegasus, who was ridden by Bellerophon in his fight
against the monster Chimaera. Bellerophon was assisted in his fight by
the gods, particularly by Athena, who was the goddess of wisdom. Other

references may also apply. A dictionary tells you that the word *chimerical* (fantastically unreal) is derived from the name of the monster. The editor may tell you that in the seventeenth and eighteenth centuries pure fantasy was regarded as being akin to madness. In the context of the time when Pope wrote, this allusion to the winged horse seems to be saying this: "If you wish to avoid madness or just foolishness in your writing, and if you wish to be favored by the goddess of wisdom, you must guide your imagination by judgment." Thus Pope's imagery works in two ways, literal and allusive, to strengthen his point that judgment is necessary in works of imagination and criticism.

You can see that reference books and annotated editions can be indispensable in guiding you to an understanding of at least some of the implications of an author's imagery. You may justifiably ask how you can learn about allusions when you don't recognize them. The answer is to read a good, annotated text and to look up all words and references that are not immediately familiar to you. There are responsible, "definitive" editions of most writers either available or in process of publication. See the card catalogue in your library to find out about these editions.

Your Theme

Your job in preparing this theme, as always, is to be alert and to employ all facilities that can aid your understanding and appreciation. You must study your poem or passage word by word. Savor each word and set up a classification of what sorts of responses the words elicit. You might set up a series of lists headed by the words *Sight, Smell, Taste, Hearing, Touch,* and *Combinations* (how could you classify the image "embalmed darkness" except by this latter category?). Then check yourself: Can you visualize a word or description? Can you recall a touch or taste similar to that which the words describe?

With images that cause visual responses you might aid your imagination by drawing sketches. Some people might object to sketching images on the grounds that it tends to limit your responses too narrowly, but if it aids you in responding to a work, it is not despicable. The following line from Shakespeare's Sonnet No. 146, for example, offers an interesting challenge to the imagination that might be aided by a sketch:

> So shalt thou [the speaker's Soul] feed on
> Death that feeds on men, . . .
>
> —line 13

Just how far does the image invite complete visualization? That is one problem faced by the student with a theme to write about this poem.

Do the metaphors *feed* and *feeds* invite a response visualizing an eater, while eating, being eaten, or should the words be read without the reader's attempting to imagine specific feeders? One student responded to these lines with the following drawing:

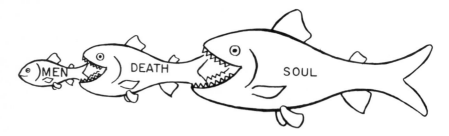

This drawing vividly shows the relationships involved, though it tends to demean Soul, Death, and Men (perhaps the student was thinking that men, in this case, are "poor fish"). Whether or not you carry your visualization this far, it is clear that Shakespeare's speaker is calling Death voracious because it seizes men for prey. But he is also asserting that the Soul can be equally voracious and more powerful than Death, even though it is also dependent on Death for its sustenance.

Whether you make a drawing or use your ability to visualize the impressions suggested by the words, you are concerned in your analysis to see the effect of imagery in the work. How does the imagery convey meaning? What particular attitudes does it communicate or suggest? (That is, how do you feel about Death and the Soul after reading the line from Shakespeare? Or how do you feel about Keats's excitement presented in "On First Looking into Chapman's Homer"?) How fully developed are the images? Do they stem from single words, or are they developed at greater length throughout a line or several lines, or perhaps even throughout the entire work? Is there a controlling image, and what is its effect? Are there many images, few images? Do the images in the work make the work particularly powerful, feeble? Why? Are there symbols? Is the story allegorical? Does the imagery at one point in the work create any special effect on other parts of the work? Does the imagery seem to develop in any special pattern? (For example, Robert Frost's poem "Out, Out—" develops a pattern of sound beginning with the noisy, snarling buzz saw and ending with the feeble heartbeat of the dying boy; after the boy's death, Frost's description of the people turning away contains no words describing sound. The references to sound and silence within the poem therefore create an image of what happens to the boy's heart.) These are the questions that you should try to answer in your theme.

The Organization of Your Theme

INTRODUCTION

In your introduction you should make a brief statement about the nature of the work you are analyzing. Related to this will be your central idea, which is the statement of the main point you wish to illustrate about the imagery (i.e., that it is mainly visual, or that it makes the poem powerful, or that it is ineffective, or some other point that your analysis has uncovered).

BODY

There are a number of approaches to discussing imagery, and you may choose whatever method, or combination of methods, you wish. Here are some possible choices:

A   Discussion of all the kinds of responses caused by the imagery. Here you should show the variety of imagery in the work and draw a conclusion about the type of imagery that predominates. Does the work appeal to all five senses? Does one type (sight, hearing, etc.) predominate? What can you conclude from your findings?

B   Discussion of the frames of reference of the imagery. Here you might show the locations from which the images are derived. Does the writer favor images from nature, from high society, from low society, from warfare, from politics, from finance, from his reading, and so on? What conclusions can you draw?

C   Discussion of the effect of one image, or series of images, on the other images and ideas in the poem. Usually you would pick an image that occurs early in the work and ask if this image acts as a controlling image over the ideas or mood (tone) of the work. Thus, the first paragraph of Swift's *Battle of the Books* (a prose work) contains an uncomplimentary image pertaining to the behavior of hungry dogs; in this way Swift conveys the impression that the whole battle between the "Ancients" and "Moderns" has a physiological origin that is anything but flattering. In an analysis of this sort, you would try to show the importance of the controlling image throughout the work.

D   Discussion of the way imagery causes suggestions and implications to appear in the work. Here you should show how far the imagery carries your imagination, and also you ought to show the limits of the imagery. Show how the imagery affects and adds to a bare paraphrase.

CONCLUSION

In your conclusion you should give your general impressions. You might state how the imagery deepened your experience of the work or your insight into the nature of literature itself. In a more thorough analysis you might compare the imagery in the work you have analyzed with the imagery appearing in works written by the author at earlier or later points in his career. Conclusions of this kind can show much about a writer's development.

Hints

Instead of trying to discuss every single image in the work, concentrate on typical, unusual, and particularly important images.

Be prepared to relate the imagery to conclusions the author apparently expected you to reach. Always emphasize the ways in which the imagery—the vehicle—brings out conclusions and attitudes—the tenor.

It is desirable and helpful to reproduce your poem or passage, double-spaced, and to number its lines. As with the theme on a specific problem, utilize the editor's line numbers when you are reproducing a passage from an extensive work. Otherwise, number from *1* to the end. Refer to these line numbers in your theme. If you are asked to analyze the imagery in an extensive passage or in a story or novel, you might reproduce several short examples from the work to be cited in your discussion.

SAMPLE THEME

A Study of the Imagery in
Shakespeare's **Richard II,**
II.i.33-70

GAUNT [*speaks*]

Methinks I am a prophet new inspired,	33
And thus expiring, do foretell of him,	34
His rash fierce blaze of riot cannot last,	35
For violent fires soon burn out themselves,	36
Small showers last long, but sudden storms are short,	37
He tires betimes, that spurs too fast betimes;	38
With eager feeding, food doth choke the feeder:	39
Light vanity, insatiate cormorant,	40
Consuming means soon preys upon itself.	41
This royal throne of kings, this sceptered isle,	42
This earth of majesty, this seat of Mars,	43
This other Eden, demi paradise,	44
This fortress built by Nature for herself,	45
Against infection, and the hand of war:	46
This happy breed of men, this little world,	47
This precious stone, set in the silver sea,	48

Which serves it in the office of a wall,   49
Or as a moat defensive to a house,   50
Against the envy of less happier lands,   51
This blessed plot, this earth, this realm, this England,   52
This nurse, this teeming womb of royal kings,   53
Feared by their breed, and famous for their birth,   54
Renowned for their deeds, as far from home,   55
For Christian service, and true chivalry,   56
As is the sepulchre in stubborn Jewry   57
Of the world's ransom, blessed Mary's son,   58
This land of such dear souls, this dear-dear land,   59
Dear for her reputation through the world,   60
Is now leased out (I die pronouncing it)   61
Like to a tenement or pelting farm.   62
England bound in with the triumphant sea,   63
Whose rocky shore beats back the envious siege   64
Of watery Neptune, is now bound in with shame,   65
With inky blots, and rotten parchment bonds.   66
That England, that was wont to conquer others,   67
Hath made a shameful conquest of itself.   68
Ah! would the scandal vanish with my life,   69
How happy then were my ensuing death? [3]   70

This image-studded speech is above all dramatic; it is said by the dying John of Gaunt to the Duke of York, his brother. Gaunt's aim is to praise England and to show the impending danger of the profligate rule of Richard II and also to imply—but only to imply—to York that Richard, although ruling legally, could be removed. The remarkable speech also demonstrates the fertility of the dying Gaunt's mind, the alienation and death of which does not bode well for Richard, particularly because he has also alienated Bolingbroke, Gaunt's son.

The passage consists of three major sections, characterized first by imagery suggesting Richard's profligacy, second, by imagery pointing out England's greatness, and third, by imagery asserting that Richard's effect on England is destructive. Dominating the entire speech are two images that are announced in the first two lines: Gaunt is dying and he expresses this fact as a metaphor of expiring—breathing the last. This image in fact controls the passage like a symbol, directing the visual imagery in the first section and also that in the third. A second image is that of the prophet, the role Shakespeare gives Gaunt on his deathbed to provide an analogical basis for the Biblical imagery in the second section.

---

3 Matthew W. Black, ed., *The Life and Death of King Richard the Second* (A New Variorum Edition of Shakespeare, ed. James McManaway [Philadelphia and London: J. B. Lippincott Co., 1955]), pp. 101-5. The spelling is here modernized.

In the first section the imagery reflects Richard's prodigality—prodigality, that is, in Gaunt's eyes. Metaphorically, Gaunt compares Richard first to a blazing fire (lines 35, 36). The basis for the image is this: the king is like a fire to his subjects, providing them with heat and light, and he should assume this role constantly. To this end, the king needs a slow, steady, life-giving supply of fuel and draft. But Richard is a blaze, and although he now is brilliant, he will soon deplete the fuel and die, perhaps after having burned or scorched his country.

This notion of dying down and tiring is pursued in the remaining images in the passage, drawn from water, travel, and food. Richard is thus compared with a destructive storm, not a life-giving small shower (37). He is like a horseman who spurs his horse too strongly and who will thus tire himself and his horse and not reach his destination (38). He is choking himself with food and is so greedy that like a cormorant, he is actually devouring himself (40, 41). These images connote a progression from natural prodigality to human foolishness and ultimately to suicidal gluttony. Both suicide and gluttony were, in Renaissance Christian values, sinful. Gaunt's condemnation of Richard as a person could not, therefore, be more emphatic.

An abrupt contrast to these images of waste is made by the images in the second section, which is a virtuoso piece of imagery in praise of England and one that is often excerpted. The section consists of a nineteen-line noun group with eighteen nouns in apposition, with their modifiers but with no principal verb. There is no grammatical movement, but there is a brilliant progression of images. Primary is the resumption of the prophetic image from line 33, which suggests the metaphorical comparison of England and the Old-Testament Eden (44). In the latter part of the section, the image from the New Testament alludes to Christ, Mary, and the doctrine of vicarious atonement (56-58). Clearly, to Gaunt, England is a Holy Land, and England should be a fulfillment of history the way the New Testament was a fulfillment of the Old Testament. Just as Christ was born to save the world, English kings should be born to a similar role. Through suggestion and implication, Gaunt's imagery here raises England to about as high a plane of estimation as one could imagine a country could reach.

In addition, the many other images in the second section attribute other glowing, noble qualities to England. The images progress from the large, majestic, and masculine to the small, domestic and feminine. The "sceptered isle" in line 42 and the "seat of Mars" in line 43 become the "blessed plot" in line 52. This garden image hearkens back to the small-shower image of line 37 and certainly to the Eden reference in line 44: the water of life should fall gently on the land and render her fertile. From this generally feminine image, Gaunt metaphorically equates England with both a nurse and a mother (the reference to "womb" is a synecdoche) of noble sons who defend the Christian faith. Ultimately, as has been shown, he makes the comparison of England and Mary. The full weight of all these images in this second section is that England is father, lord, protector, redeemer, and mother— all things to all men.

Grammatically, the third section completes the noun group in the second section by providing a principal verb for it. This final section puts the first two sections together by associating Richard and England and asserting that the association is hurting England. The verbal metaphor in line 61 is a powerful condemnation of Richard's financial manipulations: he has now leased the country itself as security for his borrowing to fight foolish wars, and the English people now are no better than tenants in their native land. The land itself has been made a "tenement or pelting farm" (62). This image of a legal stranglehold is continued in lines 65 and 66, where Richard's financial commitments (and perhaps even Richard's control of the Crown itself) is equated with "inky blots, and rotten parchment bonds." Constantly in this final section, Gaunt's speech is filled with images that contrast his idea of the naturally powerful and wealthy condition of England (it has even made the sea "triumphant") with his idea that Richard's kingship has sickened the country. He concludes by taking up, once again, the cormorant image of line 40; this time he states that England has "made a shameful conquest of itself" (68). His implication is that the condition should be removed, and if he cannot remove it by his death, someone who is still alive should remove it. Although the speech is not an incitement to rebellion, it leaves the door open to rebellion.

Gaunt's speech is a vital part of the play. The images Shakespeare gives him—more than thirty in these heavily packed lines— appeal to ideal standards in religion, government, patriotism, economics, husbandry, horsemanship, eating habits, and housekeeping. Implicit in the second section, and clearly stated in the first and third, is the idea that Richard has fallen short in all these areas. The speech is heard by York, who during much of the play stays with Richard because of belief that the King rules legally; but it offers to York an ultimate reason for switching allegiance when the good of the country demands it. When York goes, symbolically, Richard is lost, and Shakespeare may well be showing here why York was persuaded to go.

Beyond this dramatic function, Shakespeare seems to have

another aim in his selection of fertile images. He implies that the support of men like Gaunt is necessary for any ruler; men with such patriotic fervor, moral strength, and analytical insight can prove deadly foes, just as they can be stalwart friends. To lose their support, as Richard has done, is disastrous. Therefore the imagery in the speech, which prefigures the actual deposition later in the play, produces a paean to England, a cause of important dramatic action, and a lesson in political leadership.

The Theme
Analyzing Tone

11 Tone is one of the most important concepts to understand and describe in the study of literature. Ideally, tone refers to the means by which a writer conveys attitudes. Although it is a technical subject, in practice the discussion of tone becomes focussed on the attitudes themselves. For this reason, the terms *tone* and *attitude* are sometimes used synonymously. You should remember, however, that tone refers not to attitudes but to that quality of a writer's style which reveals—or creates—these attitudes. If you preserve this distinction you should be able to handle a theme about tone and should quickly appreciate all its implications for literary study.

Studying and describing tone requires the greatest alertness and subtlety, because your understanding of tone will depend largely on your ability to make inferences from the work you are reading (sometimes this process is called "reading between the lines"). Your analysis of tone is, in effect, your analysis of the author's mind at work, and through this analysis you can become aware of the vitality of literature—the profound, alive creativity of the author's mind as seen in his words. Reading a work of literature without perceiving its tone is like watching a speaker on television with the sound turned off; without tone you can guess at meaning, but cannot understand it fully.

Tone in Operation

Tone in literature has been borrowed from the phrase *tone of voice* in speech. You have certainly heard this phrase and may even have been criticized at one time or another for having said something in a certain tone of voice or for having indicated an attitude that has displeased a parent, friend, customer, or teacher. Tone of voice, in other words, is a reflection of your attitude toward the person or persons whom you are addressing and also toward the subject matter of your discussion. In the personal circumstances of speech, tone of voice is made up of many elements: the speed with which you utter your words, the enthusiasm—or lack of it—that you project into what you say, the pitch and loudness of your speech, your facial expressions, the way you hold your body, and your distance from the person to whom you are speaking.

Your attitudes are always basic to your opinions, friendships, activities, and even your deepest personal philosophy. Think briefly about the tone of these statements, which you may have heard or said: "Don't call me; I'll call you." "Oh, yes, I would be absolutely overjoyed to make the beds, do this morning's dishes, and sweep and mop the floor." Or imagine that before an examination a good friend tells you, "I hope you get the grade you deserve on the test." You may wonder about his exact meaning. To make it clear, he may accompany his words with a roguish smile which makes you see that your friendship is not without a certain degree of antagonism. He wishes you to do well, yet he would probably not grieve uncontrollably if you did not. But perhaps you realize that your friendship is sound if he feels safe in expressing his complexity of attitudes toward you. All these situations, and many more that you could supply yourself, require a consideration of tone.

As a literary comparison, let us look briefly at this passage from *Gulliver's Travels,* written by one of the great masters of tone in English literature:

> Imagine with thy self, courteous Reader, how often I then wished for the Tongue of *Demosthenes* or *Cicero,* that might have enabled me to celebrate the Praise of my own dear native Country in a Style equal to its Merits and Felicity.[1]

You have here a passage in which Gulliver is perfectly sincere about praising England, whereas Swift the satirist, behind the scenes, is just about to deliver a satiric condemnation of his England. The control of tone makes these contrasting attitudes evident and makes this passage comic. Swift controls the tone by causing Gulliver to refer to the two most famous ancient orators who were known for their ability to speak well but who were also known for their powers to condemn. He also makes Gulliver use the ambiguous phrase "equal to its Merits and Felicity" and the possibly sarcastic word "celebrate." The tone here is quite similar to that in the previously mentioned banter with the imaginary

[1] Robert A. Greenberg, ed., *Gulliver's Travels: An Annotated Text With Critical Essays* (New York: W. W. Norton & Co., Inc., 1961), II, vi, 103.

friend, with this difference: in the literary work you are not aided by the physical, conversational context of the interchange. All you have is the printed page; to interpret it properly you have only a dictionary, other reference works, and, above all, your intelligence.

Tone, of course, may be described in many ways, as there are many human moods. Here is a partial list of words that might describe tone in particular passages.

> simple, straightforward, direct, unambiguous
> complicated, complex, difficult
> forceful, powerful
> ironic, sardonic, sarcastic
> indirect, understated, evasive
> bitter, grim
> sympathetic, interested
> indifferent, unconcerned, apathetic
> antagonistic, hostile
> violent, outraged, indignant, angry
> elevated, grand, lofty
> serious, solemn, sepulchral, ghoulish
> comic, jovial, easy, friendly

A thesaurus would supply you with many more words, and it is conceivable that there are, somewhere, literary works to which all the words you discover might be applied.

Problems in Describing Tone

The study of tone is the study of the ways in which attitudes are manifested in a particular literary work. Therefore, when you write a theme about tone, you must attempt to name and describe these attitudes and analyze the means by which they are expressed. Your statements will be based upon inferences that you make from the text.

You must also attempt to describe the intensity, the force with which the attitudes are expressed. This task is difficult, but necessary, and it is one of the ways by which you can amplify your statements about the nature of the attitudes. The force of the tone depends on the intrinsic seriousness of the situation, the speaker's degree of involvement in it, and his control over his expression. You would recognize the differences in intensity between the statements in the two columns:

1	2
"This report is not what we expected."	"This report is terrible."
"Mr. Student, your paper shows promise, but it is not, as yet, up to passing standards."	"Mr. Student, your paper is a slovenly disgrace."

In describing the difference, you would necessarily concentrate on the differing *intensities* of the tones expressed in the quotations. Or, compare the intensities of tone implicit in these two quotations:

1 Written on a wall in Havana: "Yankee, go home."
2 Written on a wall in Paris: "Yankee, go home—via Air France."

These last quotations bring up another, closely related, element in the consideration of tone—namely, that of control. A writer may feel deeply about a subject, but if he gives vent to his feelings completely he is likely to create not a literary work but only an emotional display. He must always control the expression of sentiment, because his appeal must be not only to his readers' sympathies but also to their understanding. A fine example of the control of attitude is *Antony and Cleopatra* (V. ii, 241-81). Cleopatra is about to commit suicide. Just before she does, Shakespeare introduces a rustic on stage to bring her the asp. The resulting interchange between Cleopatra, serious and about to die, and the stupid but concerned clown is clearly designed to arouse laughter.

> *Enter Guardsman and Clown [with Basket]*.

GUARD — This is the man.

CLEOPATRA — Avoid, and leave him.

> *Exit Guardsman.*

Hast thou the pretty worm of Nilus there
That kills and pains not?

CLOWN — Truly I have him. But I would not be the party that should desire you to touch him, for his biting is immortal. Those that do die of it do seldom or never recover.

CLEOPATRA — Remember'st thou any that have died on't?

CLOWN — Very many, men and women too. I heard of one of them no longer than yesterday; a very honest woman, but something given to lie, as a woman should not do but in the way of honesty—how she died of the biting of it, what pain she felt. Truly, she makes a very good report o' the worm; but he that will believe all that they say shall never be saved by half that they do. But this is most falliable, the worm's an odd worm.

CLEOPATRA — Get thee hence; farewell.

CLOWN — I wish you all joy of the worm.

> *[Sets down his basket]*.

CLEOPATRA — Farewell. . . .

—lines 241-260

The problem in interpreting this scene is that of Shakespeare's attitude toward Cleopatra and toward his audience. It is likely that Shakespeare introduced the comic scene in order to keep his treatment of Cleopatra from becoming purely sentimental. He knew that one way to produce laughter is to heap misfortune upon misfortune, so that an audience will ultimately respond to additional misfortunes with laughter, not with sympathy. Cleopatra's suicide is the final misfortune, and lest his audience not respond with sorrow, Shakespeare provides the clown to siphon off, as it were, his audience's tension by giving it a legitimate release in laughter. In this way he directs a proper amount of sympathy toward Cleopatra and deepens our concern for her. The situation is complex, but Shakespeare's handling of it indicates the control of the master.

Irony

The greatest skill of the writer is often his courage to treat a serious problem in a light or comic way. By doing so he maintains proportion, shows control, and makes his work generally effective. Shakespeare must have had great confidence in his own ability to evaluate dramatic situations to succeed with this comic scene. You may remember similar situations in your own life. Have you ever had the impulse to insult a friend, parent, or a "steady" date? In friendly banter, however, you always assume that your friend will be able to see through your "insult" into your genuine fondness. Treatment like this is usually called *irony*, a term describing ambiguity or indirection. In literature, as in friendship, irony implies a compliment by the writer to the reader, for it indicates that the writer assumes skill and intelligence on his reader's part sufficient to see through the surface statement into the seriousness or levity beneath. Irony implies that the writer has great control over his material and much confidence in his readers. Sir Winston Churchill, for example, has been quoted as saying, "Democracy is the worst type of government, except all the rest." His ironic statement implies great understanding of human imperfections; it implies that man is in a process of evolving and endeavoring to perfect his political institutions; but it also implies respect for democracy and for those who love it. The statement shows great control over tone.

The major types of irony are *verbal, situational,* and *dramatic. Verbal irony* is a form of indirection or ambiguity by which the opposite of what is said is usually intended. Often, verbal irony may be described as *understatement* or *overstatement.* Thus, a soldier may describe a fierce battle by saying "We had a bit of a go at it." This is understatement. Overstatement, or hyperbole, may be seen in this description of a bad situation: "Everything is just absolutely dandy."

The term *situational irony,* or irony of situation, is usually employed to describe misguided hopes or misinterpreted motives about a given situation. Thomas Hardy was adept at creating situational irony, as in *The Return of the Native,* when Eustacia appears at the window of her home briefly and glances at the visiting Mrs. Yeobright outside. Because a former suitor is visiting Eustacia, and also because she believes that her husband Clym will answer the door, she does not admit Mrs. Yeobright. Mrs. Yeobright has seen Eustacia at the window and misinterprets Eustacia's motives; she is disheartened and leaves for home, only to meet death on the heath. All subsequent disasters in the novel stem from this incident, and their effect on the tone of the novel is that the ill consequences are much more pathetic because they could have been easily avoided.

Dramatic irony applies when a character in a drama or fictional work perceives a situation in a limited way while the audience sees it in greater perspective. The audience sees double meaning whereas the character sees only one. Perhaps the classic example of dramatic irony is found in *Oedipus Rex,* where Oedipus thinks he is about to discover that someone else murdered his father, while the audience knows all along that he himself is the murderer and that as he condemns the murderer he condemns himself. In Hemingway's story "My Old Man," dramatic irony is utilized skillfully. This story is told by a son about his father who is a jockey but who also becomes involved in deals to fix horseraces. During the first part of the story the narrator does not know the significance of the events he is describing, while the reader can see that the father is guilty of fixing races. During the latter half of the story, Hemingway subtly employs dramatic irony to focus on the son's attempts to mask from himself the significance of the father's actions and also to avoid the realization that his father has undergone physical and moral deterioration. The father's death at the end of the story, and the comments by the two "guys" about the father, finally and brutally force the boy to face the truth. Hemingway thus creates a poignant account of a loss of innocence, and he does so by using dramatic irony to show that the boy possessed innocence that could be lost.

Identifying Tone in Literature

As you have undoubtedly concluded, the study of tone is quite general. It requires a study of everything in a literary work that might contribute more than just the denotative statement. To perceive tone you must be completely alert. You must be constantly aware of the general impression that a passage leaves with you, but you must also be analytical enough to study the particular ways by which this effect is achieved. You must understand all the words; you must read the work carefully, then study the passages you select for discussion in order to determine the connotations of the words and the rhythms of the cadence groups. Anything might present an illustration of tone, and to understand the tone you must respond to everything.

Look at this passage from Lytton Strachey's biography of Florence Nightingale in *Eminent Victorians*,[2] a work known for its tone:

> Eventually the whole business of purveying to the hospitals was, in effect, carried out by Miss Nightingale. She alone, it seemed, whatever the contingency, knew where to lay her hands on what was wanted; she alone could dispense her stores with readiness; above all, she alone possessed the art of circumventing the pernicious influences of official etiquette. This was her greatest enemy, and sometimes even she was baffled by it. On one occasion 27,000 shirts, sent out at her instance by the Home Government, arrived, were landed, and were only waiting to be unpacked. But the official "Purveyor" intervened; "he could not unpack them," he said, "without a Board." Miss Nightingale pleaded in vain; the sick and wounded lay half-naked, shivering for want of clothing; and three weeks elapsed before the Board released the shirts. A little later, however, on a similar occasion, Miss Nightingale felt that she could assert her own authority. She ordered a Government consignment to be forcibly opened, while the "Purveyor" stood by, wringing his hands in departmental agony.

The tone here conveys admiration and respect for Miss Nightingale, as contrasted with contempt for the official incompetence against which she had to work. Notice the diction Lytton Strachey employs in conveying his attitude toward her: "she alone," "readiness," "even she," "pleaded," "felt that she could assert," "ordered." These words are to be contrasted with those used in description of the officialdom: "pernicious influences," "baffled," "official 'Purveyor',", "three weeks elapse before the Board released the shirts," "wringing his hands in departmental agony." When these opposite series of words are placed in the context of "the sick and wounded lay half-naked, shivering for want of clothing," their opposition is made even more apparent. Lytton Strachey does not say directly that Florence Nightingale was heroic, yet his *tone* clearly indicates that he thought she was. Diction is the principal way by which he has communicated his tone, which is clear and unambiguous.

Take another instance, this time from the Old English poem "The Wanderer," in a modern prose translation by Professor R. K. Gordon: [3]

> Whither has gone the horse? Whither has gone the man? Whither has gone the giver of treasure? Whither has gone the place of feasting? Where

2 (New York: Harcourt, Brace & World, Inc., 1918), pp. 146-47.

3 *Anglo-Saxon Poetry*, rev. ed., Everyman's Library No. 794 (New York: E. P. Dutton & Co., Inc., 1954), pp. 74-75.

are the joys of hall? Alas, the bright cup! Alas, the warrior in his corslet! Alas, the glory of the prince! How that time has passed away, has grown dark under the shadow of night, as if it had never been! Now in the place of the dear warriors stands a wall, wondrous high, covered with serpent shapes; the might of the ash-wood spears has carried off the earls, the weapon greedy for slaughter—a glorious fate; and storms beat upon these rocky slopes; the falling storm binds the earth, the terror of winter. Then comes darkness, the night shadow casts gloom, sends from the north fierce hailstorms to the terror of men. Everything is full of hardship in the kingdom of earth; the decree of fate changes the world under the heavens. Here possessions are transient, here friends are transient, here man is transient, here woman is transient; all this firm-set earth becomes empty.

The details here indicate the tone—one of despair for the prosperity of man in his earthly state. Complementing the details is a series of abstractions that indicate the effect of the hailstorms and darkness on the minds of men. This semantic interpretation is augmented by the rhythms of the original (faithfully preserved in the translation). The statements are short, even abrupt at the end. The impression is given that the earth definitely holds terror for mankind. There are no subordinate clauses in which the poet might express any qualifications or exceptions to the examples he has given. Thus, the diction, sentence structure, and rhythm contribute to the tone of despair.

Unlike the passage from *Gulliver's Travels,* which is ironic and ambiguous, the tone in these last two examples is straightforward and positive.

Our analysis of these examples was largely concerned with style, but tone may also be caused by the sheer weight of accumulated evidence. The multiplication of examples in support of a claim effects a tone of certainty, and the constant insistence on some attitude produces a tone of solid conviction. As an example, look at the sermon on hell by Father Arnall in Chapter III of Joyce's *Portrait of the Artist as a Young Man,* where the tone is firm, solid, and inescapable. Few persons can read this section without being emotionally shaken by the sheer weight of the evidence presented by Father Arnall. Or think briefly about Thoreau's assertions throughout *Walden* that our industrial civilization is lifeless and artificial. Upon reading this book, one is swayed by the tone either to assent to Thoreau's position or else to question his own position thoroughly. It is difficult to imagine that a reader could be unaffected in any way by Thoreau's tone.

It is fair to conclude that tone is an integral part of meaning and literary excellence. Tone controls responses, and your responses are essential in your literary experience. Control over tone distinguishes plain statement from artistic statement. As you analyze the tone of a work you will realize that the degree of a writer's control over tone provides a strong basis for evaluating his stature as a writer.

Your Approach to Tone

Your main problem in reading the work assigned is to determine to your satisfaction what the dominant tone is. You must therefore carefully examine not only what is said but the context in which it is said. In order to support your claim about tone, you will need to study those factors (style, structure, idea) which cause the particular tone that you have noted.

The amount of analysis you do will depend on the length of the work you are discussing. In a long work you might analyze representative passages that support your central idea. If the work is short, perhaps a short poem, you might very well attempt to analyze the entire work.

Once you have determined your interpretation of the tone, you should state that as your central idea. Then, without making distortions, you should gather material that will support your central idea. Let the material produce the idea. Do not neglect material that opposes your idea. So long as what you analyze has bearing on your central idea, you might bring in considerations of style, ambiguity, accumulation of evidence—all at one time. Just remember to point your discussion toward your basic argument.

Beyond the single statement (your central idea) about tone, you might very well discover that the tone in your literary work is made up of a complexity of moods, a progression of tones. An excellent critical article has been written describing a progression of tone in the poetry of Pope,[4] and an entire book has been written to show that a typical poem by John Donne is structurally dependent on a complex progression of attitudes.[5] In your theme, if your central idea is that there is a complexity of tone or progression of attitudes, you would construct your argument to demonstrate the validity of your claim.

The Organization of Your Theme

The main problem in your discussion of tone is that your remarks are based on inferences. You cannot, therefore, state absolutely that your author actually *held* a certain attitude; you can instead only *infer* that he held that attitude. Your theme is not biographical, but interpretive. Be aware that your inferences might result as much from your own attitudes as from those of the author. For example, recent attempts to interpret the tone of Chaucer's *Prioress's Tale* have implied that because Chaucer treats the Prioress with gentle irony

[4] Maynard Mack, "The Muse of Satire," *Yale Review* (1951), XLI, 80-92.
[5] Leonard Unger, *Donne's Poetry and Modern Criticism* (Chicago: Henry Regnery Co., 1950).

in the *General Prologue,* he was hostile to the anti-Jewish sentiment expressed in her story. It would seem that in their attempt to make Chaucer as tolerant of the Jewish faith as a modern intelligent person should be, many readers have read their own enlightenment into Chaucer's work. But if you remember that great writers generally held views that were current at their times and that their attitudes may not coincide exactly with your own, you will be properly cautious in making remarks about tone.

One further caution: keep your central idea uppermost in your reader's mind. You must inevitably talk about what has happened in the work you have read, but bring in these references *only* to illustrate and amplify your remarks about tone. Never forget your point; never descend to mere synopsis.

INTRODUCTION

State your central idea. You should not only define the tone briefly but also describe the force and conviction of the tone. Your thesis sentence should be a statement about the areas into which you plan to develop your discussion. If there are any particular obstacles to the proper determination of the tone, either in the work or in your personal attitudes, you should state these in your introduction also.

BODY

This should be a pointed discussion of the major elements in the work that caused you to arrive at your central idea. You are free to organize this section in any way you wish. Two suggested methods are: *A.* If there is a unity of tone throughout the work, you should organize the body in order to show the scope of the tone; that is, you would show that various sections of the work are similar in tone. Or you might wish to illustrate the depth of the attitudes. In this plan, you would analyze a few passages (be sure that they are representative) in order to show the characteristic methods by which the author conveyed his depth of attitude. *B.* If there is a shift of tone, or if there is a complexity of tone within the work, you might organize the body of your theme in order to mirror the shift or complexity. The sample theme asserts that there is a complexity of attitudes in the work it analyzes. This theme is organized to show how this complexity is an essential part of the meaning of the work. The tone in good writing is often complex.

CONCLUSION

The principal object of your conclusion is to relate the question of tone to your understanding and evaluation of the work.

Elements to consider in evaluation are (a) the intensity and (b) the control over attitudes.

An Analysis of the Tone in Section IX of Swift's Tale of a Tub

The tone in the "Digression concerning the Original, the Use and Improvement of *Madness* in a Commonwealth"—Section IX of *A Tale of a Tub*—is steadily and grimly ironic. The tone results from Swift's *persona's* being a madman who advocates mad views. Combining this fact with the logical inference that Swift's values are to be found in the reversal of whatever the madman says, the reader can perceive Swift's relentless irony. This irony is intensely bitter, mixed with hysterical, violent, repulsive, and sometimes indecent humor. Yet surprisingly, there is an overall note of encouragement, which results from the reverse side of this same irony.

The irony can be seen through the speaker's main idea: a madman himself, he has conceived a plan that grows logically out of his previous treatment of Jack, the "reformed" brother ("A Person whose Intellectuals were overturned, and his Brain shaken out of its Natural Position" [6]). His pet theory is that madness has produced everything and everyone that the world has ever considered "great" and "noble"; that is, military conquests, schemes of science and philosophy, great statesmen, courtiers, warriors, and men of high fashion. Since madness has caused such greatness, he says, let us have a committee to examine the madmen in Bedlam (the London house for the insane) and put them to use where they can employ their madness to the highest ends, just as society has always used madmen. That is the scheme in brief, and one can easily perceive that Swift is mocking conventional definitions of "greatness." The tone shows that Swift's values are to be found in praise of sanity, in praise of eliminating madness in high places, and in praise of making people accept balanced, sane men as their political and philosophical leaders. Although this statement gives an idea of Swift's values and attitudes, however, it falls far short of describing the power, the force, with which Swift communicates his ideas.

Mockery of human society—its popular illusions, its scientific methods, its ways of carrying out recommendations, its ways of insuring domestic tranquillity and promoting the general welfare— is the dominant mood of Swift's satire. The mockery is evident, for example, in the pseudoscientific form of the "Digression" itself.

[6] A. C. Guthkelch and David Nichol Smith, eds., *A Tale of a Tub,* 2nd ed. (London: 1958), p. 162. All page numbers refer to this edition.

Like a committee report, the plan of the "Digression" is logical; it moves from a preposterous hypothesis, quietly understated, into supporting evidence, followed by a plan for action together with specific recommendations for carrying it out. But the reader's perception of the mockery is complicated by his gnawing feeling that the preposterous is true. For the irony appears through the logic of the argument: although the hypothesis seems at first to be mad, the sequence of supporting examples is entirely logical. Is logic therefore mad? But we believe in logic. Or is the hypothesis mad? We would like to think so, but what other than madness, one might ask with the mad speaker, could cause a great king to want to "take and lose Towns; beat Armies, and be beaten; drive Princes out of their Dominions; fright Children from their Bread and Butter; burn, lay waste, plunder, dragoon, massacre Subject and Stranger, Friend and Foe, Male and Female" (p. 165)? Yet this king, Louis XIV, is acknowledged in the world's eyes to be great; and war as an instrument of foreign policy is still accepted by all nations.

The tone thus makes the reader squirm in embarrassed amazement. In the "recommendations" part of the "Digression" the tone makes him squirm again. There the speaker advances his propositions for putting madmen to use. Since he is perfectly sincere, quiet, and deferential, he arouses belief, while Swift's condemnation becomes more exact and therefore more cutting and barbed. In these quiet, pseudoreasonable words, there lurks the violent lash of the master satirist, flaying the exposed carcass of society and showing the vapidity and madness beneath the skin.

For the tone ultimately brings relentless self-awareness. Swift's madman has hit upon exactly what is wrong in the world as it is, and Swift's irony is that this madman supports it; in fact, he wishes to keep the world mad and to make it more so. But if the madman's world is our world, which we support, then what is the state of our sanity? As this madman makes his preposterous analysis, and advances his insane scheme for the "betterment" of society, Swift makes the reader understand the root causes of mankind's ills. In the speaker's erratic but scholarly way, interspersed freely with low images that reduce all illusions to the manure pile, the speaker assumes that because things are as they are, they are right, whereas the reader comes increasingly to object at the moment of assenting to what this former madhouse inmate says. This tension produces one of the most grimly comic moods in the "Digression." Seizing the idea that "great men" are made by a lucky confluence of their madness with the opportunity to use it in a socially approved way, Swift's speaker brings out one of the fundamental points in his mad argument, but, says the irony, is he not right?

. . . there is a peculiar *String* in the Harmony of Human Understanding, which in several individuals is exactly of the same Tuning. This, if you can dexterously screw up to its right Key, and then
strike gently upon it; Whenever you have the Good Fortune to light
among those of the same Pitch, they will by a secret necessary Sympathy, strike exactly at the same time. And in this one Circumstance, lies all the Skill or Luck of the Matter; for if you chance to
jar the String among those who are either above or below your own
Height, instead of subscribing to your Doctrine, they will tie you
fast, call you Mad, and feed you with Bread and Water.

—pp. 167-168

The irony leads virtually to grim despair in that anti-Apol-
lonian part of the "Digression" where the speaker advances logical
reasons for preserving a superficial view of life and its problems
and avoiding a deep analysis of them. His logic, well buttressed by
supporting examples, again creates the tone, which becomes a
combination of both the affirmative and the negative. Since looking
inside things makes people see only their ugliness, he says, it is
necessary to avoid all looking into things. Let people see the surface
only, and then they will be happy, as most people define happiness.
Let them gloss over truth; let them imagine themselves better than
they are or ever can be; let them never know themselves:

. . . He that can with *Epicurus* content his Ideas with the *Films* and
Images that fly off upon his Senses from the *Superficicies* of Things;
Such a Man truly wise, creams off Nature, leaving the Sower and the
Dregs, for Philosophy and Reason to lap up. This is the sublime and
refined Point of Felicity, called, *the Possession of being well deceived;*
The Serene Peaceful State of being a Fool among Knaves.

—p. 174

Here there is an incredible control of the violence of feeling. After
all, Swift's speaker is degrading the things that Swift himself must
hold most dear (the speaker equates Reason and Philosophy with
dogs or cats lapping up dregs), whereas the speaker concludes that
self-delusion is a normal condition. Swift's indignation is restrained;
his scalpel is sharp; his incision is clean; but will the patient, society,
be cured?

Just as the heavy irony approaches despair over the patient's
prospects, it also points the way to a cure. For if the reversal of
madness is sanity, the reversal of despair is joy. There is a way to
make society recuperate, and it is not the one put forth by the
speaker. Swift suggests the method by the reversal of values implicit
in the ironic tone. Shining through is the appeal to sanity, the
appeal to know oneself. The mood of the "Digression" brightens,
therefore, because of this passage at mid-point:

. . . For, the Brain, in its natural Position and State of Serenity, disposeth its Owner to pass his Life in the common Forms, without any Thought of subduing Multitudes to his own *Power*, his *Reasons*, or his *Visions*; and the more he shapes his Understanding by the Pattern of Human Learning, the less he is inclined to form Parties after his particular Notions; because that instructs him in his private Infirmities, as well as in the stubborn Ignorance of the People.

—p. 171

There can be optimism, implies Swift himself now, speaking through the irony. If only men will follow the "Pattern of Human Learning" and look into things, ugly as they sometimes are, they will see the truth. If only men will not delude themselves, particularly into seeking power over others, or be deceived by those who are themselves deluded, they can find truth and that middle way that will save them. Truth and moderation give the only foundation for society; anything less is madness.

The tone of despair everywhere gives way to hope, but a qualified hope, since the speaker's statement that Reason is "a very light Rider, and easily shook off" (p. 180) is undeniably right in the context of the "Digression" and of the general history of the world analyzed there. Although the melioristic mood is thus only anticipatory and incomplete, no account of the tone in Swift's "Digression on Madness" would be complete without reference to it. Without an attitude of melioration, no satire could be written, and this "Digression" is surely one of the great satires.

The Theme
Analyzing Prosody
in Poetry

12 *Prosody* is the word commonly used in reference to the study of sound and rhythm in poetry. Although sound and rhythm are the primary concern of prosodic study, these elements are never to be discussed in a vacuum; they are always an integral part of every good poem and are important only as they are related to the other parts. *Prosody* is the general word referring to sound and rhythm, but other, equally descriptive, words are *metrics, versification, mechanics of verse,* and *numbers.* (*Numbers* is not common at present, but it was current in Pope's time. Longfellow also used it.) Some persons call sound and rhythm the *music* of poetry. Whatever term your instructor might use, then, he means the study of sound and rhythm in poetry.

Your instructor will usually ask you to write a theme about prosody in order to give you the opportunity (a) to develop your sensitivity to the poet's language *as sound,* and (b) to become aware of the relationship of sound and rhythm to content. You will realize, as you make your analysis and write your theme, that the poet devoted much of his creative energy not only to the content of his poem but equally to the manner of conveying his content. This assignment will help you to become a more skilled reader, better equipped to define poetry and analyze sounds. You should also have an additional standard by which to measure the quality of poems. In short, this assignment should deepen your appreciation of a poet's achievement.

Many students, having accustomed themselves to pay attention only to the ideas and events in prose works, approach a theme on prosody with much apprehension. They feel either that the study of prosody is barren and devoid of content or that they cannot do this study because they have never done it before. But the study of prosody is not barren, and

125

there is no more reason for timidity on this assignment than on any other. With knowledge of a few terms and concepts, together with close attention to a poem, you can do a good job. There is much pleasure to be gained from analyzing a poem like Donne's "Batter My Heart" and from seeing that his style is in complete accord with his meaning. When you come to this realization you have actually encountered the living mind of the poet at work, selecting words and arranging rhythms not just by accident but by premeditated design and masterly control. You cannot appreciate poetry fully until you know something about prosody.

Your main problem in this assignment is to develop the vocabulary for discussing what you and every sensitive reader can perceive. In essence, your job is to translate the written poem into the spoken poem and then to describe the noteworthy and outstanding characteristics of the sounds. Fortunately, the study of metrics has provided you with a ready-made vocabulary for discussing what your hear. Much of your preparation for this assignment will be simply to learn the vocabulary and apply it.

Poetry and Prose: Rhythm

Poetry is difficult to define exactly. It is like prose because it employs words to convey thoughts and impressions and to tell stories, but prose is expansive—its content is characterized by the use of examples that are usually developed at some length. In addition, prose is comparatively less intense than poetry in its presentation of emotions. As a result, when you read a prose passage, your voice tends to remain within a rather narrow range of pitch; the accents and lengths of the individual words are submerged. Poetry is usually more demanding. It is more compact and more intense in its expression, and the poet consequently devotes special care to the sounds and rhythms of words and lines. When you read poetry, therefore, you must give particular attention to individual words; your units of expression will be shorter; your voice will go through a wider range of pitch. The reading of poetry generally requires more vocal activity than the reading of prose; this additional activity is a direct result of poetry's greater compactness and intensity.

Poetry and Prose: Segments

Just as poetry pays particular attention to rhythm, it requires special emphasis on the sounds of individual words and also on individual sounds composing these words. These individual sounds have been classified by modern students of language as "segments." For example, in the word *soft* there are four segments, or individual meaningful sounds, that make up the word; these segments are formed by the letters *s, o, f,* and *t.* In this word, each letter that spells (*graphs*) the word also indicates a *segment* of sound. But this is not always the case. In the word *enough,* for example, there are only four segments, formed by *e, n, ou,* and *gh;* the last two segments require two letters each.

In prose, you are likely to read by sentence lengths, minimizing the segments as you emphasize the ideas in the text. But in reading poetry you might frequently linger over various segments, if they seem to have been intended for that purpose by the poet. Imagine reading these lines without making your listeners conscious of the *s, l, m,* and *w* consonant sounds and of the *short ĭ, short ŏ,* and *short ŭ* vowel sounds:

> And more, to lulle him in his slumber soft,
> A trickling streame from high rocke tumbling downe
> And ever-drizling raine upon the loft,
> Mixt with a murmuring winde, much like the sowne
> Of swarming Bees, did cast him in a swowne:

> —Spenser, *Faerie Queene,* Canto I, Stanza 41

Try reading aloud the passage of prose you are now looking at; linger over some of the sounds; give your voice a similarly wide range of pitch. Perhaps the effect of this overreading will make you aware of some of the differences between poetry and prose. Poetry—unlike prose—invites intensive, energetic reading because of its compact, intense nature. If you can perceive these facts, you must realize that poets also have this objective in mind. You can see that a study of rhythm and segments is an integral part of poetic study.

Various Demands Upon the Sound of Poetry

From the discussion thus far, you can realize that there are three main elements that must be considered in prosodic analysis. These are *rhetoric and emotion, sound,* and *rhythm.* All are equally important, and all act at the same moment in any given poem.

RHETORIC AND EMOTION

First and foremost is the rhetorical and emotional demand. Because poetry is an art of communication through words, the poet will necessarily wish to create emphasis by arranging his phrases, sentences, and paragraphs in the most effective way. As this arrangement must affect the levels of pitch and stress and will affect the placement of pauses, the rhetorical demand is sometimes in agreement with, and sometimes at odds with, the formal rhythm of the poem, depending on the poet's will.

Also a part of the rhetorical demand is the arrangement of words into *cadence groups*. You might regard these groups as the rhythm of words resulting from their being put into phrases. In the following lines, for example, the words tend to bunch together into groups separated by extremely slight pauses:

> Into the deep reaches of that dimly lit sea
> Our spray-cased craft rammed a pathless way.

The words *Into the deep reaches* make a group of six syllables that belong together by virtue of being an adverb phrase. Similarly, *Our spray-cased craft* forms a noun group. These groups form their own indissoluble rhythmical unit that may or may not correspond to the formal, regular, or metrical demands of the poem. The kind of poetry known as *free verse* tends to make cadence groups more important than meter.

The role of emotions in poetry deserves special consideration in your study of prosody. Depending on the emotions demanded by a poem, you may raise or lower your voice, increase or decrease the speed of your pronunciation, accentuate or minimize certain sounds, and pause heavily or lightly after certain words. Emotion, in short, affects the expression with which you read a poem or passage. You can describe the effects of emotion in prosody to the extent that it affects pitch, stress, length, and pause, but you will probably find that the various tones of voice and the subtle shades of spoken expression are very difficult to describe in your theme.

SOUND

You must consider the sounds of the words themselves, both independently and as they influence each other in their order in the lines. The good poet puts words together so that their sounds will augment his meaning, not contradict it; he can use the *sounds* of his words as a form of expression. In addition to the dictionary meanings of the words within lines, and from line to line, he may use words that contain identical segments; in this way, he unifies his poem not only by developing his ideas, but also by echoing earlier sounds. Sometimes he may even use words containing sounds that are actually reminiscent of the things he is describing, as in the conclusion of the passage from Tennyson analyzed in the sample theme.

RHYTHM

Another important element is the rhythm of the words when arranged into lines of poetry. The rhythm of English is usually determined by the relationship of heavily stressed to less heavily stressed syllables.[1] In pronouncing words you give some syllables more force (loudness) than others. For convenience, you may call the syllables to which you give more force *heavily stressed,* and those to which you give less force *lightly stressed.* In most English poetry the poet has regularized the heavily and lightly stressed syllables into patterns called *feet.* He usually fills his lines with a specific number of the same feet, and that number determines the *meter* of the line. Frequently, rhetorical needs lead him to substitute other feet for the regular feet. Whether there is *substitution* or not, the number and kind of feet in each line constitute the meter of that line. Notice that the major influence here is number; that is, you measure English verse by the division of syllables according to degrees of stress.

The complex interaction of all these various demands produces what we commonly call the sounds and rhythms of a poem, and the prosodic interest created by any poem depends on the degrees of tension produced by the various demands. If all the demands were perfectly in accord, the result would be perfect regularity, and soon, perfect boredom. In most poetry, however, each element has a certain degree of independence, thereby producing effects of variation and tension. Variation is a strong cause of interest and beauty, and tension promotes interest and emotional involvement in a poem. An understanding of prosody is important in the evaluation of poetry because sound and rhythm are important in the structural and emotional complex that is poetry.

Minimum Requirements for Considering Sounds in Poetry

Although you have been speaking the language for many years, the chances are great that you have not systematically studied the sounds that you utter daily. For this reason you must be sure, before you undertake a prosodic analysis, that you have a basic approach to the analysis of sound.

The segments of words are usually divided into *vowel sounds* (including *semivowels*) and *consonant sounds.* It is important to emphasize the word *sound* as distinguished from the letters of the alphabet, for often the same letters represent different sounds. You should have some acceptable notational system for indicating sounds. Perhaps the most

[1] Martin Halpern has challenged this traditional view by claiming that in iambic verse, for example, stress alone is not the only element determining feet, but that pitch and length are equally important. If one holds this position he will discover less substitution in English poetry than if he maintains the traditional view, but he will also discover greater variety within the limits of the foot. See "On the Two Chief Metrical Modes in English," *PMLA,* LXXVII (1962), 177-86.

readily available systems of pronunciation are in the collegiate dictionaries; these systems, which have won fairly wide acceptance, take into account regional differences in pronunciation. If you have questions about syllabication and the position of stresses, you can use the dictionary as an authority. Two other systems of indicating sounds are based upon more recent scientific analyses. The first is the *International Phonetic Alphabet* as adapted for use in English, and the second is a system called *phonemic*.[2] The great virtue of these notational systems is that they are more descriptive than those in the dictionaries. The phonemic system is especially useful because it presents a satisfactory method of analyzing not only sounds but also *stress, pitch,* and *juncture.* These are the so-called "suprasegmental phonemes"; that is, they are those elements of speech production other than segments that contribute to meaning. Because both the phonetic and phonemic systems would require chapter-length explication and because the dictionary systems are readily available, the dictionaries will be the guide in the following discussion and sample theme.

VOWEL SOUNDS AND THEIR QUALITIES

There are two systems operating in the pronunciation of vowel sounds: first is *front-central-back;* second is *high-mid-low.* These terms depend on the position of the tongue during the pronunciation of a vowel sound. For your analysis of prosody, you need to consider only the extremes of *high-front* and *low-back.* Observe that the vowel sounds *ē, ĭ, ā,* are all produced in a narrow space between the tongue and the hard palate. These sounds are both *front* and *high.* By contrast, pronounce the *ä* in *arm.* Notice that your tongue is still in a front position, but that it has dropped far down in your mouth. This *ä,* in other words, is a *low front* vowel sound. Now pronounce the vowel sound *ō* as in *coal.* Notice that your tongue has stayed high, but has dropped *back* in your throat. The *ō* sound is a *high, back,* and *rounded* sound. Now pronounce the *ô* in *orphan,* and the *ōō* in *troop.* Notice that these are both *back* and *low rounded* sounds.

To a considerable degree, the context in which a word appears governs the pitch and intensity of the sounds in that word. Briefly, however, the low, back sounds tend to be lower in pitch than the front, high

2 For a lucid discussion of English phonetics, see W. Nelson Francis, *The Structure of American English* (New York: Ronald Press Co., 1958), pp. 51-118. For the phonemic system, see Francis, pp. 119-61, and Donald J. Lloyd and Harry R. Warfel, *American English in its Cultural Setting* (New York: Alfred A. Knopf, 1956), pp. 294-318. For a discussion of the contributions that linguistic study can make to the study of prosody, see Ronald Sutherland, "Structural Linguistics and English Prosody," *College English,* XX (1958), 12-17; reprinted in Harold B. Allen, ed., *Readings in Applied English Linguistics,* 2nd ed. (New York: Appleton-Century-Crofts, 1964), pp. 492-99.

sounds. For this reason, although the sounds themselves are neutral in meaning, they can be used by poets to augment light (high-front) or heavy (low-back) effects. A remarkable example of the combination of high-front and low-back vowel sounds is this couplet from Pope, which demonstrates an interweaving of front *ā* and *ē* sounds through back *ō, ä,* and *ōō* sounds, just as the river that Pope describes would weave through the cold wasteland:

> Lo where Maotis sleeps, and hardly flows
> The freezing Thanais through a waste of snows.

> *—Dunciad,* III, 87-88

SEMIVOWEL SOUNDS

The semivowels are *w, y,* and *h*. These are segments that (a) begin in a vowel position but glide into a following vowel, thus performing the function of a consonant, as in *w*ind, *u*nion, *y*es, *h*aven (but the *h* in *honor* is silent), or (b) begin the central vowel of a syllable but glide into a new position, thus in effect forming the second part of a diphthong, as in *go* (go*w*) and *weigh* (wa*y*).

CONSONANT SOUNDS

Consonant sounds themselves are meaningless unless they are put into a context. The *s,* for example, in a context of rage, can augment the rage, but in a quiet context it can produce a drowsy, sleepy effect (see the earlier example from Spenser).

When discussing consonant sounds, you must be especially aware of the differences between the letters themselves and the sounds they represent. Thus, *t*rip, *t*his, na*t*ion, *t*hrough, moun*t*ain, Be*tt*y, all have the letter *t,* but the spoken sounds are all different. *S*weet, *s*hrove, and flow*s* all have *s*'s, but these *s*'s represent different sounds.

Rhyme and Meter

Once you have acquired a method for analyzing and describing sounds, you can go on to the analysis of rhyme and meter.

RHYME

Rhyme, which refers to the recurrence of syllables that sound alike—usually in words ending lines (e.g., t*ime* and ch*ime*)—is the most easily recognized characteristic of poetry. When you describe a rhyme scheme, you should use letters (i.e., *a, b, c,* etc.). Each new letter indicates a new sound; a repeated letter indicates a rhyme. In a Shake-spearean sonnet, for example, the rhyme scheme is *abab cdcd efef gg.* The rhyme scheme of an Italian or Petrarchan sonnet is *abba abba cd cd cd.*

Whenever rhyme occurs you should analyze its effects and the way these are achieved. Observe the grammatical forms of the rhyming words. If a poet rhymes only nouns, for example, his rhymes are likely to be monotonous, for he should show some variety in the grammatical forms. You should also observe, if masculine rhyme is the norm, whether there are feminine or other rhymes, and the effect of these. Another area of study is whether the rhymes are unusual or surprising. If a poet relied on "sure returns of still expected rhymes" (like the *breeze* blowing through the *trees*), his rhymes would be obvious and dull. Observe that in the following couplet by Byron the rhyming words are verbs, and that wit and surprise result from the riddle in the first line and the meaning of the final word:

> 'Tis strange—the Hebrew noun which means "I am,"
> The English always use to govern d–n.

> —*Don Juan*, I, xiv, 111-112

Although few rhymes will provide the humor of this one, you should observe the method of rhyming in the poems you study. As you make further analyses you will be impressed with the way in which your under-standing of the craft of poetry will grow.

In connection with rhyme, the following terms are important. In *eye rhyme* or *sight rhyme* the rhyming words look the same but are pro-nounced differently (e.g., "Broken is the clock I *wind*" and "I am frozen by the *wind*"). In *slant rhyme* the rhyming vowel sounds are different in quality whereas the consonant sounds are identical (e.g., c*ould* and solit*ude*). Frequently the rhythm of a rhyme is important, and for this reason you should know the terms *masculine rhyme* (the rhyme of words on accented syllables, e.g., fl*ows*, sn*ows*), *feminine rhyme* (a rhyming trochee, e.g., *see one* and *be one;* fant*astic* and el*astic*), and *triple rhyme* (a rhyming dactyl, e.g., *easily*, br*eezily*). Masculine rhyme is ordinarily used for serious purposes, whereas feminine and triple rhyme lend them-selves easily to comic effects.

METER

Meter is the systematic regulation of poetic rhythm. In order to discover the prevailing metrical system in any poem, you *scan* that poem. The act of scanning is called *scansion.*

Your first problem in scansion is to recognize where syllables are and to distinguish one syllable from another. Experience has shown that students who in the early grades have been taught to read by the "word-recognition" method, as contrasted with the "syllable" method, often find it hard to distinguish syllables. This difficulty is unfortunate, because an understanding of syllables is the first requirement in the feeling for rhythms in poetry. You must therefore be especially cautious and realize that words like *merrier* and *terrier*, for example, are three-syllable words, as is *solitude;* another three-syllable combination is *dial hand.* If you find difficulty in perceiving the syllables in lines of poetry, a good idea is to read each word aloud separately, pronouncing every syllable, before reading the words in poetic context. The practice of reading poetry aloud is good in any event. If you have been encouraged to read for speed, you must abandon this approach when you read poetry.

The next step in preparation for your theme is to interpret *stress* or *accent.* You are concerned to show the syllables that receive major and light stress, and you need a system for showing these syllables. In scansion a heavy or primary accent is commonly indicated by an acute accent mark (´) or slash (/), whereas a light accent may be indicated by a circle or zero (°). There is no reason for absoluteness in this system, however, for your instructor might direct you to indicate heavy accents by an upright line (|) or a horizontal (−) and weak or light syllables by a horizontal (−), a cross (×), or a half circle (ᵕ). As with the determination of the number of syllables in a line you must, when you read aloud, listen carefully to hear which syllables are heavily stressed and which are lightly stressed. If you are ever in doubt, use the dictionary and the stress given there. For example, the pronunciation of the word *indeciduous* is shown as follows in the *American College Dictionary:*

$$\text{in di sij oo əs}$$
(with light accent mark over *in* and heavier accent over *sij*)

A light accent mark is placed over *in,* whereas *sij* receives a heavier accent mark. The other syllables are lightly stressed. If you found a line of poetry in which this word appeared, then, you would scan it as follows:

The in - / de - cid / u-ous trees / spring forth.

Although the demands of the poetic line may lessen the force of a heavily-stressed syllable in relation to other words in the line, you will seldom be mistaken if you rely on the dictionary.

There is a problem in determining accent because some stresses are stronger than others, and some lightly-accented syllables are stressed more than others. In fact, modern linguists have recognized three degrees of major stress. The first is *primary, major,* or *heavy,* indicated by an acute accent (´). The second is *secondary* or *medium,* shown by a circumflex accent (^). The third is *tertiary* or *light,* marked by a grave accent (\).[3]

---

[3] See Lloyd and Warfel, p. 315, or Francis, p. 153.

It seems obvious that you should recognize these differences when you scan poetry. A line like the following, by Ben Jonson, can be scanned as regular iambic pentameter:

$$\overset{\circ}{\text{If}}\;\overset{/}{\text{thou}}\;/\;\overset{\circ}{\text{wouldst}}\;\overset{/}{\text{know}}\;/\;\overset{\circ}{\text{the}}\;\overset{/}{\text{vir}}\text{-}\;/\;\overset{\circ}{\text{tues}}\;\overset{/}{\text{of}}\;/\;\overset{\circ}{\text{man-}}\overset{/}{\text{kind.}}$$

The syllables *wouldst, tues,* and *man* are all lightly stressed according to the demands of meter (see below), yet you can feel that these syllables should receive heavier emphasis than *the* and even the word *of* (*of* is a major stress according to the meter). Similarly, *thou, know,* and *virtues* accumulate stress, so that the heaviest accent of the three falls on *vir,* just as *virtues* contains the climax of the idea of the line. Yet by what the acute accent indicates, *thou, know,* and *vir* all seem to receive the same emphasis as *of.* How can you indicate these differences when you make your scansion?

If you feel confident enough of your perceptions, you might attempt to use the acute, circumflex, and grave accents to show differences among the various heavily-stressed syllables. If your ear is not highly trained, however, a more likely compromise is to use the acute accent for the heaviest major stresses, and the grave accent for less heavy major stresses. Thus, the line by Jonson might be scanned as follows:

$$\overset{\circ}{\text{If}}\;\overset{\backslash}{\text{thou}}\;/\;\overset{\circ}{\text{wouldst}}\;\overset{\backslash}{\text{know}}\;/\;\overset{\circ}{\text{the}}\;\overset{/}{\text{vir}}\text{-}\;/\;\overset{\circ}{\text{tues}}\;\overset{\backslash}{\text{of}}\;/\;\overset{\frown}{\text{man-kind.}}$$

Let us see how the opening line of Shakespeare's *Henry V* might be marked:

$$\overset{/}{\text{O!}}\;\overset{\circ}{\text{for}}\;/\;\overset{\circ}{\text{a}}\;\overset{\backslash}{\text{Muse}}\;/\;\overset{\circ}{\text{of}}\;\overset{/}{\text{fire}}\;/\;\overset{\circ}{\text{that}}\;\overset{\backslash}{\text{would}}\;/\;\overset{\circ}{\text{as-}}\overset{/}{\text{cend}}\ldots$$

If you do not use this system but employ only the acute accent and the circle, be sure in your theme to show your awareness that not all heavy stresses are equal.

Since discussion of rhythm could be endless, you should know at least the following. Rhythm in poetry is usually considered in terms of metrical *feet*. In English, the most important feet are:

1 IAMB A light stress followed by a heavy stress ($\overset{\circ}{be}$ - $\overset{/}{have}$). The iamb is the most common foot in English poetry because it is capable of great variation. Within the same line of five iambic feet, as in the examples from Jonson and Shakespeare, each foot can be slightly different in intensity from the others. In this line from Wordsworth, each foot is unique:

$$\overset{\circ}{\text{The}}\;\overset{/}{\text{winds}}\;/\;\overset{\circ}{\text{that}}\;\overset{\backslash}{\text{will}}\;/\;\overset{\circ}{\text{be}}\;\overset{/}{\text{howl-}}\;/\;\overset{\circ}{\text{ing}}\;\overset{\backslash}{\text{at}}\;/\;\overset{\circ}{\text{all}}\;\overset{/}{\text{hours.}}$$

Such variability, approximating the rhythms of actual speech, makes the foot suitable for just about any purpose, serious or light. The iambic foot therefore assists the poet in focussing attention on his ideas and emotions. If he uses it with skill, it never becomes monotonous.

2 TROCHEE A heavy accent followed by a light ($\overset{/}{u}$ - $\overset{\circ}{nit}$).

3 DACTYL A heavy followed by two lights (*mÍght - ĭ - ĕst*).

4 ANAPAEST Two lights followed by a heavy (*fŏr ă MÚse*).

5 IMPERFECT FOOT A single syllable; (/) by itself, or (o) by itself.

6 PYRRHIC Two unstressed syllables, as in *lĭke ă* / great ring.

7 SPONDEE Two heavy accents, as in *great ring*. A noticeable way to show the spondee is to connect the two syllables with a mark like a corporal's chevrons, as is done here. Spondees seem to give special difficulty in prosodic analysis. A principal reason is that quite often *pitch* is confused with *stress,* as in the following example:

> Such seems / ŏ your béau- / ŏ ty still.

Although *beauty still* may easily be spoken at one pitch, there is a definite weakening of stress over the *y,* so that *beauty* is definitely not a spondee. Similarly, in "Three winters cold," the syllables *three* and *win* are of equal, heavy stress, and should therefore be marked as a spondee; but *ters* and *cold* are not equal, since *ters,* as a part of *winters,* receives a weak stress.

Another problem with spondees occurs if they are mistaken for pyrrhic feet. A spondee is the juxtaposition of two syllables of equally *heavy* stress, not of equally *light* stress.

8 AMPHIBRACH A light, heavy, and light. *Thĕ chÉstnŭt; sŭsÚrrŭs.* This foot is not common, though in the line "Such seems your beauty still," some people could argue that *your beauty* is properly an amphibrach, followed by an imperfect foot (*still*). Amphibrachs may be seen in the opening line of the song "The Old Oaken Bucket":

> ŏ / ŏ ŏ / ŏ ŏ / ŏ ŏ / ŏ
> How dear to / my heart are / the scenes of / my childhood.

9 AMPHIMACER A heavy, light, and heavy. *MÁde ă wÁy; hÁving fÚn.* The amphimacer is not at all common; most rhythms of this sort can be explained by reference to the more common feet.

10 BACCHIUS A light followed by two heavy stresses:

> ŏ / / ŏ / / ŏ / /
> He sang well / a long while / in back rooms,

> ŏ / / ŏ / /
> But lost voice / and quit young.

Like the amphimacer, the bacchius is not common.

Segmental Poetic Devices

After you have finished your scansion, you should study the poem in order to discover any segmental poetic devices employed by the poet. The common ones follow.

ASSONANCE

In connection with vowel sounds you should become familiar with *assonance,* which is the employment in close quarters of identical vowel sounds in different words (e.g., sw*i*ft Cam*i*lla sk*i*ms). Be cautious, however, about equating sounds like the *ē* in d*e*ceived with the *ē* in tr*ee*; the *ē* in *de* is not a true long *ē,* but instead is a half-long *ē,* and some would maintain that it is a *schwa* (a sound like the *a* in *sofa*). Also, you should not select isolated instances of a sound in your description of assonance. If, for example, you find three words in the same line that include a long *ā* sound, these form a pattern and are worthy of mention as an instance of assonance; *but,* if you find a word six lines later that includes a long *ā,* this word should not be mentioned as part of the pattern. The word is too far away from the pattern to be significant.

DEVICES USING CONSONANT SOUNDS

Two common poetic devices employ consonant sounds:

1. ALLITERATION   There are three kinds of alliteration. (a) Most commonly, alliteration is regarded as the repetition of identical consonant sounds beginning syllables in relatively close patterns, for example, "*L*aborious, heavy, *b*usy, *b*old, and *b*lind," and "While *p*ensive *p*oets *p*ainful vigils keep." Used sparingly, alliteration gives strength to a poem by emphasizing key words, but too much *c*an *c*ause *c*omic consequences. (b) A special kind of alliteration is CONSONANCE, whereby words are repeated that contain the exact pattern of two or more identical consonant sounds, for example, *li*v*e, le*av*e; gr*oaned, *gr*ound; *terr*or, *terr*ier; t*o*p, *t*i*p; gr*ab, *gr*ub,* and so on. This device does not occur very often in most of the poems you will encounter, for it calls attention to itself and might detract from an important idea. (c) Another form of alliteration occurs when a poet repeats identical or similar consonant sounds that do not begin syllables but that create a pattern and thereby have prosodic importance, for example, "In the*s*e place*s* freezing bree*z*e*s* ea*s*ily cau*s*e snee*z*e*s*." (In this example both *s* and *z* are sounded as *z;* such a pattern is hard to overlook.) In "The *p*e*bb*les in the *b*u*bb*ling *p*ool," both *p* and *b* are *labial* consonant sounds (i.e., they are made by a momentary stoppage of breath at the lips); *p* is a *voiceless* stopped sound, whereas *b* is a *voiced* stopped sound. Because of the similarity, the two sounds should be mentioned as part of a pattern of alliteration.

2. ONOMATOPOEIA   Onomatopoeia is a blend of consonant and vowel sounds with rhythm to create the effect of imitating the sound of

the thing being described. Onomatopoeia is technically difficult to achieve because it depends almost entirely on context (some rare instances of onomatopoeic words like *buzz* being excepted), but it is powerful when it occurs. For example, at the end of the passage from Tennyson's *Morte D'Arthur,* which is analyzed in the sample theme, a lake is mentioned. Because our minds are directed toward the image of a lake, the *l* sounds (which, along with *r* sounds, are frequently called "liquids") may be taken to suggest the sounds of waves lapping against a shore. This combination of sense and sound is onomatopoeia.

Pause and Emphasis: Other Means of Poetic Effect

PAUSE (CAESURA)

Spoken speech is composed of groups of syllables forming intelligible units, separated by pauses that add to the intelligibility. In linguistics, these pauses are called *junctures.*[4] In poetry, the pause is called a *caesura* or *cut.* In this line by Ben Jonson, for example, there are two pauses, or *caesurae:*

Thou art not, *Penshurst,* built to envious show.

The first caesura follows *not* and the second follows *Penshurst.* In the following line by Pope there are three caesurae:

His actions', passions', being's, use and end.

You can see that poets arrange pauses judiciously in order to make their lines interesting, varied, and emphatic. In your prosodic analysis, you should make observations about the use of caesura in the poem you analyze.

For scansion, the caesura is best indicated by two diagonal lines (//) in order to distinguish it from the single diagonal lines separating feet. For most purposes these two diagonals are all you need. However, there are subtle distinctions among caesurae, and as you develop your ear you will perceive these distinctions. A pause before which the voice is not raised, such as the one between *Penshurst* and *built,* might best be shown by the two diagonals bars (//). The pause between *O* and *for* in *O! for a Muse* is also of this nature, because the pause indicates that there is more to follow immediately. But the pause at the end of a declarative sentence is different, as it usually follows a lowering of *pitch* and is therefore a definite means by which the end of a statement is indicated. Perhaps

4 For a brief and lucid account of junctures, see John Nist, *A Structural History of English* (New York: St. Martin's Press, 1966), pp. 46-48.

these caesurae, usually marked by a period or semicolon in the poem, could be marked by three diagonals (///). Then too, there is still a different caesura that immediately follows the elevation of pitch that usually indicates a question. This type might conveniently be marked with a reverse double diagonal (\\).

EMPHASIS

PITCH AND LENGTH Pitch and length are two of the most important elements in effective expression. So far as pitch indicates meaning through the raising and lowering of the voice before pauses, it can be fairly well analyzed and discussed. More difficult, however, and far more subtle, is the raising and lowering of the voice that occurs because of the dramatic requirements of a poem, or because of the need for keeping the voice interestingly modulated. This variation is subjective to the extent that it is not properly a part of essential, denotative meaning, but for the most part the poetry you read will demand various levels of pitch. If a reader is at all sensitive, he cannot read poetry at the same vocal level.

Demanding similar alertness is the perception of length or *quantity*. Length is in an anomalous position in the scansion of English poetry because it does not determine the formation of metrical feet. But length is certainly important in the sensitive reading of poetry, and you should be aware of it.

Length is inherent in the long vowel sounds, as in the words *all, raid, reed, red, road, broad, food,* and *bird.* Any of these words preceded by a word containing a short vowel sound forms an iamb (e.g., *the road*), but if two of them are together, they cause a spondee (e.g., *broad road*). Shorter vowels can be seen in the words *bat, bet, bit, bought, but, foot,* and *the.*

Although the lengths of vowels in particular words are relatively fixed, the poet can create greater or lesser lengths by the ways in which he uses words in context. Notice, for example, how Shakespeare controls length in these lines by the careful selection of words:

> . . . and then my state,
> Like to the lark at break of day arising
> From sullen earth, sings hymns at heaven's gate.

> —Sonnet No. 29, lines 10-12

As contrasted with the lengthened $\bar{a}$ of *day,* the vowel sounds in *like, lark,* and *break* are restrained by the voiceless consonant stop *k.* The greatest skill, however, is shown in the way the passage (and the entire sonnet) builds toward the phrase *sings hymns,* which contains short $\breve{i}$ vowel sounds lengthened by the nasal consonant sounds *ng* and *m* (both of which are lengthened by the voiced continuous consonant sound *z*). As the poem reaches its climax in the image, the sound also reaches its climax. There are few more glorious experiences in English poetry than reading these lines, and the cause cannot be explained only by stress. The principal cause, in the context, is length.

Needless to say, the most skillful prosodists are able to make the matters of pitch and length infallibly right, whereas lesser poets cannot control them. As you read more and more good poetry, your awareness of pitch and length will improve. A good way to hasten this improvement is to read poetry aloud, and read it aloud frequently. If it helps you, try to act out the situation of the poem as you read.

When you make your first prosodic analysis, your instructor will probably not expect much from you in the analysis of pitch and length, but as you progress in your study of poetry you should be able to indicate your perceptions in your themes. One of the marks of your increasing understanding and appreciation of poetry (and also of your ability to write about it) will be your growing awareness of pitch and length.

EMPHASIS ACHIEVED BY METRICAL VARIATION, FORMAL AND RHETORI-CAL   Most poems are written in a pattern that can readily be perceived. Thus Shakespeare's plays usually follow the pattern of *blank verse* (un-rhymed iambic pentameter) and Milton's *Paradise Lost* follows this same pattern. Such a pattern is no more than a rhythmical norm, however. For interest and emphasis (and perhaps because of the very nature of the English language) the norm is varied by the *substitution* of other feet for the normal feet and also by the rhetorical effect of such substitution.

The following line is from the "January" eclogue of Spenser's *Shepherd's Calendar*. Although the abstract pattern of the line is iambic pentameter, it is varied by the substitution of two other feet:

$$\text{/ ○ ○ /} \qquad \frown \qquad \text{○ \textbackslash} \quad \text{○ /}$$
All in / a sun - / shine day, / as did / be - fall.

In the first foot, *All in* is a trochee, and *shine day* is a spondee. This line shows formal substitution; that is, a separate, formally structured foot is substituted for one of the original feet.

Many poets, however, create the effect of substitution by a means that we shall call *rhetorical* variation. An outstanding example of this variation in an iambic pentameter line is this one by Pope:

$$\text{○ /} \quad \text{○} \quad \text{/} \quad \text{○} \quad \text{/} \quad \text{○} \quad \text{/} \quad \text{○ /}$$
His ac - / tions', // pas - / sions', // be - / ing's, // use / and end;

Ordinarily there is one caesura in a line of this type, but in this one there are three, each one producing a strong pause. The line is regularly iambic and should be scanned as regular. But in reading, the effect is different. Because of the pauses, which occur in the middles of the second, third, and fourth feet, the line is actually read as an amphibrach, a trochee, a trochee, an imperfect foot, and a regular iamb. Although lines like this one are regular, the practical effect—the rhetorical effect—is of variation and tension. In this well-known line from Shakespeare, rhetorical variation may also be seen:

> If music be the food of love, play on!

This line is regularly iambic except, perhaps, for a spondee in *play on,* but the reading of the line conflicts with the formal pattern. Thus, *If music* may be read as an amphibrach and *be the food* is in practice an anapaest. Because of the subordinate clause, the caesura does not come until after the eighth syllable. These rhetorical variations produce the effect of natural, ordinary speech, because Shakespeare has lavished a good deal of his art on the line.

In whatever poetry you study, your main concern in noting variation is to observe the abstract metrical pattern and then to note the variations on this pattern—formal and rhetorical—and the principal causes for these variations. By analyzing these causes you will greatly enhance your understanding of the poet's craft.

EMPHASIS CAUSED BY TENSION BETWEEN SENTENCE STRUCTURE AND LINES   The basic working units of expression in prose are phrases, clauses, and sentences. The same applies to poetry, with the added complexity that metrical demands frequently conflict with these units. Some poets (e.g., Milton, Chaucer, Wordsworth) create emphasis and tension in their poetry by making strong demands for sentence structure over and against an established metrical pattern. Here, for example, is a short passage from Wordsworth, laid out as prose:

> And I have felt a presence that disturbs me with the joy of elevated thoughts; a sense sublime of something far more deeply interfused, whose dwelling is the light of setting suns, and the round ocean and the living air, and the blue sky, and in the mind of man.

> —"Tintern Abbey," lines 93-99

It is difficult, yet not impossible, to perceive the actual line divisions in this example. Wordsworth is superimposing an extended sentence structure on the metrical structure, a characteristic habit that is perfectly in keeping with meditative or philosophic poetry. Similarly, Milton is famous for his extended verse paragraphs in blank verse.

Other poets, by contrast, blend their sentence structure almost completely into their rhythmical pattern. Take, for example, this passage from Pope, which is also laid out as prose:

> Nor public flame, nor private, dares to shine; nor human spark is left, nor glimpse divine! Lo! thy dread empire, Chaos, is restored; light dies be-

fore thy uncreating word: thy hand, great Anarch! lets the curtain fall; and
universal darkness buries all.

—Dunciad, IV, 651-656

The sentences are perfectly fitted to the lines, making the counting of
feet comparatively easy, and we could determine the length of each line
easily, without the aid of the rhyme. As a result, Pope and poets like him
have frequently been accused of too much "boring regularity," whereas
poets like Wordsworth and Milton have been praised for their greater
"freedom." In actuality, the principles of variation are used by all these
poets, with Wordsworth and Milton adding extensive syntactic variation
to metrical variations.

You should know the technical terms connected with these variations. If a pause occurs at the end of the line, that line is called *end-
stopped:*

A thing of beauty is a joy forever:

But if the line has no punctuation mark and runs over into the next line,
it is called *run-on.* The term used to describe run-on lines is *enjambment:*

Its loveliness increases; it will never
Pass into nothingness; but still will keep
A bower quiet for us, and a sleep
Full of sweet dreams, . . .

—Keats, "Endymion," lines 1-5

The Organization of Your Theme

You should attempt to show the operation of all
these component elements of poetry. Your theme should contain the following parts.

INTRODUCTION

This section should include a brief discussion of the
rhetorical or dramatic situation of the poem as it leads into a consideration of prosody. That is, is the poem narrative or expository in structure?
Is there a speaker? Who is he? What are his characteristics? What situation is described? What special poetic theories are apparently being
exemplified in the passage? What is the principal idea of the passage?
What is the dominant mood of the poem? The object of answering questions like these (you do not need to answer all of them, and may want
to ask others) is to make possible the evaluation of how well the prosody
of the passage lives up to the expectations aroused by the rhetorical or
dramatic situation. Discussion of these questions is therefore very im-

portant. As a structural device in your themes, the discussion will give more purpose and logic to the technical discussion to follow (the introductory discussion will also help you in your prosodic analysis of the poem or passage).

BODY

Here you should discuss the rhythm of the passage. You should discuss the basic metrical pattern and variations on it (and where the variations occur). You should also discuss the relationships of the syntactic (word order) units to the meter. Is there conflict between the two? If so, why might this conflict exist? Do you see any evidence of the poet's design therein? What is the ultimate effect of the conflict? Does it seem to be appropriate to the rhetorical situation? If there is agreement between the sentence structure and the metrical emphasis, that too is usually part of the poet's design.

You should then discuss the sound of the passage, including in your discussion the quality and length of the sounds. Usually this discussion takes into consideration assonance, alliteration, consonance, and onomatopoeia.

CONCLUSION

Here you should evaluate the success of the passage. Did the prosody seem appropriate to the rhetorical situation? Did it conflict, and if so, does that conflict provide grounds for an adverse judgment? Did the prosody augment the idea of the passage? Did it give the passage more power than the idea alone would do? In short, answer the question of how well the sounds and the rhythms succeeded in being an instrument of communication and a device by which the poet may evoke the proper emotions in the reader.

Hints

1 At the beginning of your paper you should provide a triple-spaced version of the passage under analysis. Make at least two carbon copies in order to employ them for various analytical purposes, as in the sample following, where one copy shows metrics and the others show alliteration and assonance.

2 Number each line in your example, beginning with *1*, regardless of the length of the passage.

3 In preparing your material, you should follow this procedure:
   a. Establish the formal pattern of the verse and note all the positions of formal substitutions.
      1. Indicate the separate feet by a diagonal line (/). Indicate caesurae

by a double diagonal (//). If you wish to make refinements, reserve the double diagonal for caesurae that do not affect the pitch of the voice; use a triple diagonal (///) for voice-lowering caesurae and a reverse double diagonal (\\) for voice-raising caesurae.

2. Indicate lightly stressed syllables by the circle (o), or, if your instructor prefers, by the half circle (◡) or cross (x). Show heavily stressed syllables by the acute accent or slash (′ or /) and by the grave accent (\).

b. Read the passage for rhetorical substitutions; make notes about where they occur and about how the poet creates them.

c. Discover the various segmental poetic devices. Circle letters indicating a pattern of alliteration and assonance, and draw lines indicating the connection. Different colored pencils are effective in distinguishing the various patterns, or, if you use only one pencil or pen, you might set up a system of dotted, wavy, cross-hatched, or double-cross-hatched lines in order to distinguish the patterns. The sample theme uses a system numbering the various metrical variations, though on your own work sheets you would do better to use colored pencils. Any easily recognized system that is convenient for you, however, is acceptable. It is also a good idea to circle the metrical variations (thus, anapaests and trochees might be circled to help you identify them easily when you begin to write).

4 At the bottom of your pages, provide a key to your circles and lines.

5 It is best to use a standard pronunciation guide for your discussion of sounds. You may employ one of the standard collegiate dictionaries. If you have had formal linguistic study, use the phonemic or phonetic systems; otherwise you will probably find the dictionary system more convenient.

6 Underline all sounds to which you are calling attention. If you refer to a sound within a word (e.g., the *l* sound in *calling*), underline only that sound.

7 If you prepare these versions with care, half your job is over. All you need do after this preparation is to describe what you have analyzed and noted. Here your connecting lines of the same types or colors can help you immeasurably, for the lines and colors are obvious and will help you remember important variations and devices of sound.

SAMPLE THEME

A Prosodic Analysis of Lines
232–243 of Tennyson's "Morte
D'Arthur" [5]

Metrical Variation

o o /   o /   o /   o \   o \
But the o- / ther swift- / ly strode // from ridge / to ridge, //   1
——1——

5 *The Complete Poetical Works of Tennyson,* W. J. Rolfe, ed. (Cambridge, Mass.: Houghton Mifflin Co., 1898), p. 66. All quotations from "Morte D'Arthur" are taken from this page.

Clothed with / his breath, // and look- / ing, // as / he walk'd, //   2

Lar-ger / than hu- / man // on / the fro- / zen hills. ///   3

He heard / the deep / be-hind / him, // and / a cry   4

Be-fore. /// His own / thought drove / him // like / a goad. ///   5

Dry clash'd / his har- / ness // in / the i- / cy caves   6

And bar- ren/chasms, // and all / to left / and right   7

The bare / black cliff / clang'd round / him, // as / he based   8

His feet / on juts / of slip- / pe-ry crag // that rang   9

Sharp- smit- / ten // with / the dint / of ar- / med heels— ///   10

And on / a sud- / den, // lo! // the lev- / el lake, //   11

And the / long glor- / ies / of / the win- / ter moon. ///   12

---

1 = Anapaest, or effect of anapaest.

2 = Amphibrach, or the effect of amphibrach.

3 = Spondee.

4 = Effect of imperfect feet.

5 = Pyrrhic.

6 = Trochee, or the effect of trochee.

Alliteration

But the other swiftly strode from ridge to ridge,   1

Clothed with his breath, and looking, as he walk'd,   2

Larger than human on the frozen hills.   3

He heard the deep behind him, and a cry   4

Before. His own thought drove him like a goad.   5

Dry clash'd his harness in the icy caves   6

And barren chasms, and all to left and right   7

The bare black cliff clang'd round him, as he based   8

His feet on juts of slippery crag that rang   9

Sharp-smitten with the dint of armed heels—   10

And on a sudden, lo! the level lake,   11

And the long glories of the winter moon.   12

$= S$

$= H$ aspirate

$= K$

$= B$

$= L$

Assonance

But the other swiftly strode from ridge to ridge,   1

Clothed with his breath, and looking, as he walk'd,   2

Larger than human on the frozen hills.   3

He heard the deep behind him, and a cry   4

Before. His own thought drove him like a goad.   5

Dry clash'd his harness in the icy caves   6

And barren chasms, and all to left and right   7

The bare black cliff clang'd round him, as he based   8

His feet on juts of slippery crag that rang   9

Sharp-smitten with the dint of armed heels—   10

And on a sudden, lo! the level lake,   11

And the long glories of the winter moon.   12

$$\underline{\qquad} = \bar{O} \qquad \cdots\cdots = \breve{A}$$

$$\underline{\quad-\quad} = \bar{I} \qquad ---- = \ddot{A}$$

The poem itself is a dramatic tale within a tale. The poet Hall tells the story; the narrator, Tennyson's speaker, who relates what Hall tells, has been dozing before the story, while the parson sleeps through the telling. Slightly comic as it is, this sleep also lends a dreamlike quality to the poem and enables Tennyson to achieve his "high" purpose. For the poem is about the passing of the old order (symbolized by the death of Arthur), and the old order does not pass without the regret of those who are left behind, who magnify and elevate the order to unparalleled heights. Tennyson's technique of removing the story from his own voice to Hall's makes this elevation possible and actually justifies the claim that the story is a

"Homeric" echo. In short, the poem captures the magic of the old order, and also its heroic, brave, undaunted ruggedness.

The passage selected for prosodic analysis moves in sympathy with this passing of the heroic age. The motion described is from the mountainous heights where Arthur was wounded to the level lake on which he will travel to his final rest—from the elevated to the low. It is reasonable to expect, therefore, that the passage should convey the impression of Sir Bedivere's exertion as he performs his last service for his dying monarch. The passage should be strong just as Bedivere is strong; it should uncompromisingly support the elevated and magical evocation of the poem itself; it should end on an emotional key similar to that experienced by Bedivere as he reaches his goal. My study of the passage will attempt to show the degree of Tennyson's success in achieving these aims.

The rhythm of the passage is everywhere alive to the dramatic situation I have described. The basic metrical pattern is iambic pentameter, but this pattern is highly varied. Any description of Tennyson's metrical variations is arbitrary, but with this reservation I will try to describe them.

The passage opens with an anapaest (*But the o-*), and there is another anapaest in line 9. Tennyson seems to like anapaests, for he creates their effect in many other lines by inserting a pause within an iamb and then making the heavy stress of the iamb fall onto a preposition or a conjunction that must then fit into the next iamb (which usually contains the object of the preposition), as follows:

$$\overset{\circ}{\text{and}} \overset{/}{\text{look}}\overset{\circ}{\text{ing}} \; // \; \overset{\circ}{\text{as}} \overset{\circ}{\text{he}} \overset{/}{\text{walked}}$$

$$\overset{\circ}{\text{than}} \overset{/}{\text{hu}}\overset{\circ}{\text{man}} \; // \; \overset{\circ}{\text{on}} \overset{\circ}{\text{the}} \overset{/}{\text{frozen hills}}$$

$$\overset{\circ}{\text{be}}\overset{/}{\text{hind}} \overset{\circ}{\text{him}} \; // \; \overset{\circ}{\text{and}} \overset{\circ}{\text{a}} \overset{/}{\text{cry}}$$

He creates this type of rhetorical anapaestic variation in lines 2 (twice), 4, 5, 6, 8, 10, and 12. A related variation is the frequent appearance of an amphibrachic rhythm, which is produced in lines 2, 3, 4, 6, 7, and 11. In line 11, for example, the first five syllables precede the caesura:

$$\overset{\circ}{\text{And}} \overset{\backslash}{\text{on}} \; / \; \overset{\circ}{\text{a}} \overset{\backslash}{\text{sud}}\text{-} \; / \; \overset{\circ}{\text{den,}} \; // \; \overset{/}{\text{lo!}} \; // \; . . .$$

Because *And on* seems to form a foot, *a sudden* seems to be a unit too, since there is no other syllable to go with *sudden*. Thereby a rhetorical amphibrachic rhythm is formed. Still another related variation is that of the apparently imperfect feet in lines 2, 5, 8, 10, 11, and 12. These imperfect feet are usually produced by their closeness to a caesura, as in the following:

> The bare / black cliff / clang'd round / him //

> as / he based . . . .

In this line *him* is in effect all by itself, though in theory it is the unstressed syllable in the iamb *him* // *as*. But a theoretical foot does not an actual make, and I submit that the two words do not belong together.

Perhaps the most effective metrical variation in the passage is the frequent use of spondees, which appear in lines 5, 6, 8 (twice), 10, and 12. These substitutions, occurring mainly in the section where Sir Bedivere is forcing his way down the frozen hills, permit the lines to ring out, as in:

> The bare / black cliff / clang'd round /

and

> Dry clash'd / his harness . . . .

Other, less significant, substitutions are the trochees in lines 3 and 7, and the pyrrhic in line 12. The total effect of these variations is to support the grand, free conception of the heroic action described in the lines.

Many of the variations I have described are produced by Tennyson's free handling of his sentence structure, which results in a free placement of the caesurae and in a free use of end-stopping and enjambment. It is interesting to note that four of the first five lines are end-stopped (two by commas, two by periods). Bedivere is walking but exerting himself during these lines and apparently he is making short rests to gather strength for his ordeal. The ordeal comes during the next four lines, when he makes his precarious descent; none of the lines containing this description is endstopped. Bedivere is disturbed (being goaded by "his own thought"), but he must keep going, and we may presume that the free sentence structure and the free metrical variation enforce the difficulty and mental disturbance he is experiencing. But in the last two lines, when he has reached the lake and therefore his goal, the lines "relax" with feminine caesurae exactly following the fifth syllables. In other words, the sentence structure of the last two lines is fairly regular, an effect designed perhaps to indicate the return to order and beauty after the previous, rugged chaos.

This rhythmical virtuosity is accompanied by a similar brilliance of sound. Alliteration is an obvious and startling device in these lines; some notable examples are the recurrent aspirate h's in lines 3–6 (*h*uman, *h*e, *h*eard, be*h*ind, *h*im, *h*is, *h*arness), the b's in lines 7 and 8 (*b*arren, *b*are, *b*lack), the s's in line 1 (*s*wiftly *s*trode), the k's in lines 6–9 (*c*lash'd, *c*aves, *c*hasms, *c*liff, *c*lang'd, *c*rag), and the l's in lines 11 and 12 (*l*o, *l*evel, *l*ake, *l*ong, g*l*ories). Assonance is also working throughout as a unifying device, as in the $\bar{o}$ pattern of lines 1, 2, 3, and 5 (str*o*de, cl*o*thed, fr*o*zen, *o*wn, dr*o*ve, g*o*ad), the $\breve{a}$ pattern of lines 7, 8, and 9 (ch*a*sms, cl*a*ng'd, bl*a*ck, cr*a*g, r*a*ng), the $\ddot{a}$ pattern of line 10 (sh*a*rp, *a*rmed), the $\bar{\imath}$ pattern of lines 4–7 (l*i*ke, dr*y*, *i*cy, r*i*ght). One might also remark that there are many high-front vowel sounds (i.e., $\bar{e}$, $\bar{a}$, $\breve{i}$, $\breve{a}$) in the first ten lines. But in the last two lines, which describe the level lake and the moon, Tennyson introduces a number of low, back vowels (i.e., $\breve{o}$, $\breve{u}$, $\bar{o}$, $\overset{\psi}{o}$, $\tilde{o}$, $\breve{u}$, $\overline{oo}$). The striking effect of the vowels in these last two lines can be pointed out only when they are heard immediately after the two preceding lines:

> . . . as he based
> His feet on juts of slippery crag that rang
> Sharp-smitten with the dint of armed heels—
> And on a sudden, lo! the level lake,
> And the long glories of the winter moon.
>
> —lines 8-12

As these last two lines are read, their back, low vowels make possible a lowering of vocal pitch and a certain relaxation of vocal tension, and thereby they are eminently appropriate at this point in the poem, when Sir Bedivere has attained his goal.

The last two lines are, in fact, almost totally onomatopoeic, since the liquid l sounds are definitely imitative of the gentle lapping of lake waves on a shore and in the line of the moon. There are other examples of onomatopoeia in this short passage, too. In line 2 Tennyson brings out the detail of Sir Bedivere's walking in the presumably cold air "Clothed with his breath," and in the following five lines Tennyson employs many words with the aspirate h (e.g., *h*is *h*arness); in this context, these sounds suggest Sir Bedivere's labored breath as he carries his royal burden. Similarly, the explosive stops b and k, d and t in lines 6–10 seem to be imitative of the sounds of Sir Bedivere's feet as he places them on the "juts of slippery crag."

This short passage is a mine of prosodic skill—a virtuoso piece that I do not expect to find on every page I shall read of English poetry. The sounds and the rhythms of the words and lines themselves, put into this context by Tennyson, actually speak along with the meaning; they emphasize the grandeur of Arthur and his faithful follower, and for one brief moment bring out the magic that Tennyson associated with the fading past. In the poem, the outright glory of this passage makes understandable Sir Bedivere's previous reluctance to cast away King Arthur's sword. Such glory is not to be thrown away easily; but now it is gone, and we can regain it only in our imaginations, or in Tennyson's poem.

The Theme Analyzing the Style in a Short Section of Prose

13 Style is usually understood to mean the way in which a writer employs his words, phrases, and sentences to achieve his desired effects. It should be distinguished from *structure,* which is concerned with the organization and arrangement of the work as a whole. Although *style* may be used loosely to comprise the writer's entire craft, for this theme you will be concerned with the word in its narrower sense. As you read a work of literature you become aware of its style, even though you may not be able to describe the style accurately after you have finished reading. The main obstacle to discussing style is that you do not have the descriptive vocabulary for embodying your perceptions, and so the best you can say is that the style is simply "good," "bad," "crisp," "elegant," "formal," "brilliant," or the like, with an uneasy hope that no one will ask what you mean. Perhaps your previous experience with literature and with composition has been concerned not so much with style as with content. The result is that analyzing style is like experiencing weightlessness for the first time.

Let us grant, then, that style is difficult to describe and analyze. You may have discovered, however, that critics and reviewers in the Sunday papers and elsewhere are constantly praising or condemning writers for their styles. You can see the desirability of being familiar with an approach to style, for how else can you formulate your own opinions? What do the critics look for? What does your instructor look for? What are their standards for style? What criteria do they use as a basis of judgment? Is it possible, in short, for a student to be let in on the "mysteries" of discussing style, or should these arcane matters remain in the hands of the critics, forever out of reach?

Purpose of Stylistic Analysis

The object of your theme is to make you aware of style: what it is, how to discuss it, how to evaluate it, how to relate it to the achievement of the literary work as a whole, how to define the characteristics of each writer's style. Because style is concerned with diction, phrases, sentences, and sound and rhythm—together with the relation of all these matters to the entire work under consideration—you will have to wrestle with sentences and words, and from time to time you may be thrown on your ear. But if you persist you will develop the ability to make some accurate and useful observations about a writer's style. You will learn much and will be well on the way toward a dependable means of evaluating literature.

Limitations

In your analysis you will not be able to make observations about an entire work because of limited space. To write this assignment, you need only to take a short passage—a single paragraph is best, although a passage of dialogue is also satisfactory—and use it as the basis of your observations. As with the prosodic analysis, it is usually best to select a well-written passage or else one that conveys a good deal of the writer's argument, for the author will have devoted his best skill and energy to such passages. You must be aware of the limitations in this selection, for the discussion of one paragraph does not necessarily apply to the whole work in which the paragraph appears. But if you make these points—that your method of analysis would be the same for any passage in the whole book and that the paragraph is important in the book—the generalizations you make will have implications for the entire work. The authenticity of your remarks will depend on the skill and knowledge you show in your analysis. Always beware, however, of making hasty generalizations. With these reservations, your theme about style will be of great value to you.

Main Problem

The main problem you will encounter in this assignment is how to discover your writer's style. Suppose, for example, you choose to analyze a piece of dramatic prose or a passage of dialogue from a novel; or suppose you select a passage from a novel that is told from the first-person point of view. When you speak about the style of these passages, are you describing the *writer's* style or the *speaker's* style? Suppose that you analyze, in the same work, two passages that are dissimilar in style? Did the writer's style change, or did he adapt it to fit the different places or speakers? And if he did so adapt it, what are you trying to discover by an analysis of style?

The answer seems obvious. In your analysis you are trying to determine the degree of the writer's *control* over his subject matter. Control is what matters. If you discover that your writer adheres to the same style throughout his work, that fact might lead you to conclude that he has inadequate control over his subject matter. But you should ask some further questions: does he have some definite end in view in using this one style? If so, what is it? Is he successful? The aim of your analysis is always to describe specific characteristics and to make at least partial judgments of why these characteristics appear and what they contribute to the work.

To see how this aim might be fulfilled, look at the following example, from *The Merchant of Venice,* Act I, Scene ii:

> If to do were as easy as to know what were good to do, chapels had been churches and poor men's cottages princes' palaces. It is a good divine that follows his own instructions: I can easier teach twenty what were good to be done, than to be one of the twenty to follow mine own teaching. . . .

From the style of this passage, it seems clear that Portia (the speaker) is a woman with a rapid mind, well befitting her masquerade as an intelligent lawyer-judge later in the play. Her first sentence uses simple diction in a complex structure. Of her first fourteen words, six compose infinitives and two are verbs; a total of eight words out of fourteen, or over 55 per cent serve as verbs or verbals. Her mind, in other words, is active. The first fourteen words are also part of an if-clause, dependent on the verb in the following main clause. The ability to use subordination in sentences is regarded as the mark of a good mind and a good style. Portia, too, shows an ability to use rhetoric—in this sentence the rhetorical device called *zeugma* (the use of a single word with double grammatical weight).[1] The main clause of the first sentence is equivalent to two clauses, but the verb is used only once: "chapels had been churches and poor men's cottages [had been] princes' palaces." Portia's language is exceedingly simple, but she shows a fine sense of rhetorical and logical balance.

To be contrasted with Portia's speech is this one by Ophelia in *Hamlet,* Act IV, Scene v:

[1] This definition pertains to zeugma in its simplest sense. When a word works doubly grammatically, however, it frequently takes on two meanings, so that many people regard the double meaning as essential to a definition of zeugma. Thus, in Pope's line "Or stain her honor, or her new brocade," *stain* carries double weight grammatically, and also double meaning, first as a metaphoric stain on honor, and second as a literal stain on a brocade. In this line, therefore, *stain* works as a zeugma, a metaphor, and a pun. Complications like these are not unusual, but are not essential.

> Well, God 'ild you! They say, the owl was a baker's daughter. Lord! we
> know what we are, but know not what we may be. God be at your table!

Ophelia makes this speech after she has become insane. Her words are
simple, and her sentences are disconnected. Just when she seems to become coherent (in sentence three) her thought is swiftly broken, and her
last sentence seems as random as her first. Had Shakespeare introduced
the intellectual toughness of Portia's speech here, he would not have
shown a broken mind but an alert one in all its powers. Thus he gave
Ophelia these disconnected sentences, so unlike her coherent speeches
in poetry earlier in the play.

The point about these two passages is that although they differ in
style, Shakespeare's control and artistry do not. In fact, the passages
show his mastery of dramatic prose. The study of style should aim toward
a description of the writer's ability to control his words to serve his needs.

Approaches to Style

The three chief ways to describe style are (a) the
analysis of the grammar in a passage, (b) the analysis of the rhythm and
sound, and (c) the analysis of the words, their denotation and connotation, their influences on each other in context, their symbolic values,
their functions in similes, metaphors, and other rhetorical figures.

ANALYSIS OF GRAMMAR

The nomenclature of grammar is a useful tool in
describing a writer's sentences. As you have been taught grammar, you
should not have trouble undertaking the analysis of grammar in your
passage. For example, the following sentences from the beginning of
Hemingway's *A Farewell to Arms* have been justly praised by critics:

> 1 In the late summer of that year we lived in a house in a village that
> looked across the river and the plain to the mountains. 2 In the bed of
> the river there were pebbles and boulders, dry and white in the sun, and
> the water was clear and swiftly moving and blue in the channels.
> 3 Troops went by the house and down the road and the dust they raised
> powdered the leaves of the trees. 4 The trunks of the trees too were
> dusty and the leaves fell early that year and we saw the troops marching
> along the road and the dust rising and leaves, stirred by the breeze, falling
> and the soldiers marching and afterward the road bare and white except
> for the leaves.[2]

You will observe that in this paragraph Hemingway employs the word
and many times. Of the four sentences, the last three are all compound

[2] Reprinted with the permission of Charles Scribner's Sons from *A Farewell to Arms* by Ernest Hemingway, p. 3. Copyright 1929 Charles Scribner's Sons; renewal copyright Ernest Hemingway.

sentences (independent clauses joined by *and*), whereas the first one is complex. Usually compound sentences do not demonstrate cause-and-effect or other relations and so are best used in narrative description. A number of compound sentences tend to declare, rather than to analyze (similarities between Hemingway's passage and parts of the King James Bible have been noticed in this connection). Also, compound sentences strung together may, under some circumstances, suggest resignation on the speaker's part. These remarks apply here.

In this passage there are also many prepositional phrases. There are sixteen phrases, to be exact (one with a compound object). Of these sixteen, twelve are adverbial, and of these twelve, eight modify verbs. This number is to be contrasted with the number of single-word adverbs —three. The proportion of phrases is so high that you might justifiably conclude that the characteristic method of modification in the passage is the use of phrases. Prepositional phrases usually require many *in*'s, *of*'s, and *the*'s; so a passage with many phrases would likely contain many monosyllabic words. In this passage, there are 126 words; 103 have one syllable; twenty-two have two syllables; and one has three syllables. The method of modification thus has a close relationship to the simple, rather stark diction of the passage, for if Hemingway had relied on single-word adverbs he would necessarily have used more polysyllabic words. (Notice that the three single-word adverbs are all polysyllabic: *swiftly, early, afterward*. The longest word in the passage is an adverb.)

You can see that a knowledge of grammatical terms (in this example, a knowledge of conjunctions, compound sentences, complex sentences, adverbs, phrases, nouns) aids in the analysis, description, and evaluation of style. Without this knowledge you are handicapped in discussing style.

Let us take a sentence from another writer. The following is from Theodore Dreiser's *The Titan*. It has probably never been praised by anyone:

> From New York, Vermont, New Hampshire, Maine had come a strange company, earnest, patient, determined, unschooled in even the primer of refinement, hungry for something the significance of which, when they had it, they could not even guess, anxious to be called great, determined so to be without ever knowing how.[3]

This sentence begins with a prepositional phrase used adverbially, with four objects of the preposition. Then Dreiser introduces the verb (*had come*), and then the subject of the verb (*strange company*). Immediately after the subject there are three adjectives that modify it. There is then a fourth adjective (*unschooled*) modified by an adverb phrase (*in even the primer*), and the object of the preposition is modified by an adjective

---

[3] (New York: Dell Publishing Co., Inc. [Copyright World Publishing Co.] 1959), p. 25.

phrase (*of refinement*). Then there is a fifth adjective (*hungry*) modifying the subject of the sentence. This fifth adjective has complex modification; first there is an adverb phrase (*for something*), and then the noun *something* is modified by an adjective clause, which in turn has with it an adverb clause (*the significance of which, when they had it, they could not even guess*). The original series of adjectives is resumed with *anxious,* which is modified by the adverbial infinitive *to be called great.* The adjective series ends with the seventh, *determined,* which is modified by the adverbial infinitive phrase *so to be,* which is modified by the adverbial *without ever knowing how.*

If you have been confused by this grammatical description, you will readily agree that the sentence begins simply but unusually and becomes difficult and involved. It is inverted and rhetorically dramatic; it depends for its full effect on close study in its context on the printed page, whereas the example from Hemingway could be readily followed if someone read it aloud. In Dreiser's defense, you might say that the sentence explores a difficult avenue of thought: Dreiser is describing the makeup of a giant, a *titan,* and theoretically his language should therefore be grand and sweeping. In fact, this sentence fits into his design, for its seven adjectives build up to a cumulative impression of bigness. In its way, this sentence is quite effective.

Among other things, grammatical analysis reveals the complexity or simplicity of a writer's style. You should observe whether the sentences fall into patterns. Are most of the sentences simple, compound, or complex? Why? Is there a recurrence of any rhetorical devices that can be described grammatically (e.g., parallelism, zeugma, chiasmus)? Are the sentences mainly *loose* or *periodic,* and why? Always be alert to the special characteristics of your passage. For example, you might notice that its sentences are filled with many adjectives, or with subordinate clauses. Your grammatical study should conclude by trying to answer the question of why the elements are as they are. In this way you will see the usefulness of analyzing grammar when you discuss style, for the two are inseparably identified.

A word of caution is perhaps needed. The description of grammar can become deadly and sterile if it leads to no generalizations. It is not an end in itself. But the labor of grammatical analysis can produce stimulating and sometimes startling results.

RHYTHM AND SOUND

RHYTHM Some analysts of style become vague or rapturous when they speak about the rhythm of prose. The reason is not far to seek, for prose rhythm is difficult to analyze and still more difficult to describe. If you keep your ear alert and if you combine the results of your hearing with the analysis of grammar in a passage, you can arrive at accurate and useful generalizations about prose rhythms. The rhythm of prose can seldom be accurately described by iambs, trochees, dactyls, and so on, for words that could be measured neatly by feet in poetry are actually parts of some larger rhythmic pattern in prose. The rhythm of prose, in short, is generally vaster than that of poetry, in keeping with the prose writer's general intention to develop his thoughts extensively. To feel the quality of prose rhythm, read this passage:

> . . . But when a Man's Fancy gets *astride* on his Reason, when Imagination is at Cuffs with the Senses, and common Understanding, as well as common Sense, is Kickt out of Doors; the first Proselyte he makes, is Himself, and when that is once compass'd, the Difficulty is not so great in bringing over others; A strong Delusion always operating from *without,* as vigorously as from *within.* For, Cant and Vision are to the Ear and the Eye, the same that Tickling is to the Touch. Those Entertainments and Pleasures we most value in Life, are such as *Dupe* and play the Wag with the Senses. For, if we take an Examination of what is generally understood by *Happiness,* as it has Respect, either to the Understanding or the Senses, we shall find all its Properties and Adjuncts will herd under this short Definition: That, *it is a perpetual Possession of being well Deceived.*[4]

Although these sentences could easily be scanned as iambs and anapaests, you will notice that it is more accurate to submerge many of the accents in the bigger, more important rhythmical pattern; that is,

$$\text{o} \quad \text{o} \quad \text{o} \quad \backslash \quad / \quad \text{o} \quad \text{o} \quad \text{o} \quad / \quad \text{o} \quad \text{o} \quad / \quad \text{o}$$
But when a Man's Fancy gets *astride* on his Reason,

$$\text{o} \quad \text{o} \quad \text{o} \quad \text{o} / \quad \text{o} \quad \text{o} \quad \text{o} \quad / \quad \text{o} \quad \text{o} \quad / \quad \text{o}$$
when Imagination is at Cuffs with the Senses . . .

You will immediately see that there is rhythm here but that stresses are placed on fewer syllables than in a verse passage of comparable length. Notice, in fact, that in prose the individual cadence groups, or phraseological groups, are the basic units and that the cadence groups are fitted into the separate parts making up the sentence. The groups can be analyzed with the help of the punctuation marks and the natural, though slight, pauses between subjects and predicates, compound subjects, and so on. Thus the first sentence might be laid out as follows:

But when a Man's Fancy	gets *astride* on his Reason,
when Imagination	is at Cuffs with the Senses,
and common Understanding,	
as well as common Sense,	
	is Kickt out of Doors;
the first Proselyte he makes,	
	is Himself,

4 Jonathan Swift, *A Tale of a Tub,* Second ed., A. C. Guthkelch and D. Nichol Smith, eds. (London: Oxford University Press, 1958), p. 171.

and when that is once compass'd,
the Difficulty is not so great
A strong Delusion always operating

      in bringing over others;
      from *without,*

as vigorously

      as from *within.*

With this scheme may be contrasted a rhythmic analysis of the sentence from Dreiser:

      From New York,
          Vermont,
          New Hampshire,
          Maine
      had come a strange company,

earnest,
patient,
determined,
unschooled in even the primer

      of refinement,

hungry for something

      the significance of which,
      when they had it,
      they could not even guess,

anxious to be called great,
determined so to be

      without ever knowing how.

Although it is unwise to make extensive generalizations from only these two schematic patterns, you can easily see a difference between the two. The unit lengths of Swift's sentence are longer and more evenly balanced than those in the sentence by Dreiser, where the units begin thinly but bcome longer. Your job in analyzing a prose passage is to make a similar attempt to discover and to characterize its rhythms. To assist yourself, you should read the passage aloud and listen for its rises and falls, its lengths of utterance. It is also good to have a fellow student read the passage aloud to you, so that you will be better able to observe its rhythms.

    SOUND Despite the differences between poetry and prose, the various "poetic" devices such as alliteration, assonance, and onomatopoeia may also be at work in prose (see pp. 136-37). You should be alert for them. Look at the example from Hemingway again. If you listen, you will hear that Hemingway employs assonance (e.g., sentence 3: h*ou*se, d*ow*n, p*ow*dered; sentence 2: m*o*ving, bl*ue*; sentences 3 and 4: l*ea*ves, br*ee*ze, w*e*, tr*ee*s). Or, in the first sentence of the selection from Swift's *Tale of a Tub,* there are many short $\breve{i}$ and short $\breve{a}$ sounds. In fact, there is an extremely high proportion of high and central vowels (about 80 per cent). Perhaps these sounds illustrate not only the thin and rarefied quality of the human madness the speaker is describing but also the volatile, choleric qualities of his mind. The effect of this attention to sound is to make the reader conscious of prose that is not just run-of-the-mill. Although the passages are prose, they are closely controlled and have many poetic characteristics. In commenting on the passages, you should certainly establish their similarity to poetry and should include this fact in your evaluation of the style.

DICTION—MEANING OF WORDS IN CONTEXT

This phase of stylistic study is the one in which you will probably feel most at home, for you have always been aware of the problems of meaning. You should observe, however, that a study of diction does not simply rely on dictionary definitions but goes beyond the meanings of the words to a study of their relationships in context. Words rarely exist by themselves but are in a context in which one word affects another, and your interest here should be to observe and record these relationships.

Look at the words in your passage and see where they take you. You are on an exploration and may or may not discover something valuable. Some guidelines for your itinerary might be the following questions: Are any important words repeated? Why? Are there any unusual words? Surprising words? Why? Do the words have common etymologies? (E.g., are most of the words Anglo-Saxon in origin, or are there many of Latin or Greek derivation? Consult your dictionaries for etymologies.) Does the author use many adjectives before a noun? After a noun? Why? What is the effect? Are the words in the passage mainly specific or general? Concrete or abstract? Why? (Observe in the passage from Hemingway that the words are mainly specific and concrete, whereas in that from Dreiser there are many abstract words; what is the difference in effect caused by this difference in diction?) Are any of the words allusive; that is, do they suggest other contexts, literary, historical, scientific, or whatever? What are the connotations of the words as distinguished from the denotations? Does the passage rely on these connotations? How? Is there dialect in the passage? What is its effect? You can see that your understanding of point-of-view is relevant here, for the *persona* of the piece will create the nature of the diction (characterize as narrators: Huckleberry Finn, Holden Caulfield, Jane Eyre, or the speaker of "Only the Dead Know Brooklyn" by Thomas Wolfe).

These are the main questions you will attempt to answer in your analysis of diction, though there may be others that will come naturally out of the passage you select. Your principal tools here are a dictionary, your reading experience, and your alertness. Be on the lookout for relationships, but do not invent them if they do not exist. Be ready to take the hints provided you by the author.

The Organization of Your Theme

Your theme should have the following points. In the body you may arrange your analysis into any order you wish. Please recognize that even though the theme is a general one on style, any one of the points in the body could easily be developed into an extensive theme in its own right.

INTRODUCTION

A brief description of the work from which you have selected the passage you will analyze, followed by a brief discussion of the purpose and intent of the passage you have seelcted, will suffice. Many of the questions you need to answer are in the opening section of the prosodic analysis (see p. 141). The main point to answer here, however, is "What is the relationship of my passage to the work as a whole? What was the passage trying to do, and how well did it succeed?"

BODY

In this section you should consider three points.

1. The grammar of your passage. You should also observe the lengths of the sentences, but try to make your count point toward worthwhile conclusions. By modern standards, an average sentence is about twenty-five words long. If you have five sentences of, say, a fifteen-word average, with lengths from five to twenty words, you may say that the sentences are short, terse, sparse, laconic, brief. If, on the other hand, the sentences average fifty words, you can say that they are full, round, rotund, or perhaps wordy or rambling.

2. The rhythm and sound of the passage. You may wish to integrate this discussion with your consideration of grammar and punctuation, as grammatical and phraseological units dictate rhythms. Perhaps you might be observing a long sentence characterized by many extensive rhythmical units, as in the following by Edmund Burke:

> I am convinced we have a degree of delight, and that no small one, in the real misfortunes and pains of others; for let the affection be what it will in appearance, if it does not make us shun such objects, if on the contrary it induces us to approach them, if it makes us dwell upon them, in this I conceive we must have a delight or pleasure of some species or other in contemplating objects of this kind.
>
> —*A Philosophical Enquiry Into The Origin Of Our Ideas Of The Sublime And Beautiful,* Section XIV

Or perhaps you are reading short sentences and rhythms, as in this passage from John Webster:

> Now you're brave fellows. Caesar's fortune was harder than Pompey's: Caesar died in the arms of prosperity, Pompey at the feet of disgrace.

—The Duchess of Malfi, V, v, 57-61

Study your passage carefully and observe not only the rhythms but the sounds. The sample theme, analyzing a passage from Faulkner, points out instances of alliteration and assonance. If you study your passage carefully you should make worthwhile and interesting conclusions.

3. The diction. This section might well be the longest, for you are always aware of problems of meaning. Discuss the diction in context and try to make observations about its relationship to the thought and intent of the passage.

CONCLUSION

Make a concluding evaluation of the style—a summary of your findings. How well did the passage contribute to the entire work? If it did not contribute much, did it detract?

Hints

1 This theme is designed to increase your perceptions, sensitivity, and appreciation. Listen carefully; read carefully; try to feel the full force of the passage you select.

2 Make a copy of your passage and place it at the start of your theme.

3 Number each sentence in your passage.

4 When you write, use quotations to illustrate your points. Do not just quote in a vacuum, however, but explain your point and make your analysis before or immediately after your quotation.

5 *Underline* all elements to which you wish to draw attention.

6 Always indicate the sentence numbers of your quotations.

SAMPLE THEME

An Analysis of the Prose Style in the Last Paragraph of Chapter 20 in William Faulkner's Light in August [5]

1 It is as though they had merely waited until he could find something to pant with, to be reaffirmed in triumph and desire with, with

[5] From *Light in August,* by William Faulkner (New York: The Modern Library, 1950), pp. 431-32. Copyright 1932, and renewed 1959 by William Faulkner. Reprinted by permission of Random House, Inc.

this last left of honor and pride and life. 2   He hears above his heart the thunder increase, myriad and drumming. 3   Like a long sighing of wind in trees it begins, then they sweep into sight, borne now upon a cloud of phantom dust. 4   They rush past, forward-leaning in the saddles, with brandished arms, beneath whipping ribbons from slanted and eager lances; with tumult and soundless yelling they sweep past like a tide whose crest is jagged with the wild heads of horses and the brandished arms of men like the crater of the world in explosion. 5   They rush past, are gone; the dust swirls skyward sucking, fades away into the night which has fully come. 6   Yet, leaning forward in the window, his bandaged head huge and without depth upon the twin blobs of his hands upon the ledge, it seems to him that he still hears them: the wild bugles and the clashing sabres and the dying thunder of hooves.

The passage I have selected is the concluding paragraph of the Joe Christmas-Gail Hightower story in Faulkner's *Light in August.* The paragraph, in the present tense, describes Hightower's dying thoughts, which are passing from consideration of the apotheosis of Joe Christmas to the galloping cavalry. This vision of the cavalry had earlier been Hightower's plague, but here it indicates his mental "triumph and desire." Previously vague and by some thought to be sacrilegious, the men and horses now illustrate Hightower's final vision of truth—namely, that all men are brothers and that human life at any moment is on a grand crest rushing toward a final, glorious shore. Just as Hightower's vision is affirmative and grand, so should Faulkner's style be affirmative and bold. It should illustrate the power of language, and my belief is that it does.

The grammar, for example, is carefully controlled. None of the six sentences is exactly like any of the others, although sentences 4 and 5 begin in the same way. The entire passage is framed by two complex sentences (1 and 6), and sentence 4 is a long compound-complex sentence. Sentence 2 is simple, and sentences 3 and 5 are compound (although neither of these compound sentences has a conjunction joining the two independent clauses). All the sentences show care, skill, variety, and boldness. The first sentence, for example, is unusual and interesting. At the end of the adverb clause in this sentence Faulkner uses the word *with,* ordinarily a preposition, and then repeats it at the end of the infinitive phrase, as though to emphasize his boldness:

> until he could find something to pant *with,* to be reaffirmed in triumph and desire *with,* . . . .

Then he uses *with* again immediately, but now in its ordinary position as a preposition:

> *with* this last left of honor and pride and life.

This usage gives the passage both weight and emphasis.

Another strong device in the paragraph is the use of single and parallel modifiers following the word they modify. Thus, we have

the thunder . . . , *myriad* and *drumming* . . . .

When the galloping cavalry comes by,

They rush past, (1) *forwardleaning in the saddles,* (2) *with brandished arms,* (3) *beneath whipping ribbons* . . . (sentence 4).

This pattern of "back" modifiers is one of the most characteristic in Faulkner, as is also another pattern (also shown in the quotation from sentence 4), that of grammatical units appearing in three, frequently connected by the conjunction *and,* as in:

honor *and* pride *and* life
and
the wild bugles *and* the clashing sabres *and* the dying thunder of hooves.

One might notice that in this paragraph, of six sentences, these two patterns of three occur at the beginning and the end, as though Faulkner were making a neatly balanced frame.

Balance and control, in fact, are also characteristic of the rhythms in the paragraph. The passage is full, and the pauses are correctly and judiciously placed; the voice is therefore measured into fairly full but varied cadence groups. The fullest group is the second part of sentence 4. This segment is breathtaking, perfectly in keeping with the massive advance of the galloping cavalry. With the last pause of the voice falling after *past,* there are twenty-seven words that must be spoken without a significant pause—an extremely long and full rhythmical development giving an almost panoramic sweep of the cavalry:

like a tide whose crest is jagged with the wild heads of horses and the brandished arms of men like the crater of the world in explosion.

To be contrasted with his long, broad rhythm is the almost abrupt rhythm in the next sentence:

They rush past,
    are gone;
            the dust swirls skyward sucking,
            fades away into the night
            which has fully come.

Also, since Hightower feels that he is dying, it is interesting to note the many falling (i.e., dying) rhythms in the concluding words; that is: *wild bugles, dashing sabres, dying thunder.* But the passage concludes on an up-beat, a note of resurrection, well in keeping with the movement of apotheosis developed by Faulkner throughout the entire chapter:

o /o / o o /
the dying thunder of hooves.

In accord with this almost poetic control over rhythm, the sounds of the passage have many poetic characteristics. Faulkner uses assonance and alliteration in almost every line. Assonance appears in the long $\bar{\imath}$ of find, triumph, desire, pride, life (sentence 1); the short $\breve{u}$ in thunder, drumming, rust, dust, sucking, come (2 and 5); the ou diphthong in now, and cloud (3); and the short $\breve{a}$ in saddles, brandished, and slanted (4). Alliteration appears in last left (1); hears, heart, heard, huge, hands, hears (2 and 6); and sighing, sweep, sight, swirls, skyward, sucking (3 and 5). These patterns cannot be overlooked, and coming as they do in this climactic paragraph, they greatly emphasize the grand, "poetic" vision of the expiring Hightower.

The mastery already described is also apparent in the diction, which leads from mainly abstract words in the first two sentences to mainly concrete words in the last four. Yet amid the concreteness of Hightower's vision of the cavalry, Faulkner puts words that stress its abstractness. The dust is *phantom dust,* and the yelling of the cavalrymen is *soundless.* In addition, the parallel verbs describing the movement of the horses are rather muffled and for this reason permit the suggestion that they are phantom-like to work:

they *sweep* into sight (3)
They *rush* past (4)
they *sweep* past (4)
They *rush* past (5)
        are gone (5).

The greatest virtue of Faulkner's diction in the paragraph is its active, bold vividness, however. The language is virtually fearless in these phrases:

the crater of the world in explosion (4)
this last left of honor and pride and life (1)
the dust swirls skyward sucking (5)
forwardleaning in the saddles (4)

It takes bold, original thinking, and much confidence, to use language in this way. All the phrases are new, accurate, and fresh. Other phrases are remarkably vivid. My favorites are:

the dying thunder of hooves (6)
beneath whipping ribbons from slanted and eager lances (4).

It takes something great to think of *eager* lances. But my comments are superfluous here.

All in all, this paragraph gleams out of the page. When I first read it for this theme I perhaps *sensed* this quality, but after having analyzed the grammar, rhythm, sound, and diction, I am amazed at how well the paragraph wears. Each time I reread it, I recognize more and more of the real scope of a master prose stylist, and Faulkner is that. The paragraph is alive, quick. It is a fitting and brilliant conclusion to the Joe Christmas strand of *Light in August.*

The Theme on a Literary Work as It Reflects Its Historical Period

14 Everything written, spoken, painted, or composed reflects to some degree the historical period of its composition. Indeed, we cannot open our mouths without showing attitudes, idioms, and customs of our time and place. Everything belongs in its era, whether as a revolutionary idea, reaction, or synthesis; and a major job of the disciplined reader is to understand the relationship of historical movements and artistic works. On the professional level, the record of this relationship is literary history, which is in effect the chronicling of the interaction of ideas, events, and literary modes. To study a work of literature in historical perspective is to determine the degree to which the work belongs in, and transcends, its period.

In order to carry out such a study it is necessary to have some philosophy of how literature is related to its era. You might consider first the obvious fact that as circumstances change, writers express attitudes toward these changes in literary works. One aspect of the historical approach to literature is to chronicle events and literary responses to them. In addition, you might also assume that artists themselves desire to create new ideas from existing ones and to press for improvement and reform in society. A permanent standard of judging art is its newness, that is, its status of being different, and artists are always trying to meet this standard. To the degree that writers of the past (and present) have been successful, it becomes possible to place their works in historical perspective, in the light of change at least, if not of definite progress.

Analyzing a literary work as it reflects its historical period, then, becomes the task first of determining what can be clearly deducible as coming directly out of its time, and second of deciding what is new and permanent—that is, of determining what has been created by the author of the work from ideas prevalent at the time of composition. The concern is to see both the similarity and dissimilarity of a work and its period.

Such a study of literature is valuable because it promotes the realization that ideas and ways of seeing the universe change with time and place. Too often it is easy to read texts as though they were all written last week and to attribute to writers ideas that they never had. Shakespeare as well as Swift and Pope, for example, had a number of political ideas, but they did not know about representative government as we know it today. Therefore, in considering works of theirs that touch the subject of politics, you should understand why they emphasize the importance of a just and strong monarch or the necessity of a moral aristocracy. We can enthusiastically accept their ideas that wise rulers and moral people are necessary for monarchical or aristocratic forms of government, even though we today reject these forms in favor of democracy.

The idea of reading works in historical perspective is not, however, to file them away in a historical pigeon-hole but to improve understanding of the entire work in its context. The aim is to produce accuracy of reading and of judgments and to avoid errors that result from failure to see that artists respond to their own times and frequently are bound to these times. As an example, some people have objected to Plato's ideas about an ideal republic because Plato does not rule out the custom of slavery. Therefore, they say, his ideas are invalid. Aside from the logical impossibility of this argument, simple historical consideration makes one realize that Plato had not known and did not envisage any other society but one containing slavery (this aspect of his society is, to us, dated). Once this judgment is made, most of Plato's thought assumes great relevance and importance. Historical analysis, in other words, permits you to concentrate on the more vital aspects of a work and to distinguish these from others that are imprisoned within their historical moments.

Preparing for Your Theme

The first part of your task is to read the assigned work and settle any difficulties that you may encounter in it. Next you decide what is topical about the work. Making such a decision is easy for some works, particularly those written recently. *The Grapes of Wrath,* for example, is readily seen in relation to problems of the rural, unskilled poor in America in the 1930's. Walter Van Tilburg Clark's story "The Portable Phonograph," although set under circumstances that have not come to pass, may be easily related to modern apprehensions about the disastrous effects of nuclear war.

Some modern works, however, may offer special difficulties because of their topicality; that is, some works are so closely connected with ideas and assumptions of your own that you may not readily see them in historical perspective. It is difficult to realize that our own country and age may not embody all the goals of human history. Katherine Mansfield's short story "Bliss," for example, is a searching analysis of the causes for the deterioration of a marriage. If this story seems more concerned with permanent than topical aspects of human life, you might consider that the main female character is drawn as a person who has received a certain kind of education and a certain set of values about sexual relationships. You might also consider that the institution of marriage itself is a custom that at one time was enforced by sacramental power that within this century has been losing absolute influence. Further, marriage has not always been accepted by all societies at all times as the principal form of relationship between men and women. Therefore, even in such a story, which at first seems difficult to analyze in relation to history, there are materials on which to base a theme.

Other problems might arise when the work assigned is remote either in history or in place. There is a view, for example, which holds that Shakespeare's history plays were created at least partially as a defense of the Tudor monarchs' claims on the English throne. Certainly an analysis of *Henry V* in relation to its historical period would have to take this view into account.

To the degree that works like Shakespeare's history plays are written to describe and frequently to romanticize past times, they bring up another problem, namely that of determining the relationship of noncontemporary materials to contemporary times. Browning's poem "My Last Duchess" is such a work. It was published in 1842, but its subject is a Renaissance Italian nobleman. In such works, however, the subject matter brings out ideals and attitudes of the writer, and these can then be related to the time in which the work was written, which is the only relevant time for the purpose of this theme. Thus, from the character of Browning's duke, who is callous and self-centered and who wields despotic power, it is apparent that Browning is suggesting that absolute power produces destructive results on both the individual wielding it and those around him. Specifically, Browning was writing this poem for an age that had produced Napoleon and that a year before "My Last Duchess" had seen the publication of Thomas Carlyle's lectures on *Heroes, Hero Worship, and the Heroic in History*. Browning's presentation of the duke can therefore be analyzed as something more than a dramatic study of a powerful eccentric of past times, although because of the developing concerns during the period with psychology, one could also make a good case for the poem simply as a psychological study.

The Acquisition of Necessary Background Information

A question naturally arises about the assignment to relate a work to its historical period. This is: "How do I acquire the necessary information to write the theme?"

In response to this question, it is important to realize that the major source of your information is the work itself. In your reading you can discover a great deal about the period of the author and more importantly about the place of the work in that period. You need to ask, and answer, a number of questions such as: Are historical circumstances specifically mentioned? What are they? What does the author say about them? Does the writer describe conditions with photographic detail, or is he less concerned with details and more with human problems? To what social class do the principal characters belong? What is their social and educational background? What values do they hold or represent? Are the characters religious or not? Is the principal character (or any character) an important part of the prevailing social and economic system as outlined in the work, or is he an outsider? If he is outside the system, what conditions have put and now keep him there? Are you made to feel pleased or angry with these conditions? Does the character eventually win a place in the system, or is he broken by it? What assumptions do you think the author had about the literary interests of his audience? That is, does it seem that the author wrote for a sophisticated audience, a simple-minded one, or a sensation-seeking one? What conclusions can you draw, on the basis of your answers to these and like questions, about the author's attitudes toward his times? Does he attempt to give a complete view or a partial view? Does he seem to be recommending values that are similar, or contrary, to those held during his era?

From questions such as these you will soon discover a suitable topic, for there is need here as always for narrowing the focus of your discussion. For example, a question about the fortunes of a particular character can lead to an avenue of inquiry like the following: Does the successful termination of Oliver Twist's difficulties reflect an optimistic or romantic idea about opportunities presented by nineteenth-century English society? Similarly, how can the misfortune of Tom Joad in *The Grapes of Wrath* be shown to reflect Steinbeck's views about American politics in the 1930's? Events or situations themselves can be focused in the same way. The details about Stephen's homelife in Joyce's *Portrait of the Artist as a Young Man* might suggest a topic like "The Deleterious Effect of Dublin Homelife on the Individual." Franz Kafka's description of the machine in "In the Penal Colony" might lead you to pursue a

topic of how the story reflects a disillusionment with the increasing technology and bureaucracy of the twentieth century. Your following through
on questions like these should enable you to develop an interesting and
relevant topic.

This use of the work of literature itself as an authority for your
remarks in the theme may seem open to the objection that literary works
are often not reliable as actual source material for history. Sometimes
works contain exaggerations made for comic or satiric effect, and sometimes they develop out of improbable circumstances. As history therefore
the close study of a literary work is a weak substitute for more accurate
documentation.

The answer to this objection—and an important realization for
you to make—is that the focus of this assignment *is* the work itself. Your
theme is about the historical period only as it is reflected in the work.
Your concern is not to use the work for evidence in writing history but
rather as evidence of a literary reaction to historical circumstances. Even
if there are exaggerations and caricature or if conditions reported are
brighter or blacker than life, these very aspects of the work become an
important part of the material you bring to your theme. Your aim should
not be to use the work as a filter through which you attempt to acquire
historical data but to determine to what use such observable data have
been put within the work.

To see how this approach might operate, let us take the example
of the character Hurstwood in Theodore Dreiser's novel *Sister Carrie*
(1900). Hurstwood is first seen as a successful restaurateur, but in the
course of the novel he slides down hill, eventually committing suicide
after existing for a time on the Bowery. His decline is caused and aided
by a number of accidental occurrences, mistakes in judgment, an unfor-
giving wife, and just bad luck. From these circumstances it seems clear
that Dreiser's portrait of a soul in twilight is his attempt to show that
human character, as manifested in high social position and apparent
economic success, is a product of chance happenings, including those of
birth and social class; remove the external props from a character and
you in effect destroy him. From this observation, it can be seen that this
aspect of the novel reflects a period of history in which social sciences
were beginning to grow and in which character was seen as a variable,
shifting with economic and psychological circumstances. By contrast, in
Shakespeare's *Tempest,* the character Prospero has been cast out of society for many years but is portrayed as having lost none of his kindness
and benevolence. The same is true of Perdita in *The Winter's Tale;*
brought up amid shepherds, her nobility comes to the front, her bucolic
background having no harmful effect on her character. From this comparison, it seems clear that Shakespeare took for granted assumptions
about character that Dreiser questioned, and that the ages that produced

these two writers were influential in these differences. A comparison of this type should by no means be construed as inviting the claim that one age is superior to another or one writer to another; rather, it should serve to account for differences that can be seen in literary works.

Some types of literature are more readily approached from the historical point of view than others. Usually novels, short stories, narrative poems, dramas, and essays are fairly obviously rooted in customs and ideas of their time. Many of these works can be discussed without extensive reading in secondary historical sources. By contrast, many short lyric poems are not obviously connected with their respective periods, and to write about these works you must prepare yourself with research. In any event, a certain amount of research is helpful in making your remarks about a period more authoritative, and it follows that as you acquire more knowledge about a period, the more inventive and original will be your topics.

Thus, your own previous work with American history has probably familiarized you with the fact that the beginning of the present century witnessed the intellectual as well as economic growth of our nation. This much you could bring to a study of the previously mentioned decline of Hurstwood in *Sister Carrie*. But a reading of background information about Theodore Dreiser might disclose the fact that Dreiser was embodying in his novel a concept of "Social Darwinism"; that is, a belief that the principles governing both nature and society were similar. On another topic, one might find in reading literary history that the early twentieth century was an age in which authors, in responding to new ways of looking at the universe and new theories about it, wanted to create new idioms and new forms in literature. Such knowledge might interest you sufficiently to work out a topic like "The Age of Experimentation in Literature as Reflected in *A Portrait of the Artist as a Young Man*."

So it is necessary to carry out a certain amount of research, although this research should be limited to finding more material about the topic you have selected for your theme. The first guide should be your instructor, who will be happy to answer whatever questions you may ask about the relevant period or who will direct you to books that will give you answers. Much of the knowledge you will apply for this theme will have been provided you by your instructor, through classroom discussion and lectures.

Of the books, the place to start is the introductory material provided in your text. Then you might go on to consult literary histories. For American works, start with Robert E. Spiller, Willard Thorp, Thomas H. Johnson, and Henry Seidel Canby, eds., *Literary History of the United States;* for British, see Albert C. Baugh, ed., *A Literary History of England.* Further work might be done in histories of the country and period of the author, and in general background works like J. H. Randall's

Making of the Modern Mind, E. M. W. Tillyard's *Elizabethan World Pictures,* Basil Willey's four books giving background on the seventeenth, eighteenth, and nineteenth centuries, Perry Miller's *The New England Mind,* and W. J. Cash's *The Mind of the South.* Still more can be done by consulting works listed in the selected bibliography of the edition you are using. If you need still more research, you might consult the annual *Bibliography* published each spring in the *Publications of the Modern Language Association.* Further research can be carried out, but this theme, which is not primarily a research assignment, will usually not require it.

Indeed, it is important once again to emphasize that the text itself is a major source of your knowledge of the period. Even if the reliability of the text as a source of information has been attacked (as with James Fenimore Cooper's *Leatherstocking Saga,* which was ridiculed by Mark Twain) that should not create a problem; your concern is to determine a relation of period to work that does not depend on the absolute reportorial accuracy in the work. Such inaccuracy, in fact, could form the basis for one of the ideas in your paper.

The Organization of Your Theme

In the following plan the introduction will be proportionately longer than introductions usually are, because of the need for presenting detailed information about the work and its historical period. It is possible, of course, to merge the presentation of the historical data with the discussion of the work.

INTRODUCTION

In addition to defining your central idea and thesis sentence, your aim here is to place the work in its historical period. You should identify the work, state the time of its publication, and if known, its composition. If the work, say a poem or story, was included in a collection, you should mention this fact and should also describe, briefly, the nature of the collection in order to determine whether the work is typical of the author's work. You should also include any biographical data relevant to an understanding of the work. You should also state whether there are any special problems in discussing the work, such as that it is a historical novel, or a work remote in time, or that there is some controversy about the work.

Next, you should state the pertinent historical facts concerning the events and ideas that you have selected for discussion. There is no need for extensive explication, but only for those details that are relevant. If the body of your theme is to contain references to many events, you need not detail them here but should emphasize instead the general attitudes held at the time about the events. If your work was written during or shortly after a recent war, for example, you may assume that your reader knows as much generally about this war as you do and needs only those details that will remind him of his knowledge. Thus, if you are discussing *For Whom the Bell Tolls,* you might state that the book is set in Spain during the Spanish Civil War; you might then go on to state that this war was not only a civil war, but was also seen as an ideological one involving other world powers; that many people felt idealistically committed to what they considered the cause of freedom supported by the Loyalists; that these idealists were sometimes used cynically; that the war highlighted for many the idea that life and love were impermanent and fleeting; and that the war was wasteful and destructive. There is nothing unusual about these conclusions: the point about them is that they are general statements about the period rather than detailed descriptions. The risk you run with such statements is that they can easily become platitudes; the best defense against this danger is that you express the ideas as clearly and as accurately as you are able and that you select only those details that are relevant to your topic.

BODY

After presenting historical facts, you should apply them in the following way. Of the parts listed, you may include both or one or the other.

a. A discussion of how the work embodies the facts, or of how the facts shape the work. Thus, *For Whom the Bell Tolls* not only demonstrates the idealism and fears of Jordan but is also a narrative that tests his ideals and the ideals of those like him in real life. The novel can be seen as an assertion that such ideals are needed at the present historical moment, even though they are engaged in a losing action. Similarly, in discussing "My Last Duchess," you might show that the duke's conversational manners (his pre-empting the discussion of marriage details by reflecting on the portrait of his former duchess and his stating that his "just pretense" for a dowry will be acceptable) can be related to the assertion that the poem is an effective counter-argument to contemporary claims about the need for "great men" in political life. Browning's "great man" is so preoccupied with his own greatness that he listens to no one and loses all sense of human kindness.

b. As the first part of the body is concerned with ideas, the second is devoted to a discussion of literary matters (i.e., style, structure, tone, point of view, imagery, etc.) that can be related to the period. Thus, ideas about the need for personal freedom may be related to poems written in free verse. An awareness of the changeability of human emotions and the shrinking of the significance of the individual may be related to the unusual line-formations in the poetry of E. E. Cummings and to his use of the small *i* as a personal pronoun. The modern stress on psychoanalysis may account for the stream-of-consciousness novel, and the development of the camera and the newsreel movie may be related to the chapters entitled "The Camera Eye" and "Newsreel" in the novels of John Dos Passos. What is important here is to apply the facts that you have acquired to the literary characteristics of the text.

CONCLUSION

To conclude you should try to determine which elements that you have discussed are out of date and which ones are still relevant and important. For purposes of your conclusion, you may assume that your own point of view is modern and up to date, although you should assert yourself humbly and emphasize your broadmindedness. Thus, in this section you might attempt to determine how relevant or desirable is Hemingway's assertion that the world still needs heroic character and action. Has the world bypassed the need for a military demolition expert and gone on to a need for a conversational and diplomatic expert? Is there still a need for both? Are Hemingway's values timely or out of date? Do the techniques of Dos Passos help or hinder your reading of, say, *The Big Money?* Is the manner of E. E. Cummings effective, or does it now seem eccentric? These are like the questions you might ask and attempt to answer in your conclusion.

SAMPLE THEME

A View of Nature and Individualism:
The Relationship of Wordsworth's
"Tintern Abbey Lines" and Its Time [1]

"Lines Composed a Few Miles Above Tintern Abbey, On Revisiting the Banks of the Wye During a Tour, July 13, 1798," by William Wordsworth, was first published in *Lyrical Ballads,* the collection of poems by Wordsworth and Coleridge that marked the Romantic revolution against eighteenth-century poetry. The poem itself is religious but nonsectarian: it speaks about the relationship of past, present, and future and also about the origin of the good and moral forces that influence the individual. Wordsworth says that the oc-

[1] *The Complete Poetical Works of Wordsworth*, ed. A. J. George (Boston: Houghton Mifflin Co., 1932), pp. 91-93. Parenthetical page numbers and line numbers refer to this edition.

casion of his writing was a visit he paid to Tintern Abbey while on a walking trip across England (p. 91). As he continued his journey, he composed and finished the poem, committing it to paper only after he reached Bristol. The poem is thus a reflection on a highly personal experience. The expression of the idea that such individual experience leads to the highest moral good is the principal idea tying the poem to its period, which was a time of great emphasis on individual worth and on the importance of individual effort to attain truth.

At the time the poem was written, the trend in thought had been more and more focused on the importance of the individual. Philosophy, religion, politics, science, and historical events had all converged to produce the idea that individual human beings were important. Democracy in America and the revolution in France were based on the notion that the individual should have as much liberty as possible. "Inner light" theories, about how the individual could directly apprehend the mysteries of the universe, had been common in some religious faiths for more than a century. Science had opened the book of Nature and had been reading its mysteries with the aid of the physical and mathematical theories of Newton, and also with the aid of the discoveries of chemical elements. It was natural to conclude that truth could thus be found by men directly through their own inquiries and that the avenues to truth were still open both scientifically and religiously. The modern studies of psychology, sociology, and anthropology had not yet been developed, so that the mood of optimism about breaking with the past, and thereby giving man an opportunity to flower, had not yet been attacked. Generally, many people in the age when Wordsworth wrote his poem would subscribe to the notion that a single human being, standing alone, could apprehend the truths of the universe. Science of course emphasized scientific methods of attaining truth, but religion was strong, and it emphasized prophetic, nonrational means.

It is the nonrational avenue to truth and morality that is explored fully by Wordsworth in the poem. He uses himself, or perhaps rather a noble concept of himself, as the basis of his assertions. Assuming that truth and morality are necessary qualities, and also assuming that he, the speaker, is a good individual, he proceeds to inquire into the causes for his goodness. In keeping with the general recognition of the need for independence and change during the revolutionary period, he does not mention the many cultural elements that influence character for the good, but isolates only one, namely his immediate experiences, and specifically experiences like seeing the banks of the Wye at Tintern Abbey. He concludes that his experience has improved him in two ways, first by giving him immediate pleasure, and second by providing him with retrospective pleasure.

The really major idea in the poem, and the idea that Wordsworth felt deeply and proclaimed with eloquence, is that this retrospective pleasure is a cause of restorative, creative power within the individual. Much of the first part of the poem is given over to a description of the speaker when in the state of tranquillity that produces this pleasure. Wordsworth describes it as a condition in which the "affections gently lead us on,"

> Until, the breath of this corporeal frame
> And even the motion of our human blood
> Almost suspended, we are laid asleep
> In body, and become a living soul:
> While with an eye made quiet by the power
> Of harmony, and the deep power of joy
> We see into the life of things.
>
> —lines 42-49

To the degree that Wordsworth describes his own physical state during such moments of prophetic insight, the poem is purely individual and nonhistorical. But his idea of what takes place in these moments is not personal but is in keeping with many ideas of the time; it is akin to theories of divine inspiration—inner light—and is also like the ideas of inspiration that gave the books of the Bible their authority. Then, too, Wordsworth's fellow romantic poet Keats described the idea that beauty struck the individual from a "penetralium of mystery"; that is, through a process that was nonrational and mysterious. Wordsworth's poem thus reflects the contemporary thinking that the individual was not alone; forces were acting on him that were inherent in, and simultaneous with, experience of Nature. The moral effect of this force, however, could be felt only through reflection and free association, not through scientific processes.

This attempt to interpret his own experience makes Wordsworth's poem particularly timely in his own day. He wrote from the point of view of a person highly aware of the connection between himself and the universe—the type of individual who could test the revolutionary theories. It is natural then that Wordsworth would avoid mentioning all the external influences that had been previously thought to act on a person, and would emphasize the idea that goodness could best be gained through direct experience with nature and the forces transcending nature. Wordsworth is not so revolutionary that he denies the need for faith, but his faith results from a belief in the need for a spontaneous, original, unique realignment of the individual with the universe—a faith in "nature and the language of the sense" as the "nurse,/The guide, the guardian of . . . [his] heart, and soul / Of all . . . [his] moral being" (ll. 108-11). Each man must make his own faith, and must not accept formalized, ready-made answers as codified in tradition.

Wordsworth's diction is rooted in these individual ideas. In the "Preface to the Lyrical Ballads" he stated that the language of poetry and prose should be the same. That is, poetic diction should be as clear and as close to the objects described as the nature of language permitted (pp. 791-93). Accordingly, his perception in the "Tintern Abbey Lines" of the transcendent presence in the universe is couched in simple words: "setting suns," "round ocean," "living air," "blue sky," and "mind of man." His verse patterns, too, are the result of an attempt to create a medium in which a free voice could explore the effects of experience. He avoided the couplet, which had been a favorite form in the eighteenth century. The idea was to write about present issues without hindrances either of the thought or of the poetic conventions created by men of previous ages.

Wordsworth's "Tintern Abbey Lines" can thus be seen as part of a revolutionary and individualistic set of ideas that came about at the end of the eighteenth century. The principal shortcoming of the ideas, which time has exposed, is the optimism about the ease with which the individual may become moral. The poem, however, is fresh and powerful, and by no means dated. Although Wordsworth's theory that the individual could directly experience the Spirit of the Universe is not easily confirmed today, there are many persons who believe that such experience may be gained through prayer, if not through any other means. Many people in our present age of science and technology tend to be skeptical of nonrational processes of learning and therefore admire Wordsworth's poem principally for its natural descriptions and secondarily for its hints about divine power. The full theological implications of the poem may be easily ignored. The poetic practice and the theory of language behind it, fortunately, are still in the highest repute because they adhere so successfully to common sense. The strength of the poem may yet give it greater acceptance in some future age less committed to scientific method than our own. It is not the poem that is dated, but perhaps ourselves.

The Theme
of Evaluation

15 The ultimate goal of all literary study is evaluation. Evaluation is closely allied with *judgment,* which is the faculty by which we can distinguish between good and bad, right and wrong, plausibility and implausibility, and so on. *Evaluation,* as used here, means the act of deciding what is good, bad, or mediocre. It requires a steady pursuit of the best—to be satisfied with less is to deny the best efforts of our greatest writers. Evaluation implies that there are ideal standards of excellence by which decisions about quality can be made, but it must be remembered that these standards are flexible in their application and may be applicable to works of literature written in all places and ages.

Although evaluation is the goal of literary study, description is the means by which the goal is reached. Without evaluation and appreciation, however, the description of idea, form, and style is really beside the point; it becomes a peripheral issue, a vacuum. Too often a good student will avoid making any judgments or commitments at all, although he may beautifully describe, say, the prosody of a poem. Quite frequently, too, he feels comfortable as he goes about his discussion, because description, in contrast to evaluation, is "safe"; it does not require him to "go out on a limb." Evaluation frequently requires taking a debatable position, which others might degrade. No one likes to be exposed, even by someone else's assertion that an equally valid alternative exists.

Despite the obvious dangers and difficulties of evaluation you must take positions on the works you read. Not to do so is to avoid the most vital pattern in your educational development. You yourself must learn to decide what is good and not always to rely on your instructor to tell you. If you lose yourself in pure description, or if you merely take the safe way by following someone else's judgment, you are not doing the best for yourself. You need to develop your intellectual courage. Certainly during much of your career as a student you can get by with the simple statement, "This work is a great one," because most of the works you read are literary classics. But the perfunctory comment "This is great" is not enough, for you should always try to discover just what are the grounds for judgment. Your study of the classics should certainly be more than perfunctory. You should always attempt to learn what is good in good works, so that you will have grounds for evaluating and appreciating works that are not yet accepted as classics—recent works, or works by relatively unknown authors, or lesser works by well-known authors. Remember, you will not always be taking literature classes, and when you are on your own you will want to know how to judge for yourself.

You may sometimes find that works commonly adjudged to be good do not seem good to you. If such is the case, try to live with the work for a time. If you have ever played in a band or orchestra, or sung in a chorus, you surely have found some musical compositions distasteful when you first read them through. But as you reapproached the composition day after day, and worked on it and learned it, you probably discovered that you became fond of the work and that you finally became convinced of its value. This process confirms the statement that you will learn to understand and to like a good work of art when you have the opportunity to do so. If, however, you find that despite prolonged exposure to the work, you still do not concur in the general favorable judgment, be as certain as you can that your reaction is based on rational and logically defensible grounds.

You should realize too that your ability to judge will be increased as you learn about more and more fine works. You must read and learn as much as you can, for in this way you will be establishing the qualities of good literature firmly in your mind, and, naturally, as these qualities become clearer to you, you will be able to evaluate with greater ease. Now, you have the task of evaluating a single work for your theme. This single assignment should have a definite bearing on your judgment in future years, because careful effort now will permanently improve your critical faculties. Your instructor does not expect you to judge like a great critic, but he does expect that you bring to bear on your work all the ideas about good literature that you have acquired.

The Rationale of Evaluation

There is no precise answer to the problem of how to justify an evaluation, and you would be misled if you were told that there is. Consequently evaluation is the most abstract, philosophical, and

difficult writing you will do about literature, just as it is the most necessary. We must recognize that standards of taste, social mores, and even
morals differ from society to society and age to age; nonetheless, some
works of art have been adjudged good or even great by generation after
generation, whereas others have been consigned to that vast dustbin "of
historical interest only." The student therefore asks, "By what standards
may a work be judged a good or great work?" and, "How do I make this
judgment by myself?"

The Task of Evaluation

In your theme you must ask: "Is the work I have
read good, fair, or bad?" or, "Is it beautiful or not?" You must answer this
question on artistic, not ideological grounds. In other words, you might
say that a political speech does a good job of rousing the populace to vote
a certain way, and as a result that it is a good—and here you probably
mean *effective*—speech. But in claiming that it is a great work of art you
would have to judge it on artistic grounds, not on political ones; you
would in addition have to determine whether it was important not only
for the moment but for all moments. As very few speeches transcend their
era, most speeches are not great works of art.

In admiring a work, then, you must consider whether you have been
misled by an excellence that is really minor. An atrocious piece of literature might have a superb control over form, for example, and you might
suppose it to be good. But if other considerations caused you to withhold
your total assent from the work, this supposition would be foolish. In
short, you must consider everything about the work you evaluate and not
be diverted from your object by surface beauties.

The Standards for Evaluation

There are many standards to help you evaluate a
literary work. Some of the major ones are described below, and many have
been suggested in earlier chapters. The terms involved are used and defined here in the senses to which they are usually restricted by people talking about literature. To the philosopher, the aesthetician, the student of
semantics, the words are probably charged with other meanings, and a
treatment of those meanings would necessitate a whole philosophical
treatise. It should be emphasized, however, that one cannot think intelligently or seriously about literature without using these terms, and it is
to help you interpret these words as they are generally used in regard to
literature that they are included here.

TRUTH

Although *truth* or *truthful* is used in speaking of literature to mean *realism* or *realistic* (e.g., does Flaubert give a truthful picture of Emma Bovary's society?), its meaning here is restricted carefully. To speak of the truth is to imply generality and universality. Let us take a concrete illustration.

Sophocles' *Antigone* is a play that has survived the passage of 2400 years. It concerns a society (the Greek city-state with a ruling monarch) that no longer exists; it deals with a religious belief (that the souls of the unburied dead never find rest) that passed from currency centuries ago; it involves an idea (of a curse following an entire family) accepted now only by the least educated members of our society. Wherein, then, lies the appeal, the truth, of *Antigone,* which makes it as much alive for our age as it was for the Greeks of more than 2000 years ago?

The answer is at least partly in the permanence of the human problem that Antigone faces: "How do I reconcile my duty to obey the state with my duty to obey my conscience? And if the two conflict, which do I follow?" This dilemma, and the suffering inevitable for any man caught in it, regardless of which choice he makes, is one that men have probably faced since the beginning of time; while men and states exist, this conflict between laws and conscience will endure—and so will the great statement of that problem given in *Antigone.* In short, the play embodies, lives in terms of, and comments on, one of the great *truths* of human life. It measures up, then, to one standard we use in deciding whether a work of art is good or bad, great or mediocre. But other criteria must also be considered.

AFFIRMATIVENESS

Affirmativeness means here that human beings are worth caring about and writing about, no matter how debased the condition in which they live or how totally they abuse their state. All art should be affirmative. Although many works apparently say "No" to life, most say "Yes," and a good argument can be made that the "no" works indirectly present a "yes." Thus, if a character like Macbeth or Hurstwood falls to the depths of misfortune, despair, and death, the author must demonstrate that there is a loss of some sort worth lamenting. Human worth is here affirmed even as a major character loses it. If a character like Mirabel in Congreve's play *The Way of the World* is happy and in good estate at the end of the work, the author must show that his character's qualities have justified his good fortune. Life is again affirmed. If an unworthy character is fortunate at the end, like Joe Gowland in A. J. Cronin's *The Stars Look Down,* the author still affirms human worth by suggesting a world in which such worth may become triumphant. In short, the author may portray the use and abuse of life, the love and the hate, the heights and the depths, but his vision is always that life is valuable and worthy of respect and dignity. The best works are those that make this affirmation forcefully, without being platitudinous or didactic.

"THE JOINT FORCE AND FULL RESULT OF ALL"

The above quotation is from Pope's *Essay on Criticism,* where most of what can be said about evaluation is said. Pope insisted that a critic should not judge a work simply by its parts but should judge the *whole,* the entirety of the work. You can profit from Pope's wisdom. You should carefully consider the total effect of the work, both as an artistic form and as a cause of impressions and emotions in yourself. Your total impression is important. James Joyce used the concepts "whatness" and "radiance" in describing the totality of a work; that is, when a work seems to be entirely itself, the force of its totality impresses the reader in a moment of revelation, or radiance. Although this sort of experience is almost mystical, and consequently impossible to describe, you must search your reactions after reading a work and see if you have been impressed with a sense of totality. Bear in mind that a great work may be imperfect—there may be flaws in style and organization; characters may be imperfectly drawn—but if the sum total of the work is impressive, the flaws assume minor importance. In other words, even if the author can be attacked on technical matters, the total effect of his work may overshadow the adverse criticism. Thomas Hardy and Theodore Dreiser are two authors in point; their language can frequently be shown to be at fault, but a reading of their best works reveals them to be superior novelists.

You should see, then, that one cannot judge a work as good or bad by reference to only one element within it. An interesting plot, a carefully handled structure, a touching love story, a valid moral—none of these attributes alone can justify a total judgment of "good." One can say, for example, that Dickens' *Oliver Twist* has an extremely ingenious plot and that it arouses our emotions effectively. But to evaluate the novel fully one must take into consideration several questions. Foremost among them are these: How does the character of Oliver withstand modern knowledge of child development? Could a child subjected from birth to the brutal experiences that Oliver endures develop into the person that Dickens presents? These considerations should make you realize that you cannot make a final judgment on the work as a whole without taking all its important aspects into account.

Another important phase of the "joint force and full result of all" is the way in which you become involved as you read. Most of what you read, if it has merit, will cause you to become emotionally involved with the characters and actions. You have perhaps observed that characters in some works seem real to you or that incidents are described so vividly that you feel as though you had witnessed them. In these cases you were experiencing the pleasure of involvement. The problem here is whether your pleasure was fleeting and momentary ("just kicks"), or whether it has assumed more permanence (whether it resulted from a passage that is permanently, or spiritually, satisfying).

Your question in evaluating a work, therefore, is whether your involvement was justifiable. A work that is sentimental or melodramatic may involve you in the plights of the heroes and heroines, but when you finish it you may feel let down or betrayed, because your emotions have been expended in an obviously artificial situation. Many operatic plots suffer from this defect; considered alone they should be condemned, but no one would judge them independently of the music, because music is the ultimate cause of emotional involvement in opera.

Closely integrated with the idea of involvement is the Aristotelian theory of *purgation* or *catharsis* in tragedy. How do you regard the character of Macbeth when he kills Duncan, or of Othello when he strangles Desdemona? Shakespeare causes you to become involved with both heroes, and when they perform evil deeds your own conscience cries out for them to stop. The result, when the play is over, is a "purgation" of your emotions; that is, if you experience these plays well, you will also have experienced an emotional "drain," which has been caused by your involvement with character and action. You can see that the use to which a writer puts your involvement is important in your judgment of his works.

VITALITY

It may seem strange to ask if a work seems "alive" or not, but this question is valid. A good work of literature has a life of its own and can be compared to a human being. You know that your friends are always changing and growing, and that you learn more and more about them as your friendship progresses. A work of literature can grow in the sense that your repeated experience with it will produce insights that you did not have in your previous readings. A classic example of such a work is *Huckleberry Finn,* known to children as an exciting and funny story of adventure but known to adults as a profound story about the growth of a human soul. Another example is *Gulliver's Travels,* in which critics for two centuries have been finding new insights and beauties. It is naturally difficult for you to predict the future, but if you have based your present opinion on reasonable grounds and have determined that the work is good, you may conclude that within the work there will be "food for future years." In short, you may conclude that the work is vital.

BEAUTY

This word is another chameleon. Whole books have been devoted to an attempt to define *beauty,* and the branch of philosophy named aesthetics is concerned entirely with determining what is beautiful. Briefly, however, beauty is closely allied with unity, symmetry, harmony, and proportion. To discover the relationship of parts to whole—their logical and chronological and associational functions within the work—is to perceive beauty in a work.

In the eighteenth century there was an idea that "variety within order" constituted beauty; the extent to which Pope's couplets vary within the pattern of the neoclassic couplet is an illustration of the eighteenth-century ideal. The Romantic and post-Romantic periods held that beauty could be found only through greater freedom. This belief in freedom has produced such characteristics of modern literature as originality for its own sake, experimentation in verse and prose forms, freedom of syntax, stream-of-consciousness narration, and sometimes personal diction. Despite the apparent change of emphasis, however, the concepts of unity and proportion are still valid and applicable. Studies of style, structure, point of view, tone, and imagery are therefore all means to the goal of determining whether works are beautiful. Any one of these studies is an avenue toward evaluation. Remember, however, that an excellence in any one of them does not make a work excellent. Frequently critics use such terms as "facile" and "surface excellence" to describe what they judge to be technically correct but artistically imperfect works.

YOUR PREFERENCES

Although personal likes and dislikes are the least valid criteria for judgment, they are not to be excluded. They are the principal guides to what you read, but they are valueless when purely whimsical—without any basis in thought or knowledge. They become more valuable as they reflect mature thoughts based on knowledge. The more knowledge behind a preference, the more reliable it is, because the preference then stems not from a vacuum but from a deeply ingrained basis of comparison. The word of a well-educated adult on the value of a work is naturally more reliable than that of a child. Once you realize that your personal likes become more valuable as you learn more and grow, then these likes become more useful in evaluating literature.

In writing, you should carefully distinguish between evaluating a work and merely liking or disliking it. You will readily admit that you might dislike works that everyone maintains are good; similarly, you may like some works that you would admit were worthless. You have heard people say "Everyone to his taste," or "I know what I like," and thus justify their preferences on unreasonable grounds. There is much truth, of course, in the argument that "personal taste is king," because preference definitely plays a part in evaluation and appreciation. But if you are to become a literate, disciplined reader, you will realize that pure subjectivism is wholly inadequate. Evaluation must be based on more solid grounds, grounds on which most human beings, despite personality differences, can agree.

In your theme you do not need to emphasize your likes and dislikes as a separate point, but instead your discussion should permit you to make your feelings clear by implication. The only exception occurs if you are asserting your like despite faults, or your dislike despite excellences.

The Organization of Your Theme

In your theme you will attempt to answer the question of whether the work you have studied is good or not. If so, why? If not, why not? The grounds for your evaluation must be artistic. Although some works may be good pieces of political argument, or successfully controversial, your business is to judge them as works of art.

INTRODUCTION

In the introduction you should briefly describe your evaluation, which will be your central idea, and you should describe the points by which you expect to demonstrate your idea. As the grounds for evaluation are many, you should also mention briefly those grounds that you are not going to discuss in the body of your theme.

BODY

In the body you will attempt to demonstrate the grounds for your evaluation. Your principal points will be the excellences or deficiencies of the work you are evaluating. Such excellences might be qualities of style, idea, structure, character portrayal, logic, point of view, and so on. Your discussion will analyze the probability, truth, force, or power with which the work embodies these excellences.

Avoid the descent into synopsis or analysis for its own sake. If you are showing the excellence or deficiency of a character portrayal, you must necessarily bring in a description of the character, but remember that your discussion of the character is to be pointed toward *evaluation,* not *description,* of the work as a whole. Therefore you must select details for discussion that will illustrate whether the work is good or bad. Similarly, suppose you are evaluating a sonnet of Shakespeare and mention that the imagery is superb. At this point you might introduce some of the imagery, but your purpose is not to analyze imagery as such; it should be used only for illustration. If you remember, as a cardinal rule, to keep your thematic purpose foremost, you should have little difficulty in making your discussion relate to your central idea.

CONCLUSION

The conclusion should be a statement on the total result of the work you are evaluating. Your concern here is with total impressions. This part of evaluation should underline your central idea.

SAMPLE THEME

An Evaluation of
The Catcher in the Rye

Despite some opinions to the contrary, *The Catcher in the Rye* is a good novel. It is written from the point of view of a deeply disturbed sixteen-year-old boy, Holden Caulfield, as though Holden were talking to us, the readers, directly. Throughout the novel this point of view is consistently maintained, and we believe in Holden as a realistic portrait of a certain type of adolescent. Technically perfect as the novel is in this respect, however, it would have only a surface beauty if it were *only* technically perfect. For this reason the degree to which Holden's character is realized, together with the strength of Salinger's vision, is most vital in an evaluation of the novel.

Even though it has been a few years since I was sixteen, I believe that Holden says and does what a sixteen-year-old with his background and in his circumstances would say and do. Holden is real. A good child, he finds himself faced with circumstances with which he cannot entirely cope. Jane Gallagher is a case in point. Holden has had a pleasant and innocent relationship with her, but when he learns that Stradlater has had a date with her, he senses that she might have been seduced, even though he claims that Stradlater would not "get to first base with her." [1] As a result he

[1] J. D. Salinger, *The Catcher in the Rye* (New York: New American Library, 1961), p. 74.

wants to drive this thought out of his mind. His responses to most of what happens in the story are similarly truthful. The ducks frozen out of the Central Park lagoon and the James Castle story are therefore morbid images that cling to his mind, since they symbolize to him the harshness of life. His attempts to become harsh himself— his language spiced with profanity, his experience with Sunny—all end in unhappiness. With a capacity for dreaming, Holden finds that the world ends his dreams, or else that it provides him with dirty stuff to dream about. As a result he winds up in the hands of the "psychoanalyst guy." All his feelings are perfectly in accord with what an extremely sensitive boy would feel under these same circumstances. Salinger's portrayal of Holden is therefore "true" in the best sense.

Throughout Salinger's creation of Holden there is a profound pathos. Without question Salinger makes us deeply sorry for Holden's failures, and as a result we are left with little hope at the end when we learn that Holden does not know whether he is going to succeed at school. But his "little hope" makes us review the novel with an eye toward answering the question of whether the world in which Holden finds himself is really worth success on its own terms.

Here the ambiguity of Salinger's vision, and its force as he makes us strongly involved with Holden, are brought home with incredible vigor. If one only supposes that Holden is right—that children should be kept playing in the rye, and by extension be kept from becoming adults like Maurice, to name only one bad example— then *The Catcher in the Rye* is a forceful protest against our own society. The "psychoanalyst guy" wants to make Holden "mature" enough to get along, but if being mature means being able to succeed with Sunny, or to bear the vision of Stradlater corrupting Jane, then maturity is callous and society's definition of maturity is wrong. Salinger is interested in Zen Buddhism, which is associated with the saying to the effect that "a child is a guest in the house, to be loved and respected, since he belongs to God." If this idea was in Salinger's mind when he wrote *The Catcher in the Rye,* this novel is a forceful and radical analysis of life. The idea that the child is right and the adult is wrong is fresh, invigorating, mysterious, and perhaps right.

The total effect of *The Catcher in the Rye* is that life is delicate and frail; since it can be so easily destroyed, it should be more carefully nourished. The author behind the idea has obviously thought deeply about life and has done in this novel what we may expect of the best art—namely, to give a new and challenging insight into life. Right or wrong, insights of this sort cannot be ignored; nor can *The Catcher in the Rye* be ignored.

The Theme
Reviewing a Work
of Literature

16 A theme reviewing a work of literature—the *review* —is a general essay on the quality of a literary work. It may also be thought of as a "report," a "critique," a "critical review," or simply an "essay." It is a free form, for in a review virtually everything is relevant—subject matter, technique, social and intellectual background, biographical facts, relationship to other works by the same author or by different authors, historical importance, and everything else. Because your aim in writing a review should be to judge generally the author's performance, the theme closest in purpose to the review is the theme of evaluation (Chapter 15). The review is different, however, because of its general nature. In the review, evaluation is only one of the aims, for there may be other elements of the work under surveillance that should be mentioned, special difficulties that you want to explain and special features that you want to note.

Since the review is so free, it is also a challenge to the skills you have developed thus far as a disciplined reader. Much of your college experience to date has been assimilation—the acquiring of information and the application of certain skills. Because many of your assignments have been relatively limited, your tasks have been mainly doing and not so much deciding what to do. But with a review, you are left much to your own devices; you must decide not only what to say, but what to write about. Freedom of choice—this goal should be your constant aim, and it is important for you to realize that your experience is equipping you to know more and more what to do with this freedom. You should be able to put together, to synthesize, the knowledge you are acquiring; you should not only know how to answer questions, but you should also be able to decide what questions should be asked.

Because the review is the form that gives you the greatest opportunity to exercise your ability to choose, it is perhaps the most individual kind of writing about literature. As you become more skilled, the reviews you write might become more and more personal, in the sense that your choice of topics for discussion and the material you bring to these topics will become unique. This accumulation of insight and applied facts is the cause of the interest that literary criticism can provide. Indeed, many reviewers have gained such familiarity with so much literature, and such sureness of critical perception, that their reviews have become important works worthy of independent study. Sometimes these reviewers use the work under consideration primarily as a launching pad from which they go into their own orbits. Hence, such reviews might be important personal meditations or philosophical or political discourses.

Because the review is the most personal as well as general theme about literature, and also because of a close tie with the commercial side of literature and other forms of entertainment, it is also one of the most common forms of critical writing. Most of the professional writing about literature in America today is reviewing. Newspapers, magazines, and even radio and television feature reviews. Performances of plays, musical compositions, art works, scholarly performances, scientific works, and of course works of imaginative literature are all subject to review.

The review may be thought of as the "first wave" of criticism, with other, more deeply considered criticism to follow later. One immediate problem of the review is therefore to keep it from becoming too hasty, too superficial. Alexander Pope was probably considering this problem when he wrote the following couplet about the frequency of reviews and the stupidity of some of the reviewers (in the passage, substitute "works of art" for "verse," and "reviews" for "prose"):

> A *Fool* might once *himself* alone expose,
> Now *One* in *Verse* makes many more in *Prose*.
>
> —*Essay on Criticism*, I.7,8

Of all the types of themes described in this book, the review is the one that you are most likely to be called on to write in your later, post-college careers, either by formal publications or by publications issued by professional groups or churches and clubs. You should certainly know what a good review is and should be able to write one on request. It is good to bear in mind that a good review is the product of the fusion of three elements: the attitudes and knowledge of the reviewer, the notable features of the work to be reviewed, and the audience for whom the review is written.

The Audience and Your Selection
of Material

If literature in fact attempts to reach human beings in their capacity as human beings, as Wordsworth said, then the review is the one type of critical writing that attempts to reach the broadest possible human audience. As many other academic and scientific disciplines become more refined, they also become less available to human beings, until finally specialists talk only to specialists about special problems. Whereas there is certainly a place for specialized writing about literature—and some of these later chapters have indicated how literary discussions can become technical—the student should remember that critical writing should always aim at a general, literate audience. The public that supports literature should benefit from the knowledge and best opinion of persons highly educated in literary studies. Although a product of technical methods, literary study should be used for the cultivation of public taste. The situation of the review, then, is one of the most important facing the critic. The aim should be to improve taste, to create a demand for excellence, and to approve the good and disapprove the bad.

The audience you are attempting to reach in your review is to be regarded as a group of equals who are generally about as well read and about as expert as you are. You may assume that these readers have not read the work you are reviewing, but you should also assume that they might read it or are about to start reading it. You should therefore act as an alert and perceptive commentator. You are, as it were, describing a course you have traversed for the benefit of those about to go the same course. If there are any points of interest or obstacles or detours, you should describe them. Your aim, however, is not to tell your reader so much as to make him feel that he now does not need to read the work himself. You should by no means "talk down" to him just because he is unfamiliar with the work to be reviewed, but there is no need for too technical a discussion. You should let the reader into the work a little, to tell him what he may expect to find. You should whet his curiosity, arouse his enthusiasm, make him feel that the work is indeed worthy of his spending his time in reading it himself.

The job of reaching your reader is indeed delicate, for you must strike the right note exactly; you must necessarily include a description of the events or principal ideas in the work, but you must not attempt to make your description exhaustive. Do not, for example, describe the final chapter of a book that has a surprise ending. If the author draws a number of important conclusions, do not describe every one; concentrate only on one or two, leaving the rest to your reader to discover for himself. If your subject is a book of poems, do not discuss every poem, but concentrate only on those that seem important or typical.

Perhaps the best frame of mind you can muster before you begin to write is this: imagine that you are preparing your reader to read the work himself; imagine that you are providing him with parachute and rip cord, protective clothing, and the airplane ride, but that he himself must make the jump.

The Organization of Your Theme

Your review should contain the following things, formed into a thematic structure.

INTRODUCTION

In this section you should place the work in perspective. In what period was it written? What is the nationality of the author (if he is of another nationality)? What kind of background knowledge is needed for an understanding of the work, or what kind, and how much, is supplied by the author (i.e., a knowledge of oil drilling, of conditions in the old West, etc.)? To what genre does the work belong? What general issues need explaining before you begin your discussion of the work? Although most frequently you will be asked to review a play or novel, it is good to bear in mind that you may also be reviewing techniques of acting and staging a play. If you are reviewing a new edition of an old work, you may be judging the relevance of the past to the present and also the scholarly helps provided by the editor (if you have a scholarly edition to review). Try always to show that your work has relevance to the present group of readers. Be sure to include your central idea and thesis sentence.

BODY

In the body of your theme you should try to arouse your reader's interest in the work you are reviewing or else to discourage him from reading the work if the work itself dictates this conclusion. Beyond providing the introductory information, your principal objective is to describe the strengths and weaknesses of the work. To write such a description you must call into play just about everything you have learned about analyzing literature for ideas, form, and style. In a sense, the review can be as specific as you wish to make it, for the greatest part of the body should be given to analysis. In this analysis, you may bring out your own strengths and interests as a critical reader. It may be, for example, that you have discovered in your literary studies that you have become proficient in discussing structure. If we suppose that you have observed a tightly knit structure in the work you are reviewing, you might choose to discuss that element in the body of your review, and thereby you would be appealing to your reader's response to artistic excellence. Similarly you may have enjoyed talking about imagery in poetry, and in reviewing a book of poems you might choose that for discussion. You should always recognize, however, that your discussion should be of limited extent. There is no need for a detailed, word-by-word analysis. It is not a theme of structure that you want, or one on imagery, but a review emphasizing these elements.

Special Approaches

You might also call into play certain disciplines that have interested you thus far in your college career. Your study of sociology, for example, may have led you to feel competent in handling ideas connected with that subject. Hence, in your review of a novel you might bring your sociological awareness to bear on the work as a sociological topic. A discussion of *Studs Lonigan* or *The Autobiography of Malcolm X* would benefit from such an approach. Or you may have developed an interest in psychology, and may feel especially interested in treating the characters in a work according to your understanding of psychological problems.

Discussions Governed By the Work Itself

Whatever your personal interests and specialties, however, the best guide for the subject matter of the body is the work itself, which may very well force you to make certain considerations. Obvious characteristics may necessitate the form of your discussion. In the sample theme, for example, the unusual features of the characters and the dialogue in Pinter's play *The Homecoming* literally shape the form of the review. The sample theme therefore touches on aspects of *character analysis* (Chapter 2) and *style* (Chapter 13), even though it is by no means a complete essay on either of these topics. Many readers of literature would probably also choose in a review to emphasize the characters and dialogue, but many might choose to discuss the bizarre humor, or the connection with existential philosophy, and so on.

Discussions Stemming Out of the Work Itself

In this type of review, the reviewer is less interested in pointing out features in the work reviewed than he is in presenting his own train of thought prompted by his reading of the work. A review of this type is not so much a review as it is a personal essay, which may take the form of (a) a consideration of the implications of the work, going beyond them into a more far-reaching discussion, or (b) a discussion stemming from dispute or disagreement with the conclusions or implications of the book. In this second type, the writer chooses to work from what he considers to be the flaws or shortcomings in the work being reviewed; in the first type, he considers the work as a thesis that he chooses to develop in his own way.

CONCLUSION

Your conclusion should be an attempt at evaluation of the work, certainly not as extensive as that in a theme of evaluation but at least an outline of your responses and a suggestion to your reader of how he might respond, granted that you have shown that your interests coincide approximately with his. If the body of your review has emphasized evaluation, you should close your essay with a simple résumé of your points. If you are ever asked to review a work in, say, no more than 150 words, the greatest part of the review, about 130 words, should be devoted to evaluation.

Hints

1 Whereas the discussion so far has emphasized the general audience—and this should be your aim—there are many situations in which reviewing may be done for specialized audiences. Reviews, and the organization of them, must be tailored according to the audience. To test this fact, try the following exercise. Suppose that you are going to write two reviews of the same work for two magazines designed to reach (a) a group of engineers, and (b) a religious group. It is to be assumed that these publications are aimed at persons in these groups not generally, in their capacities as men, but specifically, in their capacities as engineers or as followers of a faith. Therefore, would your reviews be the same for each group, or would one tend to emphasize practical aspects of the work and the other religious aspects? To go on, suppose also that you are writing for groups interested in problems of (a) rural America, (b) the urban poor, (c) young adult courtship, (d) national politics, (e) international relations, (f) satire, (g) literary style, or (h) humor. You see that in each case (granted that the work you are reviewing would be relevant to all these groups) the materials you select for discussion would necessarily be dictated by the group you try to reach.

2 Perhaps the greatest problem in writing a review is that of preserving a thematic structure. The form itself poses this difficulty because of the general nature of the reviewing task. Therefore you must be especially cautious to state your central idea clearly somewhere in the first paragraph and keep returning to it throughout your review.

3 Most reviewing assignments will be about recent works of literature. Remember that your task is to apply standards of good literature to the work in front of you, with the general notion of determining how well the work stands up.

4 The techniques of writing a review may be applied to assignments in other courses. In a political science course, for example, you may be asked to write reviews of three books. Your aim in writing the reviews would be to assess the worth of the books as contributions to the study of political science. The same is true for books on philosophy, psychology, sociology, history, and so on.

SAMPLE THEME

The Homecoming *and the Articulation of Silence: The Sound of One Hand Clapping* [1]

The Homecoming is in the tradition of the theatre of the absurd. To some readers, this fact may suggest grotesque characters, maimed in body and soul, who reside in garbage cans and do very little or who live in never-never lands and do very little as they wait for other characters who never appear. It may also suggest that the inarticulateness of the characters and the static action may at play's end create muteness and puzzlement in the audience. To a great extent, *The Homecoming* (1965) by the British dramatist Harold Pinter, shares these forbidding characteristics, but the play is also good theatre; in fact, it is fascinating theatre. It compels by virtue of its very inaction, and it reveals provocative insights into modern life. To gain these insights, however, the student of literature must devote himself to understanding Pinter's characters and his unusual techniques and conventions, for once these are studied, the play becomes richly suggestive and powerful.

The most dominating and pervasive character in the play is Max, a seventy-year-old ex-butcher, whose drab London home serves as the setting. Max is given no surname, an absence, like so many other absences in the play, that is part of Pinter's method to suggest the rootlessness—the aimlessness and facelessness—of modern man. The namelessness both intrigues and alienates the reader, for at the same time that he comes to know the characters intimately, he is aware of how little he knows about them and how much more he would like to know. But Pinter nevertheless presents many intimate and fascinating details: Living with Max are two of his sons, Lenny and Joey, and his sixty-three-year-old brother, Sam. Lenny is a sadist and apparently a pimp. Joey does demolition work dur-

1 Harold Pinter, *The Homecoming* (New York: Grove Press, 1965 & 1966).

ing the day and is attempting a career as a professional boxer at night. Sam is a chauffeur and also, apparently, a sodomist (at least, Max thinks he is a sodomist). The play receives its name because Teddy, Max's lethargic eldest son, who has become a professor of philosophy in America and has been away for six years, returns home with his wife Ruth, a pensive woman who formerly worked as a photographer's model.

One may expect no lessons in polite social behavior from such a set of characters. Gracious they are not. All the veneer of civilization is stripped away from them. It is almost as though Pinter has created the bare human consciousness, the stream of thoughts and reflections that are suppressed in ordinary human relationships, although they are nevertheless present. Here there are no artificial enthusiasms, no etiquette, where no kindness is; or, where there is a conventionally polite or meaningless comment, it is inappropriate, and it merely underlies the unconventionality of the situation. Thus, when Teddy unexpectedly returns home and is seen by Lenny, there is no warm greeting, no laughter, no inquiry into the past six years of separation, no merriment, no cordiality; there are only two minimally courteous but hollow "hullo's." Similarly, Teddy walks calmly away from his wife without a word of goodbye or reproach. Does the author suggest that human beings would behave thus if they did not feel compelled to follow the conventions of polite society? Is there a discrepancy between wishes and action, and if the two were fused, would human beings be like the characters in *The Homecoming*? If so, Pinter is presenting a revealing although not a happy truth about life.

The key to understanding the characters, in fact, and the cause for their appeal despite their shortcomings as fully rounded human beings, is that Pinter has made their behavior almost solely a function of their thoughts. He has taken a simple human incident, and has apparently asked this question about it: "What would happen under these circumstances if all the characters behaved exactly as they felt?" *The Homecoming* is his answer. The reader could easily envisage another set of matching incidents going on simultaneously, in which all the social graces would be causing the characters to behave conventionally. Much of the theatrical effectiveness of *The Homecoming* results from this unspoken but nevertheless real contrast between the stage action and the conventional action that might be expected under the same conditions.

One might pursue this avenue of speculation, for in the realm of suggestion and fantasy the play is a rich fabric of "could be's" and "might be's." The characters contribute to the richness of the play in many ways, one of these being their names. At the outset, we learn that Max is now old though once powerful, and that his brother, "Uncle Sam," is tired after chauffeuring people around all day. Could this be taken as Pinter's suggestion that the roles of England and America as world powers are nearing their end? Similarly, there is temptation to inquire into the meaning of the Biblical names. The dead Jessie was Max's wife and mother of his sons. Biblically, Jesse was the grandson of Ruth and the father of King David, from whose line the Messiah was to derive. Samuel (Sam) was influential in selecting David as king. According to some views, Joseph (Joey) was the father of Jesus, but according to others, he was no more than the husband of Mary (in this play, Joey gets no "gravy"; if this fact is intended as a Biblical allusion, what bizarre humor!). All these relations are of course mixed up in *The Homecoming,* and the names, except for Jessie, are common enough (and Teddy and Lenny are nonBiblical names). Because of the discussion between Lenny and Teddy, however, and also because of the general spiritual drift of Pinter's characters, the names may very well be a means of enforcing the assertion that people in the twentieth century have lost their certainty. The heroes of Biblical times are a far cry from the antiheroes of today; the world is minimal, everywhere minimal.

The play's action is similarly minimal. It would indeed be difficult to maintain that there is any action at all, as that word is usually understood, except for the brief violence at the end of the first act. The action in the second, concluding act involves not so much action as the development of an incredible scheme, hatched by the younger sons and the father, that involves Ruth. The most surprising action, which is the play's climax—if it has one—consists simply in Teddy's consenting to the scheme and his consequent departure. In short, the action is absurd.

This apparent senselessness or absurdity is also characteristic of other aspects of the play, the most obvious of which is Pinter's dialogue. The speech is sparse and laconic, interspersed with occasional rhapsodic outbursts as various characters become emotionally stimulated. Frequently the dialogue contains apparently illogical and irrelevant changes of subject, and in this regard it is perhaps more naturalistic than what appears in most other plays. Also realistic, in the sense of lifelike even though not "literary," are the many pauses that break up the speeches. These pauses are carefully written into the directions and on the stage would certainly produce a slow-moving, monolithic pace. The pauses also underline the essential solitude of most of the characters. As a particular character speaks, and hears no response, he waits a moment, then goes on, but the effect is to show that the other characters, instead of forming a responsive audience, really are part of an indifferent and self-occupied universe. Once again, the dialogue suggests, what would people say if they spoke as they really felt?

Out of such characteristics of *The Homecoming* one may find the same suggestiveness, ambiguity, and beauty of traditional literature. Symbolically, here are people living without illusions, with their ties to tradition cut; they have no reverence, as Lenny says, for the unknown, no faith. Knowledge and philosophy have filtered into irrelevant and snobbish channels, as with Teddy, and present no chance for nourishing the dessicated plants of life. The significant pauses in the speeches dramatize the conflict between man, on the one hand, and nothingness, on the other. In the world of Max and his sullen sons, there is little if anything to fill up the void—a family group with no real internal loyalty but much hostility. Through these characters and their strange dialogue and behavior, Pinter suggests that many families are such in name only, and that many homes are no more than places where people live together. To come home to such a place is not to receive warmth or love or strength with which to face the world.

In fact, *The Homecoming* is very much like a sporting event in which the team one supports is losing, except that in the play there is no winner. We see no victors dashing down the field in glory, only characters in a perpetual pose, like the retreating Teddy, of walking away from an increasing series of defeats. Certainly one cannot leave such a play in a mood of great cheer, but one must recognize that Pinter has created a world that is consistent with an important interpretation of modern life. There are many other diversionary pursuits that may provide the happy endings we enjoy witnessing, but Pinter's play is not one of these. As drama, *The Homecoming* successfully creates conflict, tension, and emotional repose. As philosophy, it creates the perplexity that a great segment of humanity is feeling today. One cannot expect more from the theatre.

Appendix A
Taking Examinations
on Literature

Taking an examination on literature is not difficult if you prepare in the right way. Preparing means (a) studying the material assigned, studying the comments made in class by your instructor and by fellow students in discussion, and studying your own thoughts; (b) anticipating the questions by writing some of your own on the material to be tested and by writing practice answers to these questions; and (c) understanding the precise function of the test in your education.

You should realize that the test is not designed to plague you or to hold down your grade. The grade you receive is in fact a reflection of your achievement in the course at the time the test is given. You have been admitted to a recognized institution of higher learning; therefore you may assume that you have the ability to do superior, satisfactory, or at least passing work. If your grades are low, the chances are great that you can improve them by studying in a coherent and systematic way. For many students, adequate preparation can make the difference between staying in school or leaving. Those students who can easily do satisfactory work might do superior work if they improve their method of preparation. From whatever level you begin, you can improve your achievement by improving your method of study.

Remember that your instructor prefers to see evidence of your improvement; he is anxious to read good examinations and would like to have them all excellent. Assuming that you write literate English, your instructor has two major concerns in evaluating your test: (a) to see the extent of your command over the subject material of the course ("How good is your retention?"), and (b) to see how well you are thinking and responding to the material ("How well are you educating yourself?"). Although you must never minimize the importance of factual command, the writing that reflects your understanding of these facts will be of prime significance in the determination of your grade. To phrase this idea another way: command over facts is important, and without it your mind cannot respond properly; but once the facts are remembered, your mental sharpness assumes prominence. Ultimately, any good test is designed to elicit the extent of your understanding at that given moment, in the belief that challenging your understanding is important to the growth of your mind. There should be no cavalier disregard of factual knowledge; without a factual basis your answers, and your mind, will amount to little.

Preparation

With these thoughts, your problem is how to prepare yourself best to have a knowledgeable and ready mind at examination time. If you simply cram facts into your head for the examination in hopes that you will be able to adjust to whatever questions are asked, you will likely flounder, and your examination will result in a boring chore for your instructor and an unsatisfactory grade for you.

Above all, keep in mind that your preparation should begin not on the night before the exam but as soon as the course begins. When each assignment is given, you should complete it by the date due, for you will understand your instructor's lecture and the classroom discussion only if you know the material being discussed. Then, about a week before the exam, you should review each assignment, preferably rereading each assignment completely. With this preparation completed, your study on the night before the exam will be fruitful, for it might be viewed as a climax of preparation, not the entire preparation itself.

Go over your notes, and as you do so, refer constantly to passages from the text that were mentioned and studied in class by your instructor. A good idea is to memorize as many significant phrases from the passages as possible; then when you are writing your exam your knowledge of a small passage can sometimes prod your memory of a long one. Also, a short quotation from the text shows your instructor that you have a good knowledge of the material. As you study, it is good to think not only about main ideas but also about technical matters, such as organization and style. Any time you have a reference in your notes (or in your memory) to technical problems, observe or recollect carefully what your instructor said about them, and about their relationship to ideas. Technique is always related to ideas, and if you show understanding of both, your exam is likely to be successful.

Your final preparation should consist of more than rereading your notes and re-examining key passages from the text. It should also contain writing and thinking, and here your ability to plan and practice your own questions and answers will be of great assistance. Make up some questions; perhaps you might rephrase a sentence from your notes into a question. Here is a brief fragment from some classroom notes on the subject of Dryden's *Absalom and Achitophel:* "A political poem—unintelligible unless one knows the politics of the time." Your sample question from this fragment might be: "Why is *Absalom and Achitophel* unintelligible without an understanding of the politics of the time?" Then you could spend fifteen or twenty minutes answering this question. Or you might look over a key passage from the text, decide what its subject is, and ask questions like "What does X say about _____ subject?" and "What is the effect of _____ in _____?" Spend as much time as possible in this way, making practice questions and answers on ideas and also on technique.

Let us try an example. Suppose you are reading Browning's "My Last Duchess." You might ask yourself this practice question about it: "Why did the Duke give orders to have his former wife killed?" Then you would begin writing an answer. About midway through you would realize that the question is difficult and ambiguous: *why* applies either to the reasons given by the Duke or to the conclusions you yourself have made. You might, as a result, recast the question into two: (1) "What reasons does the Duke reveal for having given the orders to kill his wife?" and (2) "What, in your opinion, are the reasons for which the Duke gave these orders?" You could then write a satisfactory answer to either one of these questions separately or could also make them two parts of the original question. From problems like these you would gain experience not only in asking, answering, and organizing questions, but in knowing that the phrasing of questions is important.

Your questions may, of course, be of all types. You might study the organization of a work carefully and then ask yourself about that organization. Or you might become interested in a certain character and wish to practice on a question asking for an analysis of that character. Time spent in this way can never be wasted, for as you carry on your practice *you are in fact studying with great care.* In addition, this practice will surely make the examination less of a surprise to you than it would be otherwise. The less you are surprised, the better will be your performance. Possibly you could even anticipate the questions your instructor might ask.

Sometimes another view can augment your own understanding of the material to be tested. If you find it possible to study with a fellow student, both of you can benefit from discussing what was said in class. In view of the necessity for steady preparation throughout a course, keep in mind that regular conversations (over coffee or some other beverage to your taste) well in advance of the examination are a good idea.

Questions

There are two types of questions that you will find on any examination about literature. Keep them in mind as you prepare. The first type is *factual*, or *mainly objective*, and the second is *general*, *broad*, or *mainly subjective*. In a literature course, however, very few questions are purely objective, except possibly for multiple-choice questions.

FACTUAL QUESTIONS

MULTIPLE-CHOICE QUESTIONS These are the most purely factual questions. You are familiar with them from college entrance exams and also, perhaps, from other courses. In a literature course, your instructor will most likely reserve them for short quizzes, usually on days when an assignment is due, to assure himself that you are keeping up with the reading. Multiple choice, of course, can test your knowledge of facts, and it also can test your ingenuity in perceiving subtleties of phrasing in certain choices. Multiple choice on a literature exam, however, is rare.

IDENTIFICATION QUESTIONS These questions are decidedly of more interest. They test not only your factual knowledge but also your ability to relate this knowledge to your understanding of the work assigned. This type of question will frequently be used as a check on the depth and scope of your reading. In fact, an entire exam could be composed of only identification questions, each demanding, perhaps, five minutes to write.

What might you be asked to identify? Typical examples are:

A Character, for example, Maria in Joyce's short story "Clay." You would try to indicate her position, background, her importance in the story, and especially her significance in Joyce's design. You should always emphasize the second part, for it shows your understanding.

Incidents, which may be described as follows: "A woman refuses to go on tour with a traveling show" (assuming that either *Sister Carrie* by Dreiser or *The Big Money* by Dos Passos is being tested). After you locate the incident, try to demonstrate its *significance* in the story's main design.

Things Your instructor may ask you to identify, say, an "overcoat" (Gogol's "Overcoat"), or "spunk water" (*Tom Sawyer*), or some other significant object.

Quotations Theoretically, you should remember enough of the text to identify a passage taken from it, or at least to make an informed guess. Generally, you should try to locate the quotation, if you remember it, or else to describe the probable location, and to show the ways in which the quotation is typical of the work you have read, with regard to both content and style. You can often salvage much from a momentary lapse of memory by writing a reasoned and careful explanation of your guess, even if the guess is incorrect.

TECHNICAL AND ANALYTICAL QUESTIONS AND PROBLEMS   In a scale of ascending importance, the third and most difficult type of factual question is on those matters with which this book has been concerned: technique, analysis, and problems. On your test you might be asked to discuss the *structure, tone, point of view,* or *principal idea* of a work; you might be asked about a *specific problem;* you might be asked to analyze a poem that may or may not be duplicated for your benefit (if it is not duplicated, woe to the student who has not read his assignments well). Questions like these are difficult, because they usually assume that you have a fairly technical knowledge of some important terms, while they also ask you to examine the text quite rigidly within the limitations imposed by the terms.

Obviously, technical questions will occur more frequently in advanced courses than in elementary ones, and the questions will become more subtle as the courses become more advanced. Instructors of elementary courses may frequently use main-idea or special-problem questions but will probably not use many of the others unless they specifically state their intentions to do so in advance, or unless technical terms have been studied in class.

Questions of this type are fairly long, perhaps with from fifteen to twenty-five minutes allowed for each. If you have two or more of these questions to write, try to space your time sensibly; do not devote eighty per cent of your time to one question, and only twenty per cent to the rest.

BASIS OF JUDGING FACTUAL QUESTIONS

In all factual questions, literate English being assumed, your instructor is testing (1) your factual command, and (2) your quickness in relating a part to the whole. Thus, suppose that you are identifying the incident "A woman refuses to go on tour with a traveling show." You would identify Sister Carrie as the woman, and say that she is advised by her friend, Lola, to stay in New York (where the big opportunity is) and not to go on tour, where nobody important will see her. You would also try to show that the incident occurs when Carrie is just a minor dancer, during her early years in show business. But, you should, more importantly, show that her decision leaves her in New York, where a new opportunity develops, quickly enabling Carrie to become a star. You should conclude by saying that the incident prepares the way for all Carrie's later successes and shows how far she has advanced above Hurstwood's deteriorating state, monetarily speaking. The incident can therefore be seen as one of the most significant in the entire novel.

Your answers should all take this general pattern. Always try to show the *significance* of the things you are identifying. *Significance* of course works in many directions, but in a short identification question you should always try to refer to (1) major events in the book, (2) major ideas, (3) the structure of the work, and (4) in a quotation, the style. Time is short; therefore you must be selective, but if you can set your mind toward producing answers along these lines, you will probably approach what your instructor expects.

Here are three answers that were written to an identification question. The students were asked to identify "The thing which was not," from the fourth voyage of Swift's *Gulliver's Travels*.

> *Answer 1.* This quotation serves as an example of a typical saying in the language of the Houyhnhnms. It means that the thing was false. It shows their roundabout method of saying things.
>
> *Answer 2.* This quotation is found in Chapter IV of "A Voyage to the Country of the Houyhnhnms." Gulliver is told this said quotation by his Master one of the Houyhnhnms (a horse). It is brought out when the two of them are discussing their own customs and culture, and Gulliver is telling his master how he sailed over to this country. The Master finds it hard to believe. He tells Gulliver that lying is altogether foreign to the culture of the Houyhnhnms. He says speech is for the purpose of being understood and he cannot comprehend lying and is unfamiliar with doubt. He goes on to say that if someone says "the thing which was not" the whole end of speech is defeated. I think what the master has said to Gulliver clearly illustrates Swift's thought that man should use language as a means to communicate truth or otherwise its purpose is defeated. We can also see Swift's thought that this very beautiful concept of language and its use is not taken up by man. This degrades mankind.
>
> *Answer 3. The thing which was not,* a variation on *"is* not," is used throughout the fourth voyage of *Gulliver* by the Houyhnhnm Master as a term for lying—telling a thing contrary to fact. The term is interesting because it shows a completely reasonable reaction (represented by that of the Houyhnhnm Master) toward a lie, with all the subtle variations on the word we have in English. By whatever term we use, a lie is *a thing which is not* (except in the mind of the person who tells it) and destroys the chief end of speech—truthful communication. The term is therefore an integral part of Swift's attack in *Gulliver* on the misuse of reason. A lie misleads the reason, and thereby destroys all the processes of reason (e.g., logic, science, law) by supplying it with nonexistent things. Because our civilization depends on the reasonable pursuit of truth, a lie about anything is thus actually an attack on civilization itself. Swift's Houuhynhnms have this value, then, that they provide us with a reasonable basis for judging elements in our own life, and hopefully, for improving them where reason can improve them.

The first answer is not satisfactory, since it is inaccurate in sentences 1 and 3, and does not indicate much thought about the meaning of the quotation. The second answer is satisfactory; despite faults of style, it shows knowledge of the conditions under which the quotation is made, and also indicates some understanding of the general meaning of the quotation. The third answer is superior, for it relates the quotation to Swift's satiric purposes in *Gulliver's Travels* and also shows how lying actually becomes a perversion of language and reason. The distinguishing mark of the third answer is that it shows *thorough* understanding.

One thing is clear from these sample answers: *really superior answers cannot be written if your thinking originates entirely at the time you are faced with the question;* the more thinking and practicing you do before the exam, the better your answers will be. Obviously the writer of the third answer was not caught unprepared. You should reduce surprise on an exam to an absolute minimum.

The more extended factual questions pose, in addition to the problem of showing knowledge of facts and understanding of significance, the necessity for more thoroughly developed organization. Remember that here your knowledge of essay writing is important, for the quality of your composition will inevitably determine a part, or perhaps a major share, of your instructor's evaluation of your answers.

It is therefore best to take several minutes to gather your thoughts together before you begin to write, because a ten-minute planned answer is preferable to a twenty-five minute unplanned answer. Surprising as this idea may seem, you do not need to write down every possible fact on each particular question. Of greater significance is the use to which you put the facts you know and the organization of your answer. When the questions are before you, use a sheet of scratch paper to jot down the facts you remember and your ideas about them in relation to the question. Then put them together, phrase a thesis sentence, and use your facts to illustrate or prove your thesis.

It is always necessary, particularly when you are dealing with "problem" questions, to work key phrases from the original questions into your thesis sentence. Let us suppose that you are given the question: "What are some reasons for which Dick Diver loses his professional abilities and consequently drifts into oblivion?" (Fitzgerald's *Tender is the Night*). Your answer might begin in the following way: "Dick Diver loses his professional abilities for many reasons. Fitzgerald suggests that many of his energies are taken up by Nicole, but I believe that a more comprehensive reason is the paralysis of his self-esteem resulting from his superficial life among the international set. . . ." Presumably, your answer would then proceed to discuss the view you attribute to Fitzgerald and then your own. Notice that your first sentence clearly states the aims and limits of the answer, so that your answer will be completely self-contained. Whatever your method, however, do not simply start writing without reference to the question, for if your first sentence does not describe the answer to follow, your instructor will probably feel that he is reading your answer in a vacuum, and your grade will be affected accordingly. Your best approach to tests is to regard each answer as a small essay, demanding good writing, thinking, and organizing.

For comparison, here are two paragraphs from a twenty-five minute question on Fitzgerald's story "The Rich Boy." The question was: "What do Anson's two love affairs contribute to your understanding of his character?" Both paragraphs are about Anson's first love affair, with Paula Legendre:

1

The Paula affair helps understand Anson. Paula best understood him through their relationship. Anson was searching for stability and security in life; he felt he could achieve these with Paula. This was shown through the following idea: if only he could be with Paula he would be happy. Paula saw him as a mixture of solidity and self-indulgence and cynicism. She deeply loved him, but it was impossible for him to form a lasting relationship with her. The reason for this was his drinking, and his code of superiority. This was shown in the fact that he felt hopeless despair before his pride and his self-knowledge. His superiority can be further observed through his physical and emotional relationship with Paula. His entire relationship with Paula was based on his feelings that emotion was sufficient, and why should he commit himself? Her marriage greatly affected Anson; it made a cynic out of him. His attitude toward women influenced his relationship with Dolly, too.

2

To show that Anson has a dual nature, Fitzgerald develops the Paula Legendre episode at great length. Paula represents everything that Anson's reliable side needs: conservatism, equality of social and economic position, earnestness of purpose, and love. Presumably, the lengthy, low conversations between the two are presented to illustrate the positive, substantial character of Anson. But Fitzgerald is also illustrating the weakness of Anson's character—a weakness that he brings out by the relationship with Paula. As a result of a lifelong position of unchallenged wealth and status, without any real responsibility, Anson has developed into a man of shallow and superficial emotions, even though he *knows*, consciously, what mature emotions are. Thus, he cannot face the responsibility of marriage with Paula: he gets drunk and embarrasses her; he delays proposing marriage at the logical moment in the magic of love and moonlight, and therefore he lets Paula's mood vanish forever into the night. When Paula, who despite her wealth is more stable than Anson, marries another man, Anson's serious side is deeply disturbed, but his superficial side is made happy. Unfortunately, this division has made him a perpetual child, unable to cope with adult life. These same characteristics are also enforced by Fitzgerald in the affair with Dolly Karger.

It is easy to see that Column 2 is superior to Column 1. If Column 1 were judged as part of an outside-class theme, it would be a failure, but as part of a test it would probably receive a passing grade. Column 2 is clearer; it develops its point well, and uses evidence more accurately to illustrate its point.

GENERAL QUESTIONS

Many students are fond of the *general, broad,* or *freewheeling* question, which they like to regard as *subjective,* giving them the opportunity to demonstrate their mental proficiency. These students prefer the general question to the specific question, which, they feel, forces them to remember mere, picayunish details. The reason for their preference is fairly easy to assess, for frequently students may interpret a question so broadly that they ignore the obviously intended implications of the question and devote themselves to answering some other question that was never really in the instructor's mind. Then, in later discussions with their instructor, they defend their "interpretations" and plead for higher marks. Defending a poor performance in this way is deplorable and sometimes deceitful, not to speak of its damaging effect on the purpose of education. For these reasons, many instructors avoid broad questions—and the resulting problems—entirely.

Despite abuses, however, there is a definite place for general questions, particularly on final examinations, when your instructor is interested in testing your general or "total" comprehension of the course material. You have much freedom of choice in deciding what to write, but you must constantly bear in mind that your instructor is looking for intelligence and knowledge in what you choose to say.

Considerable time is usually allowed for answering a general question, perhaps forty-five minutes or more, depending on the scope and depth that your instructor expects. He may phrase the question in a number of ways:

1. A direct question asking about philosophy, underlying attitudes, "schools" of literature or literary movements, main ideas, characteristics of style, backgrounds, and so on. Here are some typical questions in this category: "Define and characterize Metaphysical poetry," or "Discuss the influences of science on literature in the Restoration," or "Describe the dramatic prose of the Jacobean dramatists."

2. A "comment" question, usually based on an extensive quotation, borrowed from a critic or written by your instructor for the occasion, about a broad class of writers, or about a literary movement, or the like. Your instructor may ask you to treat this question broadly (taking in many writers) or he may ask you to apply the quotation to a specific writer.

3. A "suppose" question, such as "Suppose Rosalind were in Desdemona's place; what would she do when Othello accused her of infidelity?" or "What would Pope say about Joyce's *Ulysses?*"

BASIS OF JUDGING GENERAL OR
FREEWHEELING QUESTIONS

As these questions are fairly fluid, all the previous remarks about good writing apply. Organizing your material is a greater problem than it is on factual questions, because your choice of material is more free and because you must solve the initial problem not only of what you *know,* but also of what you *select.* You might say that you make your own question, because your first job is to deal with general questions in terms that you can handle; you must narrow the question, but you must be sure that you stay within its limits.

Your instructor is interested in seeing: (a) the intelligence of your selection of material, (b) the quality of your organization, (c) the adequacy and intelligence of the generalizations you make about the material, and (d) the *relevance* of the facts you select for illustration.

In questions of this sort, you must avoid inconsequentiality. It is easy to write a tissue of glittering generalities that really amount to so much nonsense, unless you are careful to illustrate their truth from the assigned material. It is also easy to misinterpret the material and bring forth evidence that does not support the otherwise valid generalizations you have made. The first fault is usually a result of inadequate knowledge; the second of inadequate logic. Any low grades will reflect either or both.

Parting Advice

Whenever you take an exam, use your common sense about answering questions. Answer the questions asked, and not some others, for your instructor is interested in seeing how well you follow directions and observe the wording of the questions. If the question begins "Why does . . ." be sure to explain *why* the subject indeed *does;* do not just describe *what* is *done.* If you are asked to describe the organization of a literary work, be sure to describe the *organization.* Remember that a principal cause of low grades on exams is that many students do nothing but write a synopsis, without ever answering the questions asked. Look at the questions carefully, and answer them, trying always to deal with the issues in them. In this way, you can insure success on your exam.

Appendix B
A Note
on Documentation

It is not the intention here to present a complete discussion of documentation but only as much as is necessary for a typical theme about literature. You will find complete discussions in most writing handbooks and guidebooks to research, and in the *MLA Style Sheet*. Whenever you have questions about documentation, always ask your instructor.

In any writing not derived purely from your own mind, you must document your facts. In writing about literature, you must base your conclusions on material in particular literary works and must document this material. If you ever refer to secondary sources, as in themes about genre or about a literary work as it reflects its historical period, you must be especially careful to document your facts (see Chapters 4 and 14). To document properly you must use illustrative material in your discussion and mention the sources for this material either in your discussion or in footnotes to it.

Illustrative Quotations

When you wish to make fairly extensive quotations in a theme, you should leave three blank lines between your own discourse and the quotation, single-space the quotation, and make a special indention for it. The following example is a fragment from a theme about John Gay's *Trivia,* an early eighteenth-century poem. Here is the physical layout of the writer's discussion and the quotation:

> In the poem Gay shows his familiarity with the practices of the many hoodlums and bullies of his time. According to him, many Londoners lived in dread. We may presume that they did not dare to walk the streets at night for fear of being mugged by a gang of toughs:

> Now is the time that rakes their revels keep;
> Kindlers of riot, enemies of sleep.
> His scattered pence the flying Nicker flings,
> And with the copper shower the casement rings.
> Who has not heard the Scourer's midnight fame?
> Who has not trembled at the Mohock's name?
>
> —lines 321-326

> If I thought Mohocks and Scourers would come after me to rob me and beat me, I would not venture out myself.

The same layout applies when you are quoting prose passages. In quoting lines of poetry, you must always remember to quote them as lines. Do not run them together. When you center the quotations as in the example, you do not need quotation marks.

If you wish to use shorter quotations, incorporate them directly into your discussion, as parts of your sentences set off by quotation marks. If you quote consecutive lines of poetry, indicate the conclusion of each line with a bar or slash (/) and begin each new line with a capital letter. Show omissions by three periods (. . .), but if your quotation is short, do not surround it with the periods. Look at the absurdity of using the three periods in a sentence like this one: "Keats asserts that '. . . a thing of beauty . . .' always gives joy." Indicate words of your own within the quotations by enclosing them in square brackets ([ ]). Here is another fragment to exemplify these practices:

> In his poem, Gay deplores the miseries of the city at night. If a person must go out, he discovers that "Where a dim gleam the paly [i.e., dim] lanthorn throws / O'er the mid pavement, heapy rubbish grows" (335-336). If a person is unlucky enough to go out riding in a coach, he may find himself "In the wide gulf" where "the shattered coach o'erthrown / Sinks with the . . . steeds" (342-343).

Always reproduce your source exactly. Because most freshman anthologies and texts modernize the spelling and punctuation in works that are old, the problem may never arise. But if you use an unmodernized text, as in many advanced courses, duplicate everything exactly as you find it. Suppose that in a seventeenth-century work you encounter the word *divers* with the meaning of the modern *diverse*. If you modernize the spelling (*divers* in this sense is now archaic), you change the accent and thereby affect the rhythm of the passage you have been reading. In prose, this change would perhaps be immaterial, but in poetry it would definitely be unfortunate. Similarly, if you start changing spelling, you should theoretically change punctuation. Or suppose you encounter a word that is no longer used; should you replace the original with a modern word with the same meaning? In other words, when do you stop modernizing and start corrupting your text? You are better off to leave it exactly as you find it.

Footnotes and Informal References

To indicate the source of all factual material you must use footnotes at the bottom of your page or at the end of your theme, or else you must, in the body of your discussion, mention the page number from the source. Although the care necessary for noting book names and page numbers often annoys many students, you should realize that footnotes and informal references exist not to cause you trouble but to help your reader. First, your reader may want to consult your source in order to assure himself that you have not misstated any facts. Second, he may dispute your conclusions and wish to see your source in order to arrive at his own conclusions. Third, he may become so interested in one of your points that he might wish to read more about it for his own pleasure or edification. For these reasons, you must show the source of all material that you use.

If you are using many sources in a research report, it is wise to document your paper formally. Use the formal apparatus in the section on research themes in your writing handbook or in the *MLA Style Sheet*. If you are using only a primary source, however, as is true of most of the theme assignments in this book, you may be guided by the following.

The first time you make a quotation from a source, or refer to the source, you should write a footnote, which should contain the following information in this order:

FOR A BOOK

1 The author's name, first name or initials first.
2 The name of the story or poem, in quotation marks.
3 The name of the book, underlined.
4 The edition, if it is indicated (e.g., "Fourth edition").
5 The name or names of the editor or editors, if any. Abbreviate *editor* by *ed., editors* by *eds.*
6 Within parentheses:
   (a) The city of publication, followed by a colon. Do not include the state or country unless the city might be confused with another (e.g., Cambridge, Mass.) or unless the city is unlikely to be known by any but natives in its particular area (e.g., Larchmont, N.Y.; Emmaeus, Pa.).
   (b) The publisher. This information is frequently not given, but it is wise to include it.[1]
   (c) The year of publication.

[1] If faced with a choice, some editors prefer citing the publisher rather than the city of publication. For identification purposes, this citation is more accurate, but as yet has not come into general use. Ask your instructor about his preferences, and be guided by his advice.

7 The page number or numbers. For books commonly reprinted (like *Gulliver's Travels*) and for well-known long poems (like *Paradise Lost*) you should include chapter or part numbers or line numbers, because many readers might locate your source in a different edition.

FOR A MAGAZINE ARTICLE

1 The author, first name or initials first.
2 The title of the article, in quotation marks.
3 The name of the magazine, underlined.
4 The volume number, in Roman numerals.
5 The year of publication, within parentheses.
6 The page number or numbers.

SAMPLE FOOTNOTES

[1] Joseph Conrad, *The Rescue: A Romance of the Shallows* (New York: Doubleday & Co., Inc., 1960), p. 103.

[2] George Milburn, "The Apostate," *An Approach to Literature,* 3rd ed., Cleanth Brooks, John Thibaut Purser, and Robert Penn Warren, eds. (New York: Appleton-Century-Crofts, Inc., 1952), p. 74.

[3] Carlisle Moore, "Conrad and the Novel as Ordeal," *Philological Quarterly,* XLII (1963), 59. (Notice that when you give a volume number, you do not put a *p.* before the page number.)

Suppose that in your theme you have mentioned the name of your book and the author. Then you should include only that material that pertains to publication, as in this example, assuming that John Gay's ballad opera *Polly* is the subject of your discussion:

[4] (London: William Heineman, Ltd., 1923), p. 16 (Act I, Sc. vii).

SUBSEQUENT REFERENCES TO FOOTNOTED SOURCE

For themes about one work of literature, you may use the following informal procedure. The principle of informal documentation is to incorporate as much documentation as possible into your discussion, in order to avoid the bother of footnoting.

1. In your first footnote, indicate that all later references to the source will be indicated in parentheses:

[1] Lucian, *True History and Lucius or the Ass,* trans. Paul Turner (Bloomington: Indiana University Press, 1958), p. 49. All parenthetical page numbers refer to this edition.

2. The next time you refer to the source, do the following:
   (a) If you are making an indented quotation, indicate the page

number, line number, or chapter number, preceded by a dash, immediately below the quotation, as follows:

> Nobody grows old there, for they all stay the age they were when they first arrived, and it never gets dark. On the other hand, it never gets really light either, and they live in a sort of perpetual twilight, such as we have just before sunrise.
>
> —p. 39

(b) If you are incorporating a quotation into your own discussion, do the following:

   i If your sentence ends with the quotation, put the reference in parentheses immediately following the quotation marks and immediately before the period concluding your sentence:

> Sidney uses the example that "the Romaine lawes allowed no person to be carried to the warres but hee that was in the Souldiers role" (p. 189).

   ii If the quotation ends near the conclusion of your sentence, put the reference in parentheses at the end of your sentence before the period:

> William Webbe states that poetry originated in the needs for "eyther exhortations to vertue, dehortations from vices, or the prayses of some laudable thing"; that is, in public needs (p. 248).

   iii If the quotation ends far away from the end of your sentence, put the reference in parentheses immediately following the quotation mark but before your own mark of punctuation:

> If we accept as a truth Thomas Lodge's statement, "Chaucer in pleasant vein can rebuke sin vncontrold" (p. 69), then satire and comedy are the most effective modes of moral persuasion in literature.

Here is a final admonition: in all cases, consult your instructor about the procedures he prefers. He is your final authority.

Appendix C

Robert Frost (1874–1963)

Desert Places

Snow falling and night falling fast, oh, fast
In a field I looked into going past,
And the ground almost covered smooth in snow,
But a few weeds and stubble showing last.

The woods around it have it—it is theirs.
All animals are smothered in their lairs.
I am too absent-spirited to count;
The loneliness includes me unawares.

And lonely as it is that loneliness
Will be more lonely ere it will be less—
A blanker whiteness of benighted snow
With no expression, nothing to express.

They cannot scare me with their empty spaces
Between stars—on stars where no human race is.
I have it in me so much nearer home
To scare myself with my own desert places.

John Donne (1572–1631)

Good Friday, 1613, Riding Westward

Let mans Soule be a Spheare, and then, in this,
The intelligence that moves, devotion is,
And as the other Spheares, by being growne
Subject to forraigne motions, lose their owne,
And being by others hurried every day,   5
Scarce in a yeare their naturall forme obey:
Pleasure or businesse, so, our Soules admit
For their first mover, and are whirld by it.
Hence is't, that I am carryed towards the West
This day, when my Soules forme bends toward the East.   10
There I should see a Sunne, by rising set,
And by that setting endlesse day beget;
But that Christ on this Crosse, did rise and fall,
Sinne had eternally benighted all.
Yet dare I almost be glad, I do not see   15
That spectacle of too much weight for mee.
Who sees Gods face, that is selfe life, must dye;
What a death were it then to see God dye?
It made his owne Lieutenant Nature shrinke,
It made his footstoole crack, and the Sunne winke.   20
Could I behold those hands which span the Poles,
And tune all Spheares at once, peirc'd with those holes?
Could I behold that endlesse height which is
Zenith to us, and our Antipodes,
Humbled below us? or that blood which is   25
The seat of all our Soules, if not of his,
Made durt of dust, or that flesh which was worne
By God, for his apparell, rag'd, and torne?
If on these things I durst not looke, durst I
Upon his miserable mother cast mine eye,   30
Who was Gods partner here, and furnish'd thus
Halfe of that Sacrifice, which ransom'd us?
Though these things, as I ride, be from mine eye,
They are present yet unto my memory,
For that looks towards them; and thou look'st towards mee,   35
O Saviour, as thou hang'st upon the tree;
I turne my backe to thee, but to receive
Corrections, till thy mercies bid thee leave.
O thinke mee worth thine anger, punish mee,
Burne off my rusts, and my deformity,   40
Restore thine Image, so much, by thy grace,
That thou may'st know mee, and I'll turne my face.

From POEMS, a collection of the works of John Donne, published 1633.

John Donne

A Feaver

Oh doe not die, for I shall hate
   All women so, when thou art gone,
That thee I shall not celebrate,
   When I remember, thou wast one.

But yet thou canst not die, I know,   5
   To leave this world behinde, is death,
But when thou from this world wilt goe,
   The whole world vapors with thy breath.

Or if, when thou, the worlds soule, goest,
   It stay, tis but thy carkasse then,   10
The fairest woman, but thy ghost,
   But corrupt wormes, the worthyest men.

O wrangling schooles, that search what fire
   Shall burne this world, had none the wit
Unto this knowledge to aspire,   15
   That this her feaver might be it?

And yet she cannot waste by this,
   Nor long beare this torturing wrong,
For such corruption needfull is
   To fuell such a feaver long.   20

These burning fits but meteors bee,
   Whose matter in thee is soone spent.
Thy beauty, and all parts, which are thee,
   Are unchangeable firmament.

Yet t'was of my minde, seising thee,   25
   Though it in thee cannot persever.
For I had rather owner bee
   Of thee one houre, than all else ever.

From POEMS, 1633.

William Wordsworth (1770–1850)

Stepping Westward

While my Fellow-traveller and I were walking by the side of Loch Ket-
terine, one fine evening after sunset, in our road to a Hut where, in the
course of our Tour, we had been hospitably entertained some weeks before, we met, in one of the loneliest parts of that solitary region, two well-

dressed Women, one of whom said to us, by way of greeting, "What, you are stepping westward?"

"What, you are stepping westward?"—"Yea."
—'T would be a *wildish* destiny,
If we, who thus together roam
In a strange Land, and far from home,
Were in this place the guests of Chance: 5
Yet who would stop, or fear to advance,
Though home or shelter he had none,
With such a sky to lead him on?

The dewy ground was dark and cold;
Behind, all gloomy to behold;   10
And stepping westward seemed to be
A kind of *heavenly* destiny:
I liked the greeting; 't was a sound
Of something without place or bound;
And seemed to give me spiritual right   15
To travel through that region bright.

The voice was soft, and she who spake
Was walking by her native lake:
The salutation had to me
The very sound of courtesy: 20
Its power was felt; and while my eye
Was fixed upon the glowing Sky,
The echo of the voice enwrought
A human sweetness with the thought
Of travelling through the world that lay   25
Before me in my endless way.

William Wordsworth

Lines Composed a Few Miles Above Tintern Abbey, on Revisiting the Banks of the Wye During a Tour, July 13, 1798

No poem of mine was composed under circumstances more pleasant for me to remember than this. I began it upon leaving Tintern, after crossing the Wye, and concluded it just as I was entering Bristol in the evening, after a ramble of four or five days, with my Sister. Not a line of it was altered, and not any part of it written down till I reached Bristol. It was published almost immediately after.

Five years have past; five summers, with the length
Of five long winters! and again I hear
These waters, rolling from their mountain-springs
With a soft inland murmur.—Once again
Do I behold these steep and lofty cliffs,   5
That on a wild secluded scene impress
Thoughts of more deep seclusion; and connect
The landscape with the quiet of the sky.
The day is come when I again repose
Here, under this dark sycamore, and view   10
These plots of cottage-ground, these orchard-tufts,
Which at this season, with their unripe fruits,
Are clad in one green hue, and lose themselves
'Mid groves and copses. Once again I see
These hedge-rows, hardly hedge-rows, little lines   15
Of sportive wood run wild: these pastoral farms,
Green to the very door; and wreaths of smoke
Sent up, in silence, from among the trees!
With some uncertain notice, as might seem
Of vagrant dwellers in the houseless woods,   20
Or of some Hermit's cave, where by his fire
The Hermit sits alone.
                These beauteous forms,
Through a long absence, have not been to me
As is a landscape to a blind man's eye:
But oft, in lonely rooms, and 'mid the din   25
Of towns and cities, I have owed to them
In hours of weariness, sensations sweet,
Felt in the blood, and felt along the heart;
And passing even into my purer mind,
With tranquil restoration:—feelings too   30
Of unremembered pleasure: such, perhaps,
As have no slight or trivial influence
On that best portion of a good man's life,
His little, nameless, unremembered, acts
Of kindness and of love. Nor less, I trust,   35
To them I may have owed another gift,
Of aspect more sublime; that blessed mood,
In which the burthen of the mystery,
In which the heavy and the weary weight
Of all this unintelligible world,   40
Is lightened:—that serene and blessed mood,
In which the affections gently lead us on,—
Until, the breath of this corporeal frame
And even the motion of our human blood
Almost suspended, we are laid asleep   45

In body, and become a living soul:
While with an eye made quiet by the power
Of harmony, and the deep power of joy,
We see into the life of things.
                                   If this
Be but a vain belief, yet, oh! how oft—   50
In darkness and amid the many shapes
Of joyless daylight; when the fretful stir
Unprofitable, and the fever of the world,
Have hung upon the beatings of my heart—
How oft, in spirit, have I turned to thee,   55
O sylvan Wye! thou wanderer thro' the woods,
How often has my spirit turned to thee!
    And now, with gleams of half-extinguished thought,
With many recognitions dim and faint,
And somewhat of a sad perplexity,   60
The picture of the mind revives again:
While here I stand, not only with the sense
Of present pleasure, but with pleasing thoughts
That in this moment there is life and food
For future years. And so I dare to hope,   65
Though changed, no doubt, from what I was when first
I came among these hills; when like a roe
I bounded o'er the mountains, by the sides
Of the deep rivers, and the lonely streams,
Wherever nature led: more like a man   70
Flying from something that he dreads, than one
Who sought the thing he loved. For nature then
(The coarser pleasures of my boyish days,
And their glad animal movements all gone by)
To me was all in all.—I cannot paint   75
What then I was. The sounding cataract
Haunted me like a passion: the tall rock,
The mountain, and the deep and gloomy wood,
Their colours and their forms, were then to me
An appetite; a feeling and a love,   80
That had no need of a remoter charm,
By thought supplied, nor any interest
Unborrowed from the eye.—That time is past,
And all its aching joys are now no more,
And all its dizzy raptures. Not for this   85
Faint I, nor mourn nor murmur; other gifts
Have followed; for such loss, I would believe,
Abundant recompense. For I have learned
To look on nature, not as in the hour
Of thoughtless youth; but hearing oftentimes   90

The still, sad music of humanity,
Nor harsh nor grating, though of ample power
To chasten and subdue. And I have felt
A presence that disturbs me with the joy
Of elevated thoughts; a sense sublime   95
Of something far more deeply interfused,
Whose dwelling is the light of setting suns,
And the round ocean and the living air,
And the blue sky, and in the mind of man;
A motion and a spirit, that impels   100
All thinking things, all objects of all thought,
And rolls through all things. Therefore am I still
A lover of the meadows and the woods,
And mountains; and of all that we behold
From this green earth; of all the mighty world   105
Of eye, and ear,—both what they half create,
And what perceive; well pleased to recognise
In nature and the language of the sense,
The anchor of my purest thoughts, the nurse,
The guide, the guardian of my heart, and soul   110
Of all my moral being.
                              Nor perchance,
If I were not thus taught, should I the more
Suffer my genial spirits to decay:
For thou art with me here upon the banks
Of this fair river; thou my dearest Friend,   115
My dear, dear Friend; and in thy voice I catch
The language of my former heart, and read
My former pleasures in the shooting lights
Of thy wild eyes. Oh! yet a little while
May I behold in thee what I was once,   120
My dear, dear Sister! and this prayer I make,
Knowing that Nature never did betray
The heart that loved her; 'tis her privilege,
Through all the years of this our life, to lead
From joy to joy: for she can so inform   125
The mind that is within us, so impress
With quietness and beauty, and so feed
With lofty thoughts, that neither evil tongues,
Rash judgments, nor the sneers of selfish men,
Nor greetings where no kindness is, nor all   130
The dreary intercourse of daily life,
Shall e'er prevail against us, or disturb
Our cheerful faith, that all which we behold
Is full of blessings. Therefore let the moon
Shine on thee in thy solitary walk;   135

And let the misty mountain-winds be free
To blow against thee: and, in after years,
When these wild ecstasies shall be matured
Into a sober pleasure; when thy mind
Shall be a mansion for all lovely forms,   140
Thy memory be as a dwelling-place
For all sweet sounds and harmonies; oh! then,
If solitude, or fear, or pain, or grief,
Should be thy portion, with what healing thoughts
Of tender joy wilt thou remember me,   145
And these my exhortations! Nor, perchance—
If I should be where I no more can hear
Thy voice, nor catch from thy wild eyes these gleams
Of past existence—wilt thou then forget
That on the banks of this delightful stream   150
We stood together; and that I, so long
A worshipper of Nature, hither came
Unwearied in that service: rather say
With warmer love—oh! with far deeper zeal
Of holier love. Nor wilt thou then forget,   155
That after many wanderings, many years
Of absence, these steep woods and lofty cliffs,
And this green pastoral landscape, were to me
More dear, both for themselves and for thy sake!

Jonathan Swift (1667–1745)

from A TALE OF A TUB

SECT. IX.

*A Digression concerning the Original,
the Use and Improvement of* Madness
in a Commonwealth

NOR shall it any ways detract from the just Reputation of this famous Sect, that its Rise and Institution are owing to such an Author as I have described *Jack* to be; A Person whose Intellectuals were overturned, and his Brain shaken out of its Natural Position; which we commonly suppose to be a Distemper, and call by the Name of *Madness* or *Phrenzy.* For, if we take a Survey of the greatest Actions that have been performed in the World, under the Influence of Single Men; which are, *The Establishment of New Empires by Conquest: The Advance and Progress of New Schemes in Philosophy; and the contriving, as well as the propagating of New Religions:* We shall find the Authors of them all, to have been Persons, whose natural Reason hath admitted great Revolutions from their Dyet, their Education, the Prevalency of some certain Temper, together with the particular Influence of Air and Climate. Besides, there is something Individual in human Minds, that easily kindles at the accidental Approach and Collision of certain Circumstances, which tho' of paltry and mean Appearance, do often flame out into the greatest Emergencies of Life. For great Turns are not always given by strong Hands, but by lucky Adaption, and at proper Seasons; and it is of no import, where the Fire was kindled, if the Vapor has once got up into the Brain. For the *upper Region* of Man, is furnished like the *middle Region* of the Air; The Materials are formed from Causes of the widest Difference, yet produce at last the same Substance and Effect. Mists arise from the Earth, Steams from Dunghils, Exhalations from the Sea, and Smoak from Fire; yet all Clouds are the same in Composition, as well as Consequences: and the Fumes issuing from a Jakes,[1] will furnish as comely and useful a Vapor, as Incense from an Altar. Thus far, I suppose will easily be granted me; and then it will follow, that as the Face of Nature never produces Rain, but when it is overcast and disturbed, so Human Understanding, seated in the Brain, must be troubled and overspread by Vapours, ascending from the lower Faculties, to water the Invention, and render it fruitful. Now, altho' these Vapours (as it hath

Jonathan Swift, A TALE OF A TUB, ed. Guthkelch and Nichol Smith, 2nd ed., 1958. Reprinted by permission of the Clarendon Press, Oxford.
1 An outdoor toilet.

been already said) are of as various Original, as those of the Skies, yet the Crop they produce, differs both in Kind and Degree, meerly according to the Soil. I will produce two Instances to prove and Explain what I am now advancing.

A certain Great Prince raised a mighty Army, filled his Coffers with infinite Treasures, provided an invincible Fleet, and all this, without giving the least Part of his Design to his greatest Ministers, or his nearest Favourites.[2] Immediately the whole World was alarmed; the neighbouring Crowns, in trembling Expectation, towards what Point the Storm would burst; the small Politicians, every where forming profound Conjectures. Some believed he had laid a Scheme for Universal Monarchy: Others, after much Insight, determined the Matter to be a Project for pulling down the *Pope,* and setting up the *Reformed* Religion, which had once been his own. Some, again, of a deeper Sagacity, sent him into *Asia* to subdue the *Turk,* and recover *Palestine.* In the midst of all these Projects and Preparations; a certain *State-Surgeon,*[3] gathering the Nature of the Disease by these Symptoms, attempted the Cure, at one Blow performed the Operation, broke the Bag, and out flew the *Vapour;* nor did any thing want to render it a compleat Remedy, only, that the Prince unfortunately happened to Die in the Performance. Now, is the Reader exceeding curious to learn, from whence this *Vapour* took its Rise, which had so long set the Nations at a Gaze? What secret Wheel, what hidden Spring could put into Motion so wonderful an Engine? It was afterwards discovered, that the Movement of this whole Machine had been directed by an absent *Female,* whose Eyes had raised a Protuberancy, and before Emission, she was removed into an Enemy's Country. What should an unhappy Prince do in such ticklish Circumstances as these? He tried in vain the Poet's never-failing Receipt of *Corpora quæque;*[4] For,

> *Idque petit corpus mens unde est saucia amore;*[5]
> *Unde feritur, eo tendit, gestitq; coire.*[6] Lucr.

HAVING to no purpose used all peaceable Endeavours, the collected part of the *Semen,* raised and enflamed, became adust,[7] converted

[2] *This was* Harry *the Great of* France (Swift's note).

[3] Ravillac, *who stabb'd* Henry *the Great in his Coach* (Swift's note).

[4] A free translation of this phrase is that one sublimates his sexual energy upon "some other body." See *Lucretius, De Rerum Natura,* trans. W. H. D. Rouse, The Loeb Classical Library (Cambridge, Mass.: Harvard University Press, 1937), p. 322 (IV, 1065).

[5] Freely, "and the body aches to possess the one whose person wounds the mind with love." *Lucretius,* p. 322 (IV, 1048).

[6] Freely again, "no matter by what person love is carried to him, he seeks out that person and is eager to make love." *Lucretius,* p. 322 (IV, 1055).

[7] *Adust,* or "burning," referred to the theory that various liquids or "humours" of the body would burn up within the system, and the smoke, or "vapours," would disturb or destroy normal mental operation.

to Choler, turned head upon the spinal Duct, and ascended to the Brain. The very same Principle that influences a *Bully* to break the Windows of a Whore, who has jilted him, naturally stirs up a Great Prince to raise mighty Armies, and dream nothing but Sieges, Battles, and Victories.

———*Teterrima belli*
Causa ———————8

THE other Instance is, what I have read somewhere, in a very antient Author, of a mighty King,9 who for the space of above thirty Years, amused himself to take and lose Towns; beat Armies, and be beaten; drive Princes out of their Dominions; fright Children from their Bread and Butter; burn, lay waste, plunder, dragoon, massacre Subject and Stranger, Friend and Foe, Male and Female. 'Tis recorded, that the Philosophers of each Country were in grave Dispute, upon Causes Natural, Moral, and Political, to find out where they should assign an original Solution of this *Phœnomenon.* At last the *Vapour* or *Spirit,* which animated the Hero's Brain, being in perpetual Circulation, seized upon that Region of the Human Body, so renown'd for furnishing the *Zibeta Occidentalis,*10 and gathering there into a Tumor, left the rest of the World for that Time in Peace. Of such mighty Consequence it is, where those Exhalations fix; and of so little, from whence they proceed. The same Spirits which in their superior Progress would conquer a Kingdom, descending upon the *Anus,* conclude in a *Fistula.*

LET us next examine the great Introducers of new Schemes in Philosophy, and search till we can find, from what Faculty of the Soul the Disposition arises in mortal Man, of taking it into his Head, to advance new Systems with such an eager Zeal, in things agreed on all hands impossible to be known: from what Seeds this Disposition springs, and to what Quality of human Nature these Grand Innovators have been indebted for their Number of Disciples. Because, it is plain, that several of the chief among them, both *Antient* and *Modern,* were usually mistaken by their Adversaries, and indeed, by all, except their own Followers, to have been Persons Crazed, or out of their Wits, having generally proceeded in the common Course of their Words and Actions, by a Method very different from the vulgar Dictates of *unrefined* Reason: agreeing for the most Part in their several Models, with their present

8 This passage is from Horace's *Satires,* I.iii, 107. The context is provided in Smith Palmer Bovie's translation, "the revolting cause / Of many a war was the crotch" (*The Satires and Epistles of Horace* [Chicago: University of Chicago Press, 1959], p. 50).

9 Louis XIV of France.

10 Paracelsus, *who was so famous for Chymistry, try'd an Experiment upon human Excrement, to make a Perfume of it, which when he had brought to Perfection,* he called Zibeta Occidentalis, or Western-Civet, *the Back Parts of Man . . . being the* West (Swift's note).

undoubted Successors in the *Academy* of *Modern Bedlam* (whose Merits
and Principles I shall farther examine in due Place.) Of this Kind were
Epicurus, Diogenes, Apollonius, Lucretius, Paracelsus, Des Cartes, and
others; who, if they were now in the World, tied fast, and separate from
their Followers, would in this our undistinguishing Age, incur manifest
Danger of *Phlebotomy,* and *Whips,* and *Chains,* and *dark Chambers,*
and *Straw.* For, what Man in the natural State, or Course of Thinking,
did ever conceive it in his Power, to reduce the Notions of all Mankind,
exactly to the same Length, and Breadth, and Height of his own? Yet
this is the first humble and civil Design of all Innovators in the Empire
of Reason. *Epicurus* modestly hoped, that one Time or other, a certain
Fortuitous Concourse of all Mens Opinions, after perpetual Justlings,
the Sharp with the Smooth, the Light and the Heavy, the Round and the
Square, would by certain *Clinamina,*[11] unite in the Notions of *Atoms*
and *Void,* as these did in the Originals of all Things. *Cartesius* reckoned
to see before he died, the Sentiments of all Philosophers, like so many
lesser Stars in his *Romantick* System, rapt and drawn within his own
Vortex. Now, I would gladly be informed, how it is possible to account
for such Imaginations as these in particular Men, without Recourse to
my *Phænomenon* of *Vapours,* ascending from the lower Faculties to overshadow the Brain, and thence distilling into Conceptions, for which the
Narrowness of our Mother-Tongue has not yet assigned any other Name,
besides that of *Madness* or *Phrenzy.* Let us therefore now conjecture how
it comes to pass, that none of these great Prescribers, do ever fail providing themselves and their Notions, with a Number of implicite Disciples.
And, I think, the Reason is easie to be assigned: For, there is a peculiar
String in the Harmony of Human Understanding, which in several individuals is exactly of the same Tuning. This, if you can dexterously screw
up to its right Key, and then strike gently upon it; Whenever you have
the Good Fortune to light among those of the same Pitch, they will by
a secret necessary Sympathy, strike exactly at the same time. And in this
one Circumstance, lies all the Skill or Luck of the Matter; for if you
chance to jar the String among those who are either above or below your
own Height, instead of subscribing to your Doctrine, they will tie you
fast, call you Mad, and feed you with Bread and Water. It is therefore
a Point of the nicest Conduct to distinguish and adapt this noble Talent,
with respect to the Differences of Persons and of Times. *Cicero* understood this very well, when writing to a Friend in *England,* with a Caution, among other Matters, to beware of being cheated by our *Hackney-
Coachmen* (who, it seems, in those days, were as arrant Rascals as they
are now) has these remarkable Words. *Est quod gaudeas te in ista loca*

11 *Clinamen* is the word used by Lucretius [ii. 292] to represent the κλίσις of
Epicurus, the bias or deviation from a straight line which was supposed to explain
the concourse of atoms (note by Guthkelch and Smith).

venisse, ubi aliquid sapere viderere.[12] For, to speak a bold Truth, it is a fatal Miscarriage, so ill to order Affairs, as to pass for a *Fool* in one Company, when in another you might be treated as a *Philosopher*. Which I desire *some certain Gentlemen of my Acquaintance,* to lay up in their Hearts, as a very seasonable *Innuendo*.

THIS, indeed, was the Fatal Mistake of that worthy Gentleman, my most ingenious Friend, Mr. *W-tt-n:* [13] A Person, in appearance ordain'd for great Designs, as well as Performances; whether you will consider his *Notions* or his *Looks*. Surely, no Man ever advanced into the Publick, with fitter Qualifications of Body and Mind, for the Propagation of a new Religion. Oh, had those happy Talents misapplied to vain Philosophy, been turned into their proper Channels of *Dreams* and *Visions,* where *Distortion* of Mind and Countenance, are of such Sovereign Use; the base detracting World would not then have dared to report, that something is amiss, that his Brain hath undergone an unlucky Shake; which even his Brother *Modernists* themselves, like Ungrates, do whisper so loud, that it reaches up to the very Garret I am now writing in.

LASTLY, Whoever pleases to look into the Fountains of *Enthusiasm,* from whence, in all Ages, have eternally proceeded such fatning Streams, will find the Spring Head to have been as *troubled* and *muddy* as the Current; Of such great Emolument, is a Tincture of this *Vapour,* which the World calls *Madness,* that without its Help, the World would not only be deprived of those two great Blessings, *Conquests* and *Systems,* but even all Mankind would unhappily be reduced to the same Belief in Things Invisible. Now, the former *Postulatum* being held, that it is of no Import from what Originals this *Vapour* proceeds, but either in what *Angles* it strikes and spreads over the Understanding, or upon what *Species* of Brain it ascends; It will be a very delicate Point, to cut the Feather, and divide the several Reasons to a Nice and Curious Reader, how this numerical Difference in the Brain, can produce Effects of so vast a Difference from the same *Vapour,* as to be the sole Point of Individuation between *Alexander the Great, Jack of Leyden,* and Monsieur *Des Cartes*. The present Argument is the most abstracted that ever I engaged in, it strains my Faculties to their highest Stretch; and I desire the Reader to attend with utmost Perpensity; For, I now proceed to unravel this knotty Point.

THERE is in Mankind a certain*   *   *   *   *
*   *   *   *   *   *   *   *   *   *
       *   *   *   *   *   *   *   *
Hic multa   *   *   *   *   *   *   *   *
desiderantur.   *   *   *   *   *   *   *   *
*   *   *   *   *   *   *   *   *   *

[12] "You may be happy that you have reached regions where you may seem to be wise," from Cicero's letter to Trebatius in Gaul (*Epistolae ad Familiares,* VII, 10).
[13] *W-tt-n* is William Wotten, a scholarly writer whom Swift disliked.

*   *   *   And this I take to be a clear Solution of the Matter.[14]

HAVING therefore so narrowly past thro' this intricate Difficulty, the Reader will, I am sure, agree with me in the Conclusion; that if the *Moderns* mean by *Madness,* only a Disturbance or Transposition of the Brain, by Force of certain *Vapours* issuing up from the lower Faculties; Then has this *Madness* been the Parent of all those mighty Revolutions, that have happened in *Empire,* in *Philosophy,* and in *Religion.* For, the Brain, in its natural Position and State of Serenity, disposeth its Owner to pass his Life in the common Forms, without any Thought of sub-duing Multitudes to his own *Power,* his *Reasons* or his *Visions;* and the more he shapes his Understanding by the Pattern of Human Learning, the less he is inclined to form Parties after his particular Notions; be-cause that instructs him in his private Infirmities, as well as in the stub-born Ignorance of the People. But when a Man's Fancy gets *astride* on his Reason, when Imagination is at Cuffs with the Senses, and common Understanding, as well as common Sense, is Kickt out of Doors; the first Proselyte he makes, is Himself, and when that is once compass'd, the Difficulty is not so great in bringing over others; A strong Delusion al-ways operating from *without,* as vigorously as from *within.* For, Cant and Vision are to the Ear and the Eye, the same that Tickling is to the Touch. Those Entertainments and Pleasures we most value in Life, are such as *Dupe* and play the Wag with the Senses. For, if we take an Examina-tion of what is generally understood by *Happiness,* as it has Respect, either to the Understanding or the Senses, we shall find all its Properties and Adjuncts will herd under this short Definition: That, *it is a per-petual Possession of being well Deceived.* And first, with Relation to the Mind or Understanding; 'tis manifest, what mighty Advantages Fiction has over Truth; and the Reason is just at our Elbow; because Imagina-tion can build nobler Scenes, and produce more wonderful Revolutions than Fortune or Nature will be at Expence to furnish. Nor is Mankind so much to blame in his Choice, thus determining him, if we consider that the Debate meerly lies between *Things past,* and *Things conceived;* and so the Question is only this; Whether Things that have Place in the *Imagination,* may not as properly be said to *Exist,* as those that are seated in the *Memory;* which may be justly held in the Affirmative, and very much to the Advantage of the former, since This is acknowledged to be the *Womb* of Things, and the other allowed to be no more than the *Grave.* Again, if we take this Definition of Happiness, and examine it

---

[14] The asterisks are part of Swift's comic apparatus, designed to ridicule the scholarly handling of manuscript texts. Swift's note on the passage is this: *Here is another Defect in the Manuscript, but I think the Author did wisely, and that the Matter which thus strained his Faculties, was not worth a Solution; and it were well if all Metaphysical Cobweb Problems were no otherwise answered.*

with Reference to the Senses, it will be acknowledged wonderfully adapt. How fade and insipid do all Objects accost us that are not convey'd in the Vehicle of *Delusion?* How shrunk is every Thing, as it appears in the Glass of Nature? So, that if it were not for the Assistance of Artificial *Mediums,* false Lights, refracted Angles, Varnish, and Tinsel; there would be a mighty Level in the Felicity and Enjoyments of Mortal Men. If this were seriously considered by the World, as I have a certain Reason to suspect it hardly will; Men would no longer reckon among their high Points of Wisdom, the Art of exposing weak Sides, and publishing Infirmities; an Employment in my Opinion, neither better nor worse than that of *Unmasking,* which I think, has never been allowed fair Usage, either in the *World* or the *Play-House.*

IN the Proportion that Credulity is a more peaceful Possession of the Mind, than Curiosity, so far preferable is that Wisdom, which converses about the Surface, to that pretended Philosophy which enters into the Depth of Things, and then comes gravely back with Informations and Discoveries, that in the inside they are good for nothing. The two Senses, to which all Objects first address themselves, are the Sight and the Touch; These never examine farther than the Colour, the Shape, the Size, and whatever other Qualities dwell, or are drawn by Art upon the Outward of Bodies; and then comes Reason officiously, with Tools for cutting, and opening, and mangling, and piercing, offering to demonstrate, that they are not of the same consistence quite thro'. Now, I take all this to be the last Degree of perverting Nature: one of whose Eternal Laws it is, to put her best Furniture forward. And therefore, in order to save the Charges of all such expensive Anatomy [15] for the Time to come; I do here think fit to inform the Reader, that in such Conclusions as these, Reason is certainly in the Right; and that in most Corporeal Beings, which have fallen under my Cognizance, the *Outside* hath been infinitely preferable to the *In:* Whereof I have been farther convinced from some late Experiments. Last Week I saw a Woman *flay'd,* and you will hardly believe, how much it altered her Person for the worse. Yesterday I ordered the Carcass of a *Beau* to be stript in my Presence; when we were all amazed to find so many unsuspected Faults under one Suit of Cloaths: Then I laid open his *Brain,* his *Heart,* and his *Spleen;* But, I plainly perceived at every Operation, that the farther we proceeded, we found the Defects encrease upon us in Number and Bulk: from all which, I justly formed this Conclusion to my self; That whatever Philosopher or Projector can find out an Art to sodder and patch up the Flaws and Imperfections of Nature, will deserve much better of Mankind, and teach us a more useful Science, than that so much in present Esteem, of widening and exposing them (like him who held *Anatomy* to be the ultimate End of *Physick.*) And he, whose Fortunes

[15] Anatomy, a medical dissection, to which Swift refers in the following passage.

and Dispositions have placed him in a convenient Station to enjoy the Fruits of this noble Art; He that can with *Epicurus* content his Ideas with the *Films* and *Images* that fly off upon his Senses from the *Superficies* of Things; Such a Man truly wise, creams off Nature, leaving the Sower and the Dregs, for Philosophy and Reason to lap up. This is the sublime and refined Point of Felicity, called, *the Possession of being well deceived;* The Serene Peaceful State of being a Fool among Knaves.

BUT to return to *Madness.* It is certain, that according to the System I have above deduced; every *Species* thereof proceeds from a Redundancy of *Vapour;* therefore, as some Kinds of *Phrenzy* give double Strength to the Sinews, so there are of other *Species,* which add Vigor, and Life, and Spirit to the Brain: Now, it usually happens, that these active Spirits, getting Possession of the Brain, resemble those that haunt other waste and empty Dwellings, which for want of Business, either vanish, and carry away a Piece of the House, or else stay at home and fling it all out of the Windows. By which are mystically display'd the two principal Branches of *Madness,* and which some Philosophers not considering so well as I, have mistook to be different in their Causes, over-hastily assigning the first to Deficiency, and the other to Redundance.

I think it therefore manifest, from what I have here advanced, that the main Point of Skill and Address, is to furnish Employment for this Redundancy of *Vapour,* and prudently to adjust the Seasons of it; by which means it may certainly become of Cardinal and Catholick Emolument in a Commonwealth. Thus one Man chusing a proper Juncture, leaps into a Gulph, from thence proceeds a Hero, and is called the Saver of his Country; Another atchieves the same Enterprise, but unluckily timing it, has left the Brand of *Madness,* fixt as a Reproach upon his Memory; Upon so nice a Distinction are we taught to repeat the Name of *Curtius* with Reverence and Love; that of *Empedocles,* with Hatred and Contempt. Thus, also it is usually conceived, that the Elder *Brutus* only personated the *Fool* and *Madman,* for the Good of the Publick: but this was nothing else, than a Redundancy of the same *Vapor,* long misapplied, called by the *Latins, Ingenium par negotiis:* [16] Or, (to translate it as nearly as I can) a sort of   * *Tacit.* *Phrenzy,* never in its right Element, till you take it up in Business of the State.

UPON all which, and many other Reasons of equal Weight, though not equally curious; I do here gladly embrace an Opportunity I have long sought for, of Recommending it as a very noble Undertaking, to Sir E———d S———r, Sir C———r M———ve, Sir J———n B———ls, J———n H———w, Esq; and other Patriots concerned,

---

[16] "Equal to business," that is, a mind capable of performing dull administrative duties. Tacitus, *Annals,* VI. 39 and XVI. 18, uses the phrase.

that they would move for Leave to bring in a Bill, for appointing Commissioners to Inspect into *Bedlam,* and the Parts adjacent; who shall be empowered to *send for Persons, Papers, and Records:* to examine into the Merits and Qualifications of every Student and Professor; to observe with utmost Exactness their several Dispositions and Behaviour; by which means, duly distinguishing and adapting their Talents, they might produce admirable Instruments for the several Offices in a State,   *   *   * *Civil* and *Military;* proceeding in such Methods as I shall here humbly propose. And, I hope the Gentle Reader will give some Allowance to my great Solicitudes in this important Affair, upon Account of that high Esteem I have ever born that honourable Society, whereof I had some Time the Happiness to be an unworthy Member.

IS any Student tearing his Straw in piece-meal, Swearing and Blaspheming, biting his Grate, foaming at the Mouth, and emptying his Pispot in the Spectator's Faces? Let the Right Worshipful, the *Commissioners of Inspection,* give him a Regiment of Dragoons, and send him into *Flanders* among the *Rest.* Is another eternally talking, sputtering, gaping, bawling, in a Sound without Period or Article? What wonderful Talents are here mislaid! Let him be furnished immediately with a green Bag and Papers, and *three Pence* in his Pocket,[17] and away with Him to *Westminster-Hall.* You will find a Third, gravely taking the Dimensions of his Kennel; A Person of Foresight and Insight, tho' kept quite in the Dark; for why, like *Moses, Ecce cornuta erat ejus facies.*[18] He walks duly in one Pace, intreats your Penny with due Gravity and Ceremony; talks much of hard Times, and Taxes, and the *Whore of Babylon;* Bars up the woodden Window of his Cell constantly at eight a Clock: Dreams of *Fire,* and *Shop-lifters,* and *Court-Customers,* and *Priviledg'd Places.* Now, what a Figure would all these Acquirements amount to, if the Owner were sent into the *City* among his Brethren! Behold a Fourth, in much and deep Conversation with himself, biting his Thumbs at proper Junctures; His Countenance chequered with Business and Design; sometimes walking very fast, with his Eyes nailed to a Paper that he holds in his Hands: A great Saver of Time, somewhat thick of Hearing, very short of Sight, but more of Memory. A Man ever in Haste, a great Hatcher and Breeder of Business, and excellent at the Famous Art of *whispering Nothing.* A huge Idolater of Monosyllables and Procrastination; so ready to *Give* his Word to every Body, that he never *keeps* it. One that has forgot the common *Meaning* of Words, but an admirable Retainer of the *Sound.* Extreamly subject to the *Loosness,* for his *Occasions* are perpetually *calling him away.* If you approach his Grate in his familiar Intervals; *Sir,* says he, *Give me a Penny, and I'll*

---

17 *A lawyer's Coach-hire* (Swift's note).
18 Cornutus, *is either Horned or Shining, and by this Term,* Moses *is described in the vulgar* Latin *of the Bible* (Swift's note).

sing you a Song: But give me the Penny first. (Hence comes the common Saying, and commoner Practice of parting with Money for a *Song.*) What a compleat System of *Court-Skill* is here described in every Branch of it, and all utterly lost with wrong Application? Accost the Hole of another Kennel, first stopping your Nose, you will behold a surley, gloomy, nasty, slovenly Mortal, raking in his own Dung, and dabling in his Urine. The best Part of his Diet, is the Reversion of his own Ordure, which exspiring into Steams, whirls perpetually about, and at last re-infunds. His Complexion is of a dirty Yellow, with a thin scattered Beard, exactly agreeable to that of his Dyet upon its first Declination; like other Insects, who having their Birth and Education in an Excrement, from thence borrow their Colour and their Smell. The Student of this Apartment is very sparing in his Words, but somewhat over-liberal of his Breath; He holds his Hand out ready to receive your Penny, and immediately upon Receipt, withdraws to his former Occupations. Now, is it not amazing to think, the Society of *Warwick-Lane,*[19] should have no more Concern, for the Recovery of so useful a Member, who, if one may judge from these Appearances, would become the greatest Ornament to that Illustrious Body? Another Student struts up fiercely to your Teeth, puffing with his Lips, half squeezing out his Eyes, and very graciously holds you out his Hand to kiss. The *Keeper* desires you not to be afraid of this Professor, for he will do you no Hurt: To him alone is allowed the Liberty of the Anti-Chamber, and the *Orator* of the Place gives you to understand, that this solemn Person is a *Taylor* run mad with Pride. This considerable Student is adorned with many other Qualities, upon which, at present, I shall not farther enlarge. — — — — *Heark in your Ear* — — — — — — — — — — — — —[20] I am strangely mistaken, if all his Address, his Motions, and his Airs, would not then be very natural, and in their proper Element.

I shall not descend so minutely, as to insist upon the vast Number of *Beaux, Fidlers, Poets,* and *Politicians,* that the World might recover by such a Reformation; But what is more material, besides the clear Gain redounding to the Commonwealth, by so large an Acquisition of Persons to employ, whose Talents and Acquirements, if I may be so bold to affirm it, are now buried, or at least misapplied: It would be a mighty Advantage accruing to the Publick from this Enquiry, that all these would very much excel, and arrive at great Perfection in their several Kinds; which, I think, is manifest from what I have already shewn; and shall inforce by this one plain Instance; That even, I my self, the Author of these momentous Truths, am a Person, whose Imaginations are hard-mouth'd,

[19] The Royal College of Physicians was in Warwick Lane from 1674 to 1825 (note by Guthkelch and Smith).

[20] *I cannot conjecture what the Author means here, or how this Chasm could be fill'd, tho' it is capable of more than one Interpretation* (Swift's note).

and exceedingly disposed to run away with his *Reason,* which I have observed from long Experience, to be a very light Rider, and easily shook off; upon which Account, my Friends will never trust me alone, without a solemn Promise, to vent my Speculations in this, or the like manner, for the universal Benefit of Human kind; which, perhaps, the gentle, courteous, and candid Reader, brimful of that *Modern* Charity and Tenderness, usually annexed to his *Office,* will be very hardly persuaded to believe.

1704

D. H. Lawrence (1885–1930)

The Horse Dealer's Daughter

"WELL, Mabel, and what are you going to do with yourself?" asked Joe, with foolish flippancy. He felt quite safe himself. Without listening for an answer, he turned aside, worked a grain of tobacco to the tip of his tongue, and spat it out. He did not care about anything, since he felt safe himself.

The three brothers and the sister sat round the desolate breakfast-table, attempting some sort of desultory consultation. The morning's post had given the final tap to the family fortunes, and all was over. The dreary dining-room itself, with its heavy mahogany furniture, looked as if it were waiting to be done away with.

But the consultation amounted to nothing. There was a strange air of ineffectuality about the three men, as they sprawled at table, smoking and reflecting vaguely on their own condition. The girl was alone, a rather short, sullen-looking young woman of twenty-seven. She did not share the same life as her brothers. She would have been good-looking, save for the impressive fixity of her face, 'bull-dog', as her brothers called it.

There was a confused tramping of horses' feet outside. The three men all sprawled round in their chairs to watch. Beyond the dark holly bushes that separated the strip of lawn from the high-road, they could see a cavalcade of shire horses swinging out of their own yard, being taken for exercise. This was the last time. These were the last horses that would go through their hands. The young men watched with critical, callous look. They were all frightened at the collapse of their lives, and

From THE COMPLETE SHORT STORIES OF D. H. LAWRENCE. Copyright 1922 by Thomas B. Seltzer, Inc., 1950 by Frieda Lawrence. Reprinted by permission of The Viking Press, Inc.

the sense of disaster in which they were involved left them no inner freedom.

Yet they were three fine, well-set fellows enough. Joe, the eldest, was a man of thirty-three, broad and handsome in a hot, flushed way. His face was red, he twisted his black moustache over a thick finger, his eyes were shallow and restless. He had a sensual way of uncovering his teeth when he laughed, and his bearing was stupid. Now he watched the horses with a glazed look of helplessness in his eyes, a certain stupor of downfall.

The great draught-horses swung past. They were tied head to tail, four of them, and they heaved along to where a lane branched off from the high-road, planting their great hoofs floutingly in the fine black mud, swinging their great rounded haunches sumptuously, and trotting a few sudden steps as they were led into the lane, round the corner. Every movement showed a massive, slumbrous strength, and a stupidity which held them in subjection. The groom at the head looked back, jerking the leading rope. And the cavalcade moved out of sight up the lane, the tail of the last horse, bobbed up tight and stiff, held out taut from the swinging great haunches as they rocked behind the hedges in a motion-like sleep.

Joe watched with glazed hopeless eyes. The horses were almost like his own body to him. He felt he was done for now. Luckily he was engaged to a woman as old as himself, and therefore her father, who was steward of a neighbouring estate, would provide him with a job. He would marry and go into harness. His life was over, he would be a subject animal now.

He turned uneasily aside, the retreating steps of the horses echoing in his ears. Then, with foolish restlessness, he reached for the scraps of bacon-rind from the plates, and making a faint whistling sound, flung them to the terrier that lay against the fender. He watched the dog swallow them, and waited till the creature looked into his eyes. Then a faint grin came on his face, and in a high, foolish voice he said:

"You won't get much more bacon, shall you, you little b——?"

The dog faintly and dismally wagged its tail, then lowered its haunches, circled round, and lay down again.

There was another helpless silence at the table. Joe sprawled uneasily in his seat, not willing to go till the family conclave was dissolved. Fred Henry, the second brother, was erect, clean-limbed, alert. He had watched the passing of the horses with more *sang-froid*. If he was an animal, like Joe, he was an animal which controls, not one which is controlled. He was master of any horse, and he carried himself with a well-tempered air of mastery. But he was not master of the situations of life. He pushed his coarse brown moustache upwards, off his lip, and glanced irritably at his sister, who sat impassive and inscrutable.

"You'll go and stop with Lucy for a bit, shan't you?" he asked. The girl did not answer.

"I don't see what else you can do," persisted Fred Henry.

"Go as a skivvy," Joe interpolated laconically.

The girl did not move a muscle.

"If I was her, I should go in for training for a nurse," said Malcolm, the youngest of them all. He was the baby of the family, a young man of twenty-two, with a fresh, jaunty *museau*.

But Mabel did not take any notice of him. They had talked at her and round her for so many years, that she hardly heard them at all.

The marble clock on the mantelpiece softly chimed the half-hour, the dog rose uneasily from the hearth-rug and looked at the party at the breakfast-table. But still they sat on in ineffectual conclave.

"Oh, all right," said Joe suddenly, apropos of nothing. "I'll get a move on."

He pushed back his chair, straddled his knees with a downward jerk, to get them free, in horsey fashion, and went to the fire. Still he did not go out of the room; he was curious to know what the others would do or say. He began to charge his pipe, looking down at the dog and saying in a high, affected voice:

"Going wi' me? Going wi' me are ter? Tha'rt goin' further than tha counts on just now, dost hear?"

The dog faintly wagged its tail, the man stuck out his jaw and covered his pipe with his hands, and puffed intently, losing himself in the tobacco, looking down all the while at the dog with an absent brown eye. The dog looked up at him in mournful distrust. Joe stood with his knees stuck out, in real horsey fashion.

"Have you had a letter from Lucy?" Fred Henry asked of his sister.

"Last week," came the neutral reply.

"And what does she say?"

There was no answer.

"Does she *ask* you to go and stop there?" persisted Fred Henry.

"She says I can if I like."

"Well, then, you'd better. Tell her you'll come on Monday."

This was received in silence.

"That's what you'll do then, is it?" said Fred Henry, in some exasperation.

But she made no answer. There was a silence of futility and irritation in the room. Malcolm grinned fatuously.

"You'll have to make up your mind between now and next Wednesday," said Joe loudly, "or else find yourself lodgings on the kerbstone."

The face of the young woman darkened, but she sat on immutable.

"Here's Jack Fergusson!" exclaimed Malcolm, who was looking aimlessly out of the window.

"Where?" exclaimed Joe loudly.

"Just gone past."

"Coming in?"

Malcolm craned his neck to see the gate.

"Yes," he said.

There was a silence. Mabel sat on like one condemned, at the head of the table. Then a whistle was heard from the kitchen. The dog got up and barked sharply. Joe opened the door and shouted:

"Come on."

After a moment a young man entered. He was muffled up in over-coat and a purple woollen scarf, and his tweed cap, which he did not remove, was pulled down on his head. He was of medium height, his face was rather long and pale, his eyes looked tired.

"Hello, Jack! Well, Jack!" exclaimed Malcolm and Joe. Fred Henry merely said: "Jack."

"What's doing?" asked the newcomer, evidently addressing Fred Henry.

"Same. We've got to be out by Wednesday. Got a cold?"

"I have—got it bad, too."

"Why don't you stop in?"

"*Me* stop in? When I can't stand on my legs, perhaps I shall have a chance." The young man spoke huskily. He had a slight Scotch accent.

"It's a knock-out, isn't it," said Joe, boisterously, "if a doctor goes round croaking with a cold. Looks bad for the patients, doesn't it?"

The young doctor looked at him slowly.

"Anything the matter with *you*, then?" he asked sarcastically.

"Not as I know of. Damn your eyes, I hope not. Why?"

"I thought you were very concerned about the patients, wondered if you might be one yourself."

"Damn it, no, I've never been patient to no flaming doctor, and hope I never shall be," returned Joe.

At this point Mabel rose from the table, and they all seemed to become aware of her existence. She began putting the dishes together. The young doctor looked at her, but did not address her. He had not greeted her. She went out of the room with the tray, her face impassive and unchanged.

"When are you off then, all of you?" asked the doctor.

"I'm catching the eleven-forty," replied Malcolm. "Are you goin' down wi' th' trap, Joe?"

"Yes, I've told you I'm going down wi' th' trap, haven't I?"

"We'd better be getting her in then. So long, Jack, if I don't see you before I go," said Malcolm, shaking hands.

He went out, followed by Joe, who seemed to have his tail between his legs.

"Well, this is the devil's own," exclaimed the doctor, when he was left alone with Fred Henry. "Going before Wednesday, are you?"

"That's the orders," replied the other.

"Where, to Northampton?"

"That's it."

"The devil!" exclaimed Fergusson, with quiet chagrin.

And there was silence between the two.

"All settled up, are you?" asked Fergusson.

"About."

There was another pause.

"Well, I shall miss yer, Freddy, boy," said the young doctor.

"And I shall miss thee, Jack," returned the other.

"Miss you like hell," mused the doctor.

Fred Henry turned aside. There was nothing to say. Mabel came in again, to finish clearing the table.

"What are *you* going to do, then, Miss Pervin?" asked Fergusson. "Going to your sister's, are you?"

Mabel looked at him with her steady, dangerous eyes, that always made him uncomfortable, unsettling his superficial ease.

"No," she said.

"Well, what in the name of fortune *are* you going to do? Say what you mean to do," cried Fred Henry, with futile intensity.

But she only averted her head, and continued her work. She folded the white table-cloth, and put on the chenille cloth.

"The sulkiest bitch that ever trod!" muttered her brother.

But she finished her task with perfectly impassive face, the young doctor watching her interestedly all the while. Then she went out.

Fred Henry stared after her, clenching his lips, his blue eyes fixing in sharp antagonism, as he made a grimace of sour exasperation.

"You could bray her into bits, and that's all you'd get out of her," he said, in a small, narrowed tone.

The doctor smiled faintly.

"What's she *going* to do, then?" he asked.

"Strike me if *I* know!" returned the other.

There was a pause. Then the doctor stirred.

"I'll be seeing you to-night, shall I?" he said to his friend.

"Ay—where's it to be? Are we going over to Jessdale?"

"I don't know. I've got such a cold on me. I'll come round to the 'Moon and Stars', anyway."

"Let Lizzie and May miss their night for once, eh?"

"That's it—if I feel as I do now."

"All's one——"

The two young men went through the passage and down to the back door together. The house was large, but it was servantless now, and desolate. At the back was a small bricked house-yard and beyond that a big square, gravelled fine and red, and having stables on two sides. Sloping, dank, winter-dark fields stretched away on the open sides.

But the stables were empty. Joseph Pervin, the father of the family, had been a man of no education, who had become a fairly large horse dealer. The stables had been full of horses, there was a great turmoil and come-and-go of horses and of dealers and grooms. Then the kitchen was full of servants. But of late things had declined. The old man had married a second time, to retrieve his fortunes. Now he was dead and everything was gone to the dogs, there was nothing but debt and threatening.

For months, Mabel had been servantless in the big house, keeping the home together in penury for her ineffectual brothers. She had kept house for ten years. But previously it was with unstinted means. Then, however brutal and coarse everything was, the sense of money had kept her proud, confident. The men might be foul-mouthed, the women in the kitchen might have had reputations, her brothers might have illegitimate children. But so long as there was money, the girl felt herself established, and brutally proud, reserved.

No company came to the house, save dealers and coarse men. Mabel had no associates of her own sex, after her sister went away. But she did not mind. She went regularly to church, she attended to her father. And she lived in the memory of her mother, who had died when she was fourteen, and whom she had loved. She had loved her father, too, in a different way, depending upon him, and feeling secure in him, until at the age of fifty-four he married again. And then she had set hard against him. Now he had died and left them all hopelessly in debt.

She had suffered badly during the period of poverty. Nothing, however, could shake the curious, sullen, animal pride that dominated each member of the family. Now, for Mabel, the end had come. Still she would not cast about her. She would follow her own way just the same. She would always hold the keys of her own situation. Mindless and persistent, she endured from day to day. Why should she think? Why should she answer anybody? It was enough that this was the end, and there was no way out. She need not pass any more darkly along the main street of the small town, avoiding every eye. She need not demean herself any more, going into the shops and buying the cheapest food. This was at an end. She thought of nobody, not even of herself. Mindless and persistent, she seemed in a sort of ecstasy to be coming nearer to her fulfilment, her own glorification, approaching her dead mother, who was glorified.

In the afternoon she took a little bag, with shears and sponge and a small scrubbing-brush, and went out. It was a grey, wintry day, with saddened, dark green fields and an atmosphere blackened by the smoke of foundries not far off. She went quickly, darkly along the causeway, heeding nobody, through the town to the churchyard.

There she always felt secure, as if no one could see her, although as a matter of fact she was exposed to the stare of everyone who passed along under the churchyard wall. Nevertheless, once under the shadow of the great looming church, among the graves, she felt immune from the world, reserved within the thick churchyard wall as in another country.

Carefully she clipped the grass from the grave, and arranged the pinky white, small chrysanthemums in the tin cross. When this was done, she took an empty jar from a neighbouring grave, brought water, and carefully, most scrupulously sponged the marble headstone and the coping-stone.

It gave her sincere satisfaction to do this. She felt in immediate contact with the world of her mother. She took minute pains, went through the park in a state bordering on pure happiness, as if in performing this task she came into a subtle, intimate connection with her mother. For the life she followed here in the world was far less real than the world of death she inherited from her mother.

The doctor's house was just by the church. Fergusson, being a mere hired assistant, was slave to the country-side. As he hurried now to attend to the out-patients in the surgery, glancing across the graveyard with his quick eye, he saw the girl at her task at the grave. She seemed so intent and remote, it was like looking into another world. Some mystical element was touched in him. He slowed down as he walked, watching her as if spellbound.

She lifted her eyes, feeling him looking. Their eyes met. And each looked again at once, each feeling, in some way, found out by the other. He lifted his cap and passed on down the road. There remained distinct in his consciousness, like a vision, the memory of her face, lifted from the tombstone in the churchyard, and looking at him with slow, large, portentous eyes. It *was* portentous, her face. It seemed to mesmerise him. There was a heavy power in her eyes which laid hold of his whole being, as if he had drunk some powerful drug. He had been feeling weak and done before. Now the life came back into him, he felt delivered from his own fretted, daily self.

He finished his duties at the surgery as quickly as might be, hastily filling up the bottles of the waiting people with cheap drugs. Then, in perpetual haste, he set off again to visit several cases in another part of his round, before tea-time. At all times he preferred to walk if he could, but particularly when he was not well. He fancied the motion restored him.

The afternoon was falling. It was grey, deadened, and wintry, with a slow, moist, heavy coldness sinking in and deadening all the faculties. But why should he think or notice? He hastily climbed the hill and turned across the dark green fields, following the black cinder-track. In the distance, across a shallow dip in the country, the small town was clustered like smouldering ash, a tower, a spire, a heap of low, raw, extinct houses. And on the nearest fringe of the town, sloping into the dip, was Oldmeadow, the Pervins' house. He could see the stables and the outbuildings distinctly, as they lay towards him on the slope. Well, he would not go there many more times! Another resource would be lost to him, another place gone: the only company he cared for in the alien, ugly little town he was losing. Nothing but work, drudgery, constant hastening from dwelling to dwelling among the colliers and the iron-workers. It wore him out, but at the same time he had a craving for it. It was a stimulant to him to be in the homes of the working people, moving, as it were, through the innermost body of their life. His nerves were excited and gratified. He could come so near, into the very lives of the rough, inarticulate, powerfully emotional men and women. He grumbled, he said he hated the hellish hole. But as a matter of fact it excited him, the contact with the rough, strongly-feeling people was a stimulant applied direct to his nerves.

Below Oldmeadow, in the green, shallow, soddened hollow of fields, lay a square, deep pond. Roving across the landscape, the doctor's quick eye detected a figure in black passing through the gate of the field, down towards the pond. He looked again. It would be Mabel Pervin. His mind suddenly became alive and attentive.

Why was she going down there? He pulled up on the path on the slope above, and stood staring. He could just make sure of the small black figure moving in the hollow of the failing day. He seemed to see her in the midst of such obscurity, that he was like a clairvoyant, seeing rather with the mind's eye than with ordinary sight. Yet he could see her positively enough, whilst he kept his eye attentive. He felt, if he looked away from her, in the thick, ugly falling dusk, he would lose her altogether.

He followed her minutely as she moved, direct and intent, like something transmitted rather than stirring in voluntary activity, straight down the field towards the pond. There she stood on the bank for a moment. She never raised her head. Then she waded slowly into the water.

He stood motionless as the small black figure walked slowly and deliberately towards the centre of the pond, very slowly, gradually moving deeper into the motionless water, and still moving forward as the water got up to her breast. Then he could see her no more in the dusk of the dead afternoon.

"There!" he exclaimed. "Would you believe it?"

And he hastened straight down, running over the wet, soddened fields, pushing through the hedges, down into the depression of callous wintry obscurity. It took him several minutes to come to the pond. He stood on the bank, breathing heavily. He could see nothing. His eyes seemed to penetrate the dead water. Yes, perhaps that was the dark shadow of her black clothing beneath the surface of the water.

He slowly ventured into the pond. The bottom was deep, soft clay, he sank in, and the water clasped dead cold round his legs. As he stirred he could smell the cold, rotten clay that fouled up into the water. It was objectionable in his lungs. Still, repelled and yet not heeding, he moved deeper into the pond. The cold water rose over his thighs, over his loins, upon his abdomen. The lower part of his body was all sunk in the hideous cold element. And the bottom was so deeply soft and uncertain, he was afraid of pitching with his mouth underneath. He could not swim, and was afraid.

He crouched a little, spreading his hands under the water and moving them round, trying to feel for her. The dead cold pond swayed upon his chest. He moved again, a little deeper, and again, with his hands underneath, he felt all around under the water. And he touched her clothing. But it evaded his fingers. He made a desperate effort to grasp it.

And so doing he lost his balance and went under, horribly, suffocating in the foul earthy water, struggling madly for a few moments. At last, after what seemed an eternity, he got his footing, rose again into the air and looked around. He gasped, and knew he was in the world. Then he looked at the water. She had risen near him. He grasped her clothing, and drawing her nearer, turned to take his way to land again.

He went very slowly, carefully, absorbed in the slow progress. He rose higher, climbing out of the pond. The water was now only about his legs; he was thankful, full of relief to be out of the clutches of the pond. He lifted her and staggered on to the bank, out of the horror of wet, grey clay.

He laid her down on the bank. She was quite unconscious and running with water. He made the water come from her mouth, he worked to restore her. He did not have to work very long before he could feel the breathing begin again in her; she was breathing naturally. He worked a little longer. He could feel her live beneath his hands; she was coming back. He wiped her face, wrapped her in his overcoat, looked round into the dim, dark grey world, then lifted her and staggered down the bank and across the fields.

It seemed an unthinkably long way, and his burden so heavy he felt he would never get to the house. But at last he was in the stable-yard, and then in the house-yard. He opened the door and went into the house. In the kitchen he laid her down on the hearth-rug and called. The house was empty. But the fire was burning in the grate.

Then again he kneeled to attend to her. She was breathing regularly, her eyes were wide open and as if conscious, but there seemed something missing in her look. She was conscious in herself, but unconscious of her surroundings.

He ran upstairs, took blankets from a bed, and put them before the fire to warm. Then he removed her saturated, earthy-smelling clothing, rubbed her dry with a towel, and wrapped her naked in the blankets. Then he went into the dining-room, to look for spirits. There was a little whisky. He drank a gulp himself, and put some into her mouth.

The effect was instantaneous. She looked full into his face, as if she had been seeing him for some time, and yet had only just become conscious of him.

"Dr. Fergusson?" she said.

"What?" he answered.

He was divesting himself of his coat, intending to find some dry clothing upstairs. He could not bear the smell of the dead, clayey water, and he was mortally afraid for his own health.

"What did I do?" she asked.

"Walked into the pond," he replied. He had begun to shudder like one sick, and could hardly attend to her. Her eyes remained full on him, he seemed to be going dark in his mind, looking back at her helplessly. The shuddering became quieter in him, his life came back to him, dark and unknowing, but strong again.

"Was I out of my mind?" she asked, while her eyes were fixed on him all the time.

"Maybe, for the moment," he replied. He felt quiet, because his strength had come back. The strange fretful strain had left him.

"Am I out of my mind now?" she asked.

"Are you?" he reflected a moment. "No," he answered truthfully, "I don't see that you are." He turned his face aside. He was afraid now, because he felt dazed, and felt dimly that her power was stronger than his, in this issue. And she continued to look at him fixedly all the time. "Can you tell me where I shall find some dry things to put on?" he asked.

"Did you dive into the pond for me?" she asked.

"No," he answered. "I walked in. But I went in overhead as well."

There was silence for a moment. He hesitated. He very much wanted to go upstairs to get into dry clothing. But there was another desire in him. And she seemed to hold him. His will seemed to have gone to sleep, and left him, standing there slack before her. But he felt warm inside himself. He did not shudder at all, though his clothes were sodden on him.

"Why did you?" she asked.

"Because I didn't want you to do such a foolish thing," he said.

"It wasn't foolish," she said, still gazing at him as she lay on the floor, with a sofa cushion under her head. "It was the right thing to do. *I* knew best, then."

"I'll go and shift these wet things," he said. But still he had not the power to move out of her presence, until she sent him. It was as if she had the life of his body in her hands, and he could not extricate himself. Or perhaps he did not want to.

Suddenly she sat up. Then she became aware of her own immediate condition. She felt the blankets about her, she knew her own limbs. For a moment it seemed as if her reason were going. She looked round, with wild eye, as if seeking something. He stood still with fear. She saw her clothing lying scattered.

"Who undressed me?" she asked, her eyes resting full and inevitable on his face.

"I did," he replied, "to bring you round."

For some moments she sat and gazed at him awfully, her lips parted.

"Do you love me, then?" she asked.

He only stood and stared at her, fascinated. His soul seemed to melt.

She shuffled forward on her knees, and put her arms round him, round his legs, as he stood there, pressing her breasts against his knees and thighs, clutching him with strange, convulsive certainty, pressing his thighs against her, drawing him to her face, her throat, as she looked up at him with flaring, humble eyes of transfiguration, triumphant in first possession.

"You love me," she murmured, in strange transport, yearning and triumphant and confident. "You love me. I know you love me, I know."

And she was passionately kissing his knees, through the wet clothing, passionately and indiscriminately kissing his knees, his legs, as if unaware of everything.

He looked down at the tangled wet hair, the wild, bare, animal shoulders. He was amazed, bewildered, and afraid. He had never thought of loving her. He had never wanted to love her. When he rescued her and restored her, he was a doctor, and she was a patient. He had had no single personal thought of her. Nay, this introduction of the personal element was very distasteful to him, a violation of his professional honour. It was horrible to have her there embracing his knees. It was horrible. He revolted from it, violently. And yet—and yet—he had not the power to break away.

She looked at him again, with the same supplication of powerful love, and that same transcendent, frightening light of triumph. In view of the delicate flame which seemed to come from her face like a light, he was powerless. And yet he had never intended to love her. He had never intended. And something stubborn in him could not give way.

"You love me," she repeated, in a murmur of deep, rhapsodic assurance. "You love me."

Her hands were drawing him, drawing him down to her. He was afraid, even a little horrified. For he had, really, no intention of loving her. Yet her hands were drawing him towards her. He put out his hand quickly to steady himself, and grasped her bare shoulder. A flame seemed to burn the hand that grasped her soft shoulder. He had no intention of loving her: his whole will was against his yielding. It was horrible. And yet wonderful was the touch of her shoulders, beautiful the shining of her face. Was she perhaps mad? He had a horror of yielding to her. Yet something in him ached also.

He had been staring away at the door, away from her. But his hand remained on her shoulder. She had gone suddenly very still. He looked down at her. Her eyes were now wide with fear, with doubt, the light was dying from her face, a shadow of terrible greyness was returning. He could not bear the touch of her eyes' question upon him, and the look of death behind the question.

With an inward groan he gave way, and let his heart yield towards her. A sudden gentle smile came on his face. And her eyes, which never left his face, slowly, slowly filled with tears. He watched the strange water rise in her eyes, like some slow fountain coming up. And his heart seemed to burn and melt away in his breast.

He could not bear to look at her any more. He dropped on his knees and caught her head with his arms and pressed her face against his throat. She was very still. His heart, which seemed to have broken, was burning with a kind of agony in his breast. And he felt her slow, hot tears wetting his throat. But he could not move.

He felt the hot tears wet his neck and the hollows of his neck, and he remained motionless, suspended through one of man's eternities. Only now it had become indispensable to him to have her face pressed close to him; he could never let her go again. He could never let her head go away from the close clutch of his arm. He wanted to remain like that for ever, with his heart hurting him in a pain that was also life to him. Without knowing, he was looking down on her damp, soft brown hair.

Then, as it were suddenly, he smelt the horrid stagnant smell of that water. And at the same moment she drew away from him and looked at him. Her eyes were wistful and unfathomable. He was afraid of them, and he fell to kissing her, not knowing what he was doing. He wanted her eyes not to have that terrible, wistful, unfathomable look.

When she turned her face to him again, a faint delicate flush was glowing, and there was again dawning that terrible shining of joy in her eyes, which really terrified him, and yet which he now wanted to see, because he feared the look of doubt still more.

"You love me?" she said, rather faltering.

"Yes." The word cost him a painful effort. Not because it wasn't true. But because it was too newly true, the *saying* seemed to tear open again his newly-torn heart. And he hardly wanted it to be true, even now.

She lifted her face to him, and he bent forward and kissed her on the mouth, gently, with the one kiss that is an eternal pledge. And as he kissed her his heart strained again in his breast. He never intended to love her. But now it was over. He had crossed over the gulf to her, and all that he had left behind had shrivelled and become void.

After the kiss, her eyes again slowly filled with tears. She sat still, away from him, with her face drooped aside, and her hands folded in her lap. The tears fell very slowly. There was complete silence. He too sat there motionless and silent on the hearth-rug. The strange pain of his heart that was broken seemed to consume him. That he should love her? That this was love! That he should be ripped open in this way! Him, a doctor! How they would all jeer if they knew! It was agony to him to think they might know.

In the curious naked pain of the thought he looked again to her. She was sitting there drooped into a muse. He saw a tear fall, and his heart flared hot. He saw for the first time that one of her shoulders was quite uncovered, one arm bare, he could see one of her small breasts; dimly, because it had become almost dark in the room.

"Why are you crying?" he asked, in an altered voice.

She looked up at him, and behind her tears the consciousness of her situation for the first time brought a dark look of shame to her eyes.

"I'm not crying, really," she said, watching him, half frightened.

He reached his hand, and softly closed it on her bare arm.

"I love you! I love you!" he said in a soft, low vibrating voice, unlike himself.

She shrank, and dropped her head. The soft, penetrating grip of his hand on her arm distressed her. She looked up at him.

"I want to go," she said. "I want to go and get you some dry things."

"Why?" he said. "I'm all right."

"But I want to go," she said. "And I want you to change your things."

He released her arm, and she wrapped herself in the blanket, looking at him rather frightened. And still she did not rise.

"Kiss me," she said wistfully.

He kissed her, but briefly, half in anger.

Then, after a second, she rose nervously, all mixed up in the blanket. He watched her in her confusion as she tried to extricate herself and wrap herself up so that she could walk. He watched her relentlessly, as she knew. And as she went, the blanket trailing, and as he saw a glimpse of her feet and her white leg, he tried to remember her as she was when he had wrapped her in the blanket. But then he didn't want to remember, because she had been nothing to him then, and his nature revolted from remembering her as she was when she was nothing to him.

A tumbling, muffled noise from within the dark house startled him.

Then he heard her voice: "There are clothes." He rose and went to the foot of the stairs, and gathered up the garments she had thrown down. Then he came back to the fire, to rub himself down and dress. He grinned at his own appearance when he had finished.

The fire was sinking, so he put on coal. The house was now quite dark, save for the light of a street-lamp that shone in faintly from beyond the holly trees. He lit the gas with matches he found on the mantelpiece. Then he emptied the pockets of his own clothes, and threw all his wet things in a heap into the scullery. After which he gathered up her sodden clothes, gently, and put them in a separate heap on the coppertop in the scullery.

It was six o'clock on the clock. His own watch had stopped. He ought to go back to the surgery. He waited, and still she did not come down. So he went to the foot of the stairs and called:

"I shall have to go."

Almost immediately he heard her coming down. She had on her best dress of black voile, and her hair was tidy, but still damp. She looked at him—and in spite of herself, smiled.

"I don't like you in those clothes," she said.

"Do I look a sight?" he answered.

They were shy of one another.

"I'll make you some tea," she said.

"No, I must go."

"Must you?" And she looked at him again with the wide, strained, doubtful eyes. And again, from the pain of his breast, he knew how he loved her. He went and bent to kiss her, gently, passionately, with his heart's painful kiss.

"And my hair smells so horrible," she murmured in distraction. "And I'm so awful, I'm so awful! Oh no, I'm too awful." And she broke into bitter, heart-broken sobbing. "You can't want to love me, I'm horrible."

"Don't be silly, don't be silly," he said, trying to comfort her, kissing her, holding her in his arms. "I want you, I want to marry you, we're going to be married, quickly, quickly—to-morrow if I can."

But she only sobbed terribly, and cried:

"I feel awful. I feel awful. I feel I'm horrible to you."

"No, I want you, I want you," was all he answered, blindly, with that terrible intonation which frightened her almost more than her horror lest he should *not* want her.

1922

Thomas Hardy (1840–1928)

The Three Strangers

AMONG the few features of agricultural England which retain an appearance but little modified by the lapse of centuries may be reckoned the high, grassy and furzy downs, coombs, or ewe-leases, as they are indifferently called, that fill a large area of certain counties in the south and southwest. If any mark of human occupation is met with hereon, it usually takes the form of the solitary cottage of some shepherd.

Fifty years ago such a lonely cottage stood on such a down, and may possibly be standing there now. In spite of its loneliness, however, the spot, by actual measurement, was not more than five miles from a county-town. Yet that affected it little. Five miles of irregular upland, during the long inimical seasons, with their sleets, snows, rains, and mists, afford withdrawing space enough to isolate a Timon or a Nebuchadnezzar; much less, in fair weather, to please that less repellent tribe, the poets, philosophers, artists, and others who "conceive and meditate of pleasant things."

Some old earthen camp or barrow, some clump of trees, at least some starved fragment of ancient hedge is usually taken advantage of in the erection of these forlorn dwellings. But, in the present case, such a kind of shelter had been disregarded. Higher Crowstairs, as the house was called, stood quite detached and undefended. The only reason for its precise situation seemed to be the crossing of two footpaths at right angles hard by, which may have crossed there and thus for a good five hundred years. Hence the house was exposed to the elements on all sides. But, though the wind up here blew unmistakably when it did blow, and the rain hit hard whenever it fell, the various weathers of the winter season were not quite so formidable on the coomb as they were imagined to be by dwellers on low ground. The raw rimes were not so pernicious as in the hollows, and the frosts were scarcely so severe. When the shephed and his family who tenanted the house were pitied for their sufferings from the exposure, they said that upon the whole they were less inconvenienced by "wuzzes and flames" (hoarses and phlegms) than when they had lived by the stream of a snug neighboring valley.

The night of March 28, 182–, was precisely one of the nights that were wont to call forth these expressions of commiseration. The level rainstorm smote walls, slopes, and hedges like the clothyard shafts of Senlac and Crécy. Such sheep and outdoor animals as had no shelter stood with their buttocks to the winds; while the tails of little birds trying to roost on some scraggy thorn were blown inside-out like umbrellas. The gable-end of the cottage was stained with wet, and the eavesdroppings flapped against the wall. Yet never was commiseration for the shepherd more misplaced. For that cheerful rustic was entertaining a large party in glorification of the christening of his second girl.

The guests had arrived before the rain began to fall, and they were all now assembled in the chief or living room of the dwelling. A glance into the apartment at eight o'clock on this eventful evening would have resulted in the opinion that it was as cozy and comfortable a nook as could be wished for in boisterous weather. The calling of its inhabitant was proclaimed by a number of highly polished sheep crooks without stems that were hung ornamentally over the fireplace, the curl of each shining crook varying from the antiquated type engraved in the patri-archal pictures of old family Bibles to the most approved fashion of the last local sheep-fair. The room was lighted by half a dozen candles hav-ing wicks only a trifle smaller than the grease which enveloped them, in candlesticks that were never used but at high-days, holy-days, and family feasts. The lights were scattered about the room, two of them standing on the chimney piece. This position of candles was in itself significant. Candles on the chimney piece always meant a party.

On the hearth, in front of a back-brand to give substance, blazed a fire of thorns, that crackled "like the laughter of the fool."

Nineteen persons were gathered here. Of these, five women, wear-ing gowns of various bright hues, sat in chairs along the wall; girls shy and not shy filled the window-bench; four men, including Charley Jake the hedge-carpenter, Elijah New the parish-clerk, and John Pitcher, a neighboring dairyman, the shepherd's father-in-law, lolled in the settle; a young man and maid, who were blushing over tentative *pourparlers* on a life-companionship, sat beneath the corner-cupboard; and an elderly engaged man of fifty or upward moved restlessly about from spots where his betrothed was not to the spot where she was. Enjoyment was pretty general, and so much the more prevailed in being unhampered by con-ventional restrictions. Absolute confidence in each other's good opinion begat perfect ease, while the finishing stroke of manner, amounting to a truly princely serenity, was lent to the majority by the absence of any expression or trait denoting that they wished to get on in the world, enlarge their minds, or do any eclipsing thing whatever—which nowadays so generally nips the bloom and *bonhomie* of all except the two extremes of the social scale.

Shepherd Fennel had married well, his wife being a dairyman's daughter from a vale at a distance, who brought fifty guineas in her pocket—and kept them there, till they should be required for minister-ing to the needs of a coming family. This frugal woman had been some-what exercised as to the character that should be given to the gathering. A sit-still party had its advantages; but an undisturbed position of ease in chairs and settles was apt to lead on the men to such an unconscionable deal of toping that they would sometimes fairly drink the house dry. A dancing-party was the alternative; but this, while avoiding the foregoing objection on the score of good drink, had a counterbalancing disadvantage in the matter of good victuals, the ravenous appetites engendered by the exercise causing immense havoc in the buttery. Shepherdess Fennel fell back upon the intermediate plan of mingling short dances with short periods of talk and singing, so as to hinder any ungovernable rage in either. But this scheme was entirely confined to her own gentle mind: the shepherd himself was in the mood to exhibit the most reckless phases of hospitality.

The fiddler was a boy of those parts, about twelve years of age, who had a wonderful dexterity in jigs and reels, though his fingers were so small and short as to necessitate a constant shifting for the high notes, from which he scrambled back to the first position with sounds not of unmixed purity of tone. At seven the shrill tweedle-dee of this youngster had begun, accompanied by a booming ground-bass from Elijah New, the parish-clerk, who had thoughtfully brought with him his favorite musical instrument, the serpent. Dancing was instantaneous, Mrs. Fennel privately enjoining the players on no account to let the dance exceed the length of a quarter of an hour.

But Elijah and the boy, in the excitement of their position, quite forgot the injunction. Moreover, Oliver Giles, a man of seventeen, one of the dancers, who was enamored of his partner, a fair girl of thirty-three rolling years, had recklessly handed a new crown-piece to the musicians, as a bribe to keep going as long as they had muscle and wind. Mrs. Fennel, seeing the steam begin to generate on the countenances of her guests, crossed over and touched the fiddler's elbow and put her hand on the serpent's mouth. But they took no notice, and fearing she might lose her character of genial hostess if she were to interfere too markedly, she retired and sat down helpless. And so the dance whizzed on with cumulative fury, the performers moving in their planet-like courses, direct and retrograde, from apogee to perigee, till the hand of the well-kicked clock at the bottom of the room had traveled over the circumference of an hour.

While these cheerful events were in course of enactment within Fennel's pastoral dwelling, an incident having considerable bearing on the party had occurred in the gloomy night without. Mrs. Fennel's concern about the growing fierceness of the dance corresponded in point of time with the ascent of a human figure to the solitary hill of Higher Crowstairs from the direction of the distant town. This personage strode on through the rain without a pause, following the little-worn path which, further on in its course, skirted the shepherd's cottage.

It was nearly the time of full moon, and on this account, though the sky was lined with a uniform sheet of dripping cloud, ordinary objects out of doors were readily visible. The sad, wan light revealed the lonely pedestrian to be a man of supple frame; his gait suggested that he had somewhat passed the period of perfect and instinctive agility, though not so far as to be otherwise than rapid of motion when occasion required. At a rough guess, he might have been about forty years of age. He appeared tall, but a recruiting sergeant, or other person accustomed to the judging of men's heights by the eye, would have discerned that this was chiefly owing to his gauntness, and that he was not more than five-feet-eight or nine.

Notwithstanding the regularity of his tread, there was caution in it, as in that of one who mentally feels his way; and despite the fact that it was not a black coat nor a dark garment of any sort that he wore, there was something about him which suggested that he naturally belonged to the black-coated tribes of men. His clothes were of fustian, and his boots hobnailed, yet in his progress he showed not the mud-accustomed bearing of hobnailed and fustianed peasantry.

By the time that he had arrived abreast of the shepherd's premises the rain came down, or rather came along, with yet more determined violence. The outskirts of the little settlement partially broke the force of wind and rain, and this induced him to stand still. The most salient of the shepherd's domestic erections was an empty sty at the forward corner of his hedgeless garden, for in these latitudes the principle of masking the homelier features of your establishment by a conventional frontage was unknown. The traveler's eye was attracted to this small building by the pallid shine of the wet slates that covered it. He turned aside, and, finding it empty, stood under the pent-roof for shelter.

While he stood, the boom of the serpent within the adjacent house, and the lesser strains of the fiddler, reached the spot as an accompaniment to the surging hiss of the flying rain on the sod, its louder beating on the cabbage-leaves of the garden, on the eight or ten beehives just discernible by the path, and its dripping from the eaves into a row of buckets and pans that had been placed under the walls of the cottage. For at Higher Crowstairs, as at all such elevated domiciles, the grand difficulty of housekeeping was an insufficiency of water; and a casual rainfall was utilized by turning out, as catchers, every utensil that the house contained. Some queer stories might be told of the contrivances for economy in suds and dishwaters that are absolutely necessitated in upland habitations during the droughts of summer. But at this season there were no such exigencies; a mere acceptance of what the skies bestowed was sufficient for an abundant store.

At last the notes of the serpent ceased and the house was silent. This cessation of activity aroused the solitary pedestrian from the reverie into which he had elapsed, and, emerging from the shed, with an apparently new intention, he walked up the path to the house-door. Arrived here, his first act was to kneel down on a large stone beside the row of vessels, and to drink a copious draught from one of them. Having quenched his thirst, he rose and lifted his hand to knock, but paused with his eye upon the panel. Since the dark surface of the wood revealed absolutely nothing, it was evident that he must be mentally looking through the door, as if he wished to measure thereby all the possibilities that a house of this sort might include, and how they might bear upon the question of his entry.

In his indecision he turned and surveyed the scene around. Not a soul was anywhere visible. The garden path stretched downward from his feet, gleaming like the track of a snail; the roof of the little well (mostly dry), the well-cover, the top rail of the garden-gate, were varnished with the same dull liquid glaze; while, far away in the vale, a faint white-ness of more than usual extent showed that the rivers were high in the meads. Beyond all this winked a few bleared lamplights through the beating drops—lights that denoted the situation of the county-town from which he had appeared to come. The absence of all notes of life in that direction seemed to clinch his intentions, and he knocked at the door.

Within, a desultory chat had taken the place of movement and musical sound. The hedge-carpenter was suggesting a song to the company, which nobody just then was inclined to undertake, so that the knock afforded a not unwelcome diversion.

"Walk in!" said the shepherd, promptly.

The latch clicked upward, and out of the night our pedestrian appeared upon the door-mat. The shepherd arose, snuffed two of the nearest candles, and turned to look at him.

Their light disclosed that the stranger was dark in complexion and not unprepossessing as to feature. His hat, which for a moment he did not remove, hung low over his eyes, without concealing that they were large, open, and determined, moving with a flash rather than a glance round the room. He seemed pleased with his survey, and, baring his shaggy head, said, in a rich, deep voice: "The rain is so heavy, friends, that I ask leave to come in and rest awhile."

"To be sure, Stranger," said the shepherd. "And faith, you've been lucky in choosing your time, for we are having a bit of a fling for a glad cause—though, to be sure, a man could hardly wish that glad cause to happen more than once a year."

"Nor less," spoke up a woman. "For 'tis best to get your family over and done with, as soon as you can, so as to be all the earlier out of the fag o't."

"And what may be this glad cause?" asked the stranger.

"A birth and christening," said the shepherd.

The stranger hoped his host might not be made unhappy either by too many or too few of such episodes and, being invited by a gesture to a pull at the mug, he readily acquiesced. His manner, which, before entering, had been so dubious, was now altogether that of a careless and candid man.

"Late to be traipsing athwart this coomb—hey?" said the engaged man of fifty.

"Late it is, Master, as you say.—I'll take a seat in the chimney corner, if you have nothing to urge against it, Ma'am; for I am a little moist on the side that was next the rain."

Mrs. Shepherd Fennel assented, and made room for the self-invited comer, who, having got completely inside the chimney corner, stretched out his legs and arms with the expansiveness of a person quite at home.

"Yes, I am rather cracked in the vamp," he said freely, seeing that the eyes of the shepherd's wife fell upon his boots, "and I am not well fitted either. I have had some rough times lately, and have been forced to pick up what I can get in the way of wearing, but I must find a suit better fit for working-days when I reach home."

"One of hereabouts?" she inquired.

"Not quite that—further up the country."

"I thought so. And so be I; and by your tongue you come from my neighborhood."

"But you would hardly have heard of me," he said quickly. "My time would be long before yours, Ma'am, you see."

This testimony to the youthfulness of his hostess had the effect of stopping her cross-examination.

"There is only one thing more wanted to make me happy," continued the newcomer, "and that is a little baccy, which I am sorry to say I am out of."

"I'll fill your pipe," said the shepherd.

"I must ask you to lend me a pipe likewise."

"A smoker, and no pipe about 'ee?"

"I have dropped it somewhere on the road."

The shepherd filled and handed him a new clay pipe, saying, as he did so, "Hand me your baccy-box—I'll fill that too, now I am about it."

The man went through the movement of searching his pockets.

"Lost that too?" said his entertainer, with some surprise.

"I am afraid so," said the man with some confusion. "Give it to me in a screw of paper." Lighting his pipe at the candle with a suction that drew the whole flame into the bowl, he resettled himself in the corner and bent his looks upon the faint steam from his damp legs, as if he wished to say no more.

Meanwhile the general body of guests had been taking little notice of this visitor by reason of an absorbing discussion in which they were engaged with the band about a tune for the next dance. The matter being settled, they were about to stand up when an interruption came in the shape of another knock at the door.

At sound of the same the man in the chimney corner took up the poker and began stirring the brands as if doing it thoroughly were the one aim of his existence; and a second time the shepherd said, "Walk in!" In a moment another man stood upon the straw-woven door-mat. He too was a stranger.

This individual was one of a type radically different from the first. There was more of the commonplace in his manner, and a certain jovial cosmopolitanism sat upon his features. He was several years older than the first arrival, his hair being slightly frosted, his eyebrows bristly, and his whiskers cut back from his cheeks. His face was rather full and flabby, and yet it was not altogether a face without power. A few grog-blossoms marked the neighborhood of his nose. He flung back his long drab great-coat, revealing that beneath it he wore a suit of cinder-gray shade throughout, large heavy seals, of some metal or other that would take a polish, dangling from his fob as his only personal ornament. Shaking the water drops from his low-crowned glazed hat, he said, "I must ask for a few minutes' shelter, comrades, or I shall be wetted to my skin before I get to Casterbridge."

"Make yourself at home, Master," said the shepherd, perhaps a trifle less heartily than on the first occasion. Not that Fennel had the least tinge of niggardliness in his composition; but the room was far from large, spare chairs were not numerous, and damp companions were not altogether desirable at close quarters for the women and girls in their bright-colored gowns.

However, the second comer, after taking off his greatcoat, and hanging his hat on a nail in one of the ceiling-beams as if he had been specially invited to put it there, advanced and sat down at the table. This had been pushed so closely into the chimney corner, to give all available room to the dancers, that its inner edge grazed the elbow of the man who had ensconced himself by the fire; and thus the two strangers were brought into close companionship. They nodded to each other by way of breaking the ice of unacquaintance, and the first stranger handed his neighbor the family mug—a huge vessel of brown ware, having its upper edge worn away like a threshold by the rub of whole generations of thirsty lips that had gone the way of all flesh, and bearing the following inscription burnt upon its rotund side in yellow letters:

THERE IS NO FUN
UNTiL i CUM.

The other man, nothing loth, raised the mug to his lips, and drank on, and on, and on—till a curious blueness overspread the countenance of the shepherd's wife, who had regarded with no little surprise the first stranger's free offer to the second of what did not belong to him to dispense.

"I knew it!" said the toper to the shepherd with much satisfaction. "When I walked up your garden before coming in, and saw the hives all of a row, I said to myself, 'Where there's bees there's honey, and where there's honey there's mead.' But mead of such a truly comfortable sort as this I really didn't expect to meet in my older days." He took yet another pull at the mug, till it assumed an ominous elevation.

"Glad you enjoy it!" said the shepherd warmly.

"It is goodish mead," assented Mrs. Fennel, with an absence of enthusiasm which seemed to say that it was possible to buy praise for one's cellar at too heavy a price. "It is trouble enough to make—and really I hardly think we shall make any more. For honey sells well, and we ourselves can make shift with a drop o' small mead and metheglin for common use from the comb-washings."

"Oh, but you'll never have the heart!" reproachfully cried the stranger in cinder-gray, after taking up the mug a third time and setting it down empty. "I love mead, when 'tis old like this, as I love to go to church o' Sundays, or to relieve the needy any day of the week."

"Ha, ha, ha!" said the man in the chimney corner, who, in spite of the taciturnity induced by the pipe of tobacco, could not or would not refrain from this slight testimony to his comrade's humor.

Now the old mead of those days, brewed of the purest first-year or maiden honey, four pounds to the gallon—with its due complement of white of eggs, cinnamon, ginger, cloves, mace, rosemary, yeast, and processes of working, bottling, and cellaring—tasted remarkably strong; but it did not taste so strong as it actually was. Hence, presently, the stranger in cinder-gray at the table, moved by its creeping influence, unbuttoned his waistcoat, threw himself back in his chair, spread his legs, and made his presence felt in various ways.

"Well, well, as I say," he resumed, "I am going to Casterbridge, and to Casterbridge I must go. I should have been almost there by this time; but the rain drove me into your dwelling, and I'm not sorry for it."

"You don't live in Casterbridge?" said the shepherd.

"Not as yet; though I shortly mean to move there."

"Going to set up in trade, perhaps?"

"No, no," said the shepherd's wife. "It is easy to see that the gentleman is rich, and don't want to work at anything."

The cinder-gray stranger paused, as if to consider whether he would accept that definition of himself. He presently rejected it by answering, "Rich is not quite the word for me, Dame. I do work, and I must work. And even if I only get to Casterbridge by midnight I must begin work there at eight tomorrow morning. Yes, het or wet, blow or snow, famine or sword, my day's work tomorrow must be done."

"Poor man! Then, in spite o' seeming, you be worse off than we," replied the shepherd's wife.

" 'Tis the nature of my trade, men and maidens. 'Tis the nature of my trade more than my poverty. . . . But really and truly I must up and off, or I shan't get a lodging in the town." However, the speaker did not move, and directly added, "There's time for one more draught of friendship before I go; and I'd perform it at once if the mug were not dry."

"Here's a mug o' small," said Mrs. Fennel. "Small, we call it, though to be sure 'tis only the first wash o' the combs."

"No," said the stranger, disdainfully. "I won't spoil your first kindness by partaking o' your second."

"Certainly not," broke in Fennel. "We don't increase and multiply every day, and I'll fill the mug again." He went away to the dark place under the stairs where the barrel stood. The shepherdess followed him.

"Why should you do this?" she said, reproachfully, as soon as they were alone. "He's emptied it once, though it held enough for ten people; and now he's not contented wi' the small, but must needs call for more o' the strong! And a stranger unbeknown to any of us. For my part, I don't like the look o' the man at all."

"But he's in the house, my honey; and 'tis a wet night, and a christening. Daze it, what's a cup of mead more or less? There'll be plenty more next bee-burning."

"Very well—this time, then," she answered, looking wistfully at the barrel. "But what is the man's calling, and where is he one of, that he should come in and join us like this?"

"I don't know. I'll ask him again."

The catastrophe of having the mug drained dry at one pull by the stranger in cinder-gray was effectually guarded against this time by Mrs. Fennel. She poured out his allowance in a small cup, keeping the large one at a discreet distance from him. When he had tossed off his portion the shepherd renewed his inquiry about the stranger's occupation.

The latter did not immediately reply, and the man in the chimney corner, with sudden demonstrativeness, said, "Anybody may know my trade—I'm a wheelwright."

"A very good trade for these parts," said the shepherd.

"And anybody may know mine—if they've the sense to find it out," said the stranger in cinder-gray.

"You may generally tell what a man is by his claws," observed the hedge-carpenter, looking at his own hands. "My fingers be as full of thorns as an old pincushion is of pins."

The hands of the man in the chimney corner instinctively sought the shade, and he gazed into the fire as he resumed his pipe. The man at the table took up the hedge-carpenter's remark, and added smartly, "True; but the oddity of my trade is that, instead of setting a mark upon me, it sets a mark upon my customers."

No observation being offered by anybody in elucidation of this enigma, the shepherd's wife once more called for a song. The same obstacles presented themselves as at the former time—one had no voice, another had forgotten the first verse. The stranger at the table, whose soul had now risen to a good working temperature, relieved the difficulty by exclaiming that, to start the company, he would sing himself. Thrusting one thumb into the armhole of his waistcoat, he waved the other hand in the air, and, with an extemporizing gaze at the shining sheep-crooks above the mantelpiece, began:

> *O my trade it is the rarest one,*
> > *Simple shepherds all—*
> *My trade is a sight to see;*
> *For my customers I tie, and take them up on high,*
> *And waft 'em to a far countree!*

The room was silent when he had finished the verse—with one exception, that of the man in the chimney corner, who at the singer's word, "Chorus!" joined him in a deep bass voice of musical relish:

> *And waft 'em to a far countree!*

Oliver Giles, John Pitcher the dairyman, the parish-clerk, the engaged man of fifty, the row of young women against the wall, seemed lost in thought not of the gayest kind. The shepherd looked meditatively on the ground, the shepherdess gazed keenly at the singer, and with some suspicion; she was doubting whether this stranger were merely singing an old song from recollection, or was composing one there and then for the occasion. All were as perplexed at the obscure revelation as the guests at Belshazzar's Feast, except the man in the chimney corner, who quietly said, "Second verse, stranger," and smoked on.

The singer thoroughly moistened himself from his lips inward, and went on with the next stanza as requested:

> *My tools are but common ones,*
> > *Simple shepherds all—*
> *My tools are no sight to see:*
> *A little hempen string, and a post whereon to swing,*
> *Are implements enough for me!*

Shepherd Fennel glanced round. There was no longer any doubt that the stranger was answering his question rhythmically. The guests one and all started back with suppressed exclamations. The young woman engaged to the man of fifty fainted halfway, and would have proceeded, but finding him wanting in alacrity for catching her she sat down trembling.

"Oh, he's the ——!" whispered the people in the background, mentioning the name of an ominous public officer. "He's come to do it! 'Tis to be at Casterbridge jail tomorrow—the man for sheep-stealing—the poor clockmaker we heard of, who used to live away at Shottsford and had no work to do—Timothy Summers, whose family were astarving, and so he went out of Shottsford by the highroad, and took a sheep in open daylight, defying the farmer and the farmer's wife and the farmer's lad, and every man jack among 'em. He" (and they nodded toward the stranger of the deadly trade) "is come from up the country to do it because there's not enough to do in his own county-town, and he's got the place here now our own county-man's dead; he's going to live in the same cottage under the prison wall."

The stranger in cinder-gray took no notice of this whispered string of observations, but again wetted his lips. Seeing that his friend in the chimney corner was the only one who reciprocated his joviality in any way, he held out his cup toward that appreciative comrade, who also held out his own. They clinked together, the eyes of the rest of the room hanging upon the singer's actions. He parted his lips for the third verse; but at that moment another knock was audible upon the door. This time the knock was faint and hesitating.

The company seemed scared; the shepherd looked with consternation toward the entrance, and it was with some effort that he resisted his alarmed wife's deprecatory glance, and uttered for the third time the welcoming words, "Walk in!"

The door was gently opened, and another man stood upon the mat. He, like those who had preceded him, was a stranger. This time it was a short, small personage, of fair complexion, and dressed in a decent suit of dark clothes.

"Can you tell me the way to ——?" he began: when, gazing round the room to observe the nature of the company among whom he had fallen, his eyes lighted on the stranger in cinder-gray. It was just at the instant when the latter, who had thrown his mind into his song with such a will that he scarcely heeded the interruption, silenced all whispers and inquiries by bursting into his third verse:

> *Tomorrow is my working day,*
>> *Simple shepherds all—*
> *Tomorrow is a working day for me:*
> *For the farmer's sheep is slain, and the lad who did it ta'en,*
> *And on his soul may God ha' merc-y!*

The stranger in the chimney corner, waving cups with the singer so heartily that his mead splashed over on the hearth, repeated in his bass voice as before:

And on his soul may God ha' merc-y!

All this time the third stranger had been standing in the door-way. Finding now that he did not come forward or go on speaking, the guests particularly regarded him. They noticed to their surprise that he stood before them the picture of abject terror—his knees trembling, his hand shaking so violently that the door-latch by which he supported himself rattled audibly: his white lips were parted, and his eyes fixed on the merry officer of justice in the middle of the room. A moment more and he had turned, closed the door, and fled.

"What a man can it be?" said the shepherd.

The rest, between the awfulness of their late discovery and the odd conduct of this third visitor, looked as if they knew not what to think, and said nothing. Instinctively they withdrew further and further from the grim gentleman in their midst, whom some of them seemed to take for the Prince of Darkness himself, till they formed a remote circle, an empty space of floor being left between them and him—

. . . *circulas, cujus centrum diabolus.**

The room was so silent—though there were more than twenty people in it—that nothing could be heard but the patter of the rain against the window-shutters, accompanied by the occasional hiss of a stray drop that fell down the chimney into the fire, and the steady puffing of the man in the corner, who had now resumed his pipe of long clay.

The stillness was unexpectedly broken. The distant sound of a gun reverberated through the air—apparently from the direction of the county-town.

"Be jiggered!" cried the stranger who had sung the song, jumping up.

"What does that mean?" asked several.

"A prisoner escaped from the jail—that's what it means."

All listened. The sound was repeated, and none of them spoke but the man in the chimney corner, who said quietly, "I've often been told that in this county they fire a gun at such times; but I never heard it till now."

"I wonder if it is *my* man?" murmured the personage in cinder-gray.

"Surely it is!" said the shepherd involuntarily. "And surely we've

* . . . *circles, whose center [is] the devil.*

zeed him! That little man who looked in at the door by now, and quiv-
ered like a leaf when he zeed ye and heard your song!"

"His teeth chattered, and the breath went out of his body," said the
dairyman.

"And his heart seemed to sink within him like a stone," said Oliver
Giles.

"And he bolted as if he'd been shot at," said the hedge-carpenter.

"True—his teeth chattered, and his heart seemed to sink; and he
bolted as if he'd been shot at," slowly summed up the man in the chimney
corner.

"I didn't notice it," remarked the hangman.

"We were all awondering what made him run off in such a fright,"
faltered one of the women against the wall, "and now 'tis explained!"

The firing of the alarm-gun went on at intervals, low and sul-
lenly, and their suspicions became a certainty. The sinister gentleman in
cinder-gray roused himself. "Is there a constable here?" he asked, in thick
tones. "If so, let him step forward."

The engaged man of fifty stepped quavering out from the wall, his
betrothed beginning to sob on the back of the chair.

"You are a sworn constable?"

"I be, Sir."

"Then pursue the criminal at once, with assistance, and bring him
back here. He can't have gone far."

"I will, Sir, I will—when I've got my staff. I'll go home and get it,
and come sharp here, and start in a body."

"Staff!—never mind your staff; the man'll be gone!"

"But I can't do nothing without my staff—can I, William, and John,
and Charles Jake? No; for there's the king's royal crown apainted on en
in yaller and gold, and the lion and the unicorn, so as when I raise en
up and hit my prisoner, 'tis made a lawful blow thereby. I wouldn't
'tempt to take up a man without my staff—no, not I. If I hadn't the law
to gie me courage, why, instead o' my taking up him he might take up
me!"

"Now, I'm a king's man myself, and can give you authority enough
for this," said the formidable officer in gray. "Now then, all of ye, be
ready. Have ye any lanterns?"

"Yes—have ye any lanterns?—I demand it!" said the constable.

"And the rest of you able-bodied—"

"Able-bodied men—yes—the rest of ye!" said the constable.

"Have you some good stout staves and pitchforks—"

"Staves and pitchforks—in the name o' the law! And take 'em in
yer hands and go in quest, and do as we in authority tell ye!"

Thus aroused, the men prepared to give chase. The evidence was, indeed, though circumstantial, so convincing, that but little argument was needed to show the shepherd's guests that after what they had seen it would look very much like connivance if they did not instantly pursue the unhappy third stranger, who could not as yet have gone more than a few hundred yards over such uneven country.

A shepherd is always well provided with lanterns; and, lighting these hastily, and with hurdle-staves in their hands, they poured out of the door, taking a direction along the crest of the hill, away from the town, the rain having fortunately a little abated.

Disturbed by the noise, or possibly by unpleasant dreams of her baptism, the child who had been christened began to cry heart-brokenly in the room overhead. These notes of grief came down through the chinks of the floor to the ears of the women below, who jumped up one by one, and seemed glad of the excuse to ascend and comfort the baby, for the incidents of the last half-hour greatly oppressed them. Thus in the space of two or three minutes the room on the ground-floor was deserted quite.

But it was not for long. Hardly had the sound of footsteps died away when a man returned round the corner of the house from the direction the pursuers had taken. Peeping in at the door, and seeing nobody there, he entered leisurely. It was the stranger of the chimney corner, who had gone out with the rest. The motive of his return was shown by his helping himself to a cut piece of skimmer-cake that lay on a ledge beside where he had sat, and which he had apparently forgotten to take with him. He also poured out half a cup more mead from the quantity that remained, ravenously eating and drinking these as he stood. He had not finished when another figure came in just as quietly—his friend in cinder-gray.

"Oh—you here?" said the latter, smiling. "I thought you had gone to help in the capture." And this speaker also revealed the object of his return by looking solicitously round for the fascinating mug of old mead.

"And I thought you had gone," said the other, continuing his skimmer-cake with some effort.

"Well, on second thoughts, I felt there were enough without me," said the first confidentially, "and such a night as it is, too. Besides, 'tis the business o' the Government to take care of its criminals—not mine."

"True; so it is. And I felt as you did, that there were enough without me."

"I don't want to break my limbs running over the humps and hollows of this wild country."

"Nor I neither, between you and me."

"These shepherd-people are used to it—simple-minded souls, you know, stirred up to anything in a moment. They'll have him ready for me before the morning, and no trouble to me at all."

"They'll have him, and we shall have saved ourselves all labor in the matter."

"True, true. Well, my way is to Casterbridge; and 'tis as much as my legs will do to take me that far. Going the same way?"

"No, I am sorry to say! I have to get home over there" (he nodded indefinitely to the right), "and I feel as you do, that it is quite enough for my legs to do before bedtime."

The other had by this time finished the mead in the mug, after which, shaking hands heartily at the door, and wishing each other well, they went their several ways.

In the meantime the company of pursuers had reached the end of the hog's-back elevation which dominated this part of the down. They had decided on no particular plan of action; and, finding that the man of the baleful trade was no longer in their company, they seemed quite unable to form any such plan now. They descended in all directions down the hill, and straightway several of the party fell into the snare set by Nature for all misguided midnight ramblers over this part of the cretaceous formation. The "lanchets," or flint slopes, which belted the escarpment at intervals of a dozen yards, took the less cautious ones unawares, and losing their footing on the rubbly steep they slid sharply downward, the lanterns rolling from their hands to the bottom, and there lying on their sides till the horn was scorched through.

When they had again gathered themselves together, the shepherd, as the man who knew the country best, took the lead, and guided them round these treacherous inclines. The lanterns, which seemed rather to dazzle their eyes and warn the fugitive than to assist them in the exploration, were extinguished, due silence was observed; and in this more rational order they plunged into the vale. It was a grassy, briery, moist defile, affording some shelter to any person who had sought it; but the party perambulated it in vain, and ascended on the other side. Here they wandered apart, and after an interval closed together again to report progress. At the second time of closing in they found themselves near a lonely ash, the single tree on this part of the coomb, probably sown there by a passing bird some fifty years before. And here, standing a little to one side of the trunk, as motionless as the trunk itself appeared the man they were in quest of, his outline being well defined against the sky beyond. The band noiselessly drew up and faced him.

"Your money or your life!" said the constable sternly to the still figure.

"No, no," whispered John Pitcher. "'Tisn't our side ought to say that. That's the doctrine of vagabonds like him, and we be on the side of the law."

"Well, well," replied the constable, impatiently; "I must say something, mustn't I? and if you had all the weight o' this undertaking upon your mind, perhaps you'd say the wrong thing, too!—Prisoner at the bar, surrender in the name of the Father—the Crown, I mane!"

The man under the tree seemed now to notice them for the first time, and, giving them no opportunity whatever for exhibiting their courage, he strolled slowly toward them. He was, indeed, the little man, the third stranger; but his trepidation had in a great measure gone.

"Well, travelers," he said, "did I hear you speak to me?"

"You did; you've got to come and be our prisoner at once!" said the constable. "We arrest 'ee on the charge of not biding in Casterbridge jail in a decent proper manner to be hung tomorrow morning. Neighbors, do your duty, and seize the culpet!"

On hearing the charge, the man seemed enlightened, and, saying not another word, resigned himself with preternatural civility to the search-party, who, with their staves in their hands, surrounded him on all sides, and marched him back toward the shepherd's cottage.

It was eleven o'clock by the time they arrived. The light shining from the open door, a sound of men's voices within, proclaimed to them as they approached the house that some new events had arisen in their absence. On entering they discovered the shepherd's living-room to be invaded by two officers from Casterbridge jail, and a well-known magistrate who lived at the nearest county-seat, intelligence of the escape having become generally circulated.

"Gentlemen," said the constable, "I have brought back your man—not without risk and danger; but everyone must do his duty! He is inside this circle of able-bodied persons, who have lent me useful aid, considering their ignorance of Crown work.—Men, bring forward your prisoner!" And the third stranger was led to the light.

"Who is this?" said one of the officials.

"The man," said the constable.

"Certainly not," said the turnkey; and the first corroborated his statement.

"But how can it be otherwise?" asked the constable. "Or why was he so terrified at sight o' the singing instrument of the law who sat there?" Here he related the strange behavior of the third stranger on entering the house during the hangman's song.

"Can't understand it," said the officer coolly. "All I know is that it is not the condemned man. He's quite a different character from this one; a gauntish fellow, with dark hair and eyes, rather good-looking, and with a musical bass voice that if you heard it once you'd never mistake as long as you lived."

"Why, souls—'twas the man in the chimney corner!"

"Hey—what?" said the magistrate, coming forward after inquiring particulars from the shepherd in the background. "Haven't you got the man after all?"

"Well, Sir," said the constable, "he's the man we were in search of, that's true; and yet he's not the man we were in search of. For the man we were in search of was not the man we wanted, Sir, if you understand my everyday way; for 'twas the man in the chimney corner!"

"A pretty kettle of fish altogether!" said the magistrate. "You had better start for the other man at once."

The prisoner now spoke for the first time. The mention of the man in the chimney corner seemed to have moved him as nothing else could do. "Sir," he said, stepping forward to the magistrate, "take no more trouble about me. The time is come when I may as well speak. I have done nothing; my crime is that the condemned man is my brother. Early this afternoon I left home at Shottsford to tramp it all the way to Casterbridge jail to bid him farewell. I was benighted, and called here to rest and ask the way. When I opened the door I saw before me the very man, my brother, that I thought to see in the condemned cell at Casterbridge. He was in this chimney corner; and jammed close to him, so that he could not have got out if he had tried, was the executioner who'd come to take his life, singing a song about it and not knowing that it was his victim who was close by, joining in to save appearances. My brother looked a glance of agony at me, and I know he meant, 'Don't reveal what you see; my life depends on it.' I was so terror-struck that I could hardly stand, and, not knowing what I did, I turned and hurried away."

The narrator's manner and tone had the stamp of truth, and his story made a great impression on all around. "And do you know where your brother is at the present time?" asked the magistrate.

"I do not. I have never seen him since I closed this door."

"I can testify to that, for we've been between ye ever since," said the constable.

"Where does he think to fly to?—what is his occupation?"

"He's a watch-and-clock-maker, Sir."

"'A said 'a was a wheelwright—a wicked rogue," said the constable.

"The wheels of clocks and watches he meant, no doubt," said Shepherd Fennel. "I thought his hands were palish for's trade."

"Well, it appears to me that nothing can be gained by retaining this poor man in custody," said the magistrate; "your business lies with the other, unquestionably."

And so the little man was released off-hand; but he looked nothing the less sad on that account, it being beyond the power of magistrate or constable to raze out the written troubles in his brain, for they concerned another whom he regarded with more solicitude than himself. When this was done, and the man had gone his way, the night was found to be so far advanced that it was deemed useless to renew the search before the next morning.

Next day, accordingly, the quest for the clever sheep-stealer became general and keen, to all appearance at least. But the intended punishment was cruelly disproportioned to the transgression, and the sympathy of a great many country-folk in that district was strongly on the side of the fugitive. Moreover, his marvelous coolness and daring in hob-and-nobbing with the hangman, under the unprecedented circumstances of the shepherd's party, won their admiration. So that it may be questioned if all those who ostensibly made themselves so busy in exploring woods and fields and lanes were quite so thorough when it came to the private examination of their own lofts and outhouses. Stories were afloat of a mysterious figure being occasionally seen in some old overgrown trackway or other, remote from turnpike roads, but when a search was instituted in any of these suspected quarters nobody was found. Thus the days and weeks passed without tidings.

In brief, the bass-voiced man of the chimney corner was never recaptured. Some said that he went across the sea, others that he did not, but buried himself in the depths of a populous city. At any rate, the gentleman in cinder-gray never did his morning's work at Casterbridge, nor met anywhere at all, for business purposes, the genial comrade with whom he had passed an hour of relaxation in the lonely house on the coomb.

The grass has long been green on the graves of Shepherd Fennel and his frugal wife; the guests who made up the christening party have mainly followed their entertainers to the tomb; the baby in whose honor they all had met is a matron in the sere and yellow leaf. But the arrival of the three strangers at the shepherd's that night, and the details connected therewith, is a story as well-known as ever in the country about Higher Crowstairs.

1888

Index